lonely planet walking guide

Bushwalking
in Australia

D0110438

ISBN 0-86442-171-0

9 780864 421715

Australia RRP $16.95
USA $12.95
UK £7.95
Canada $16.95
Singapore $22.95

2nd Edition

Bushwalking
in Australia

John Chapman
Monica Chapman

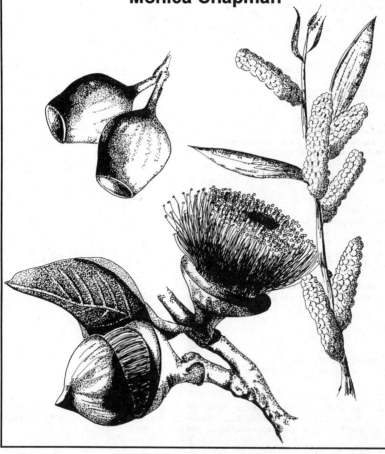

Bushwalking in Australia

2nd edition

Published by
 Lonely Planet Publications
 Head Office: PO Box 617, Hawthorn, Vic 3122, Australia
 Branches: PO Box 2001A, Berkeley, CA 94702, USA and London, UK

Printed by
 Colorcraft Ltd, Hong Kong

Photographs by
 All photographs by John Chapman or Monica Chapman except:
 Glenn van der Knijff (GvdK)
 Tony Wheeler (TW)
 Jeff Williams (JW)

 Front cover: Looking towards the Breadknife, Warrumbungles (John Chapman)
 Back cover: At the side of Cradle Mountain, The Overland Track (John Chapman)

First Published
 May 1988

This Edition
 November 1992

National Library of Australia Cataloguing in Publication Data

Chapman, John.
 Bushwalking in Australia.

 2nd ed.
 Includes index.
 ISBN 0 86442 171 0.

 1. Hiking – Australia – Guidebooks. 2. Australia – Guidebooks.
 I. Chapman, Monica. II. Title. (Series: Lonely Planet walking guide).

919.40463

John Chapman

John has a wealth of experience in the Australian bush and has walked extensively in Victoria, Tasmania and New South Wales. He has shared some of this knowledge in magazine and newspaper articles, and in bushwalking guidebooks. He enjoys both colour and black & white photography, and has exhibited internationally. John is also a keen ski tourer and rockclimber who has led many treks in the Nepal and India Himalaya.

Monica Chapman

Monica has been involved in local bushwalking clubs for many years. She has held several committee positions, including that of president, and has lead numerous bushwalks. She is currently President of the Federation of Victorian Walking Clubs and is a member of Search & Rescue. Monica has explored most of Victoria, some of New South Wales and walked in south-west Tasmania several times. She has also visited Bali and trekked in Nepal. Monica is a keen photographer, enjoys ski touring and occasionally even rockclimbs!

Together they have travelled and walked extensively throughout Australia researching this book. It is the culmination of several years of work.

Acknowledgements

Thanks to all those who contributed to this project: the national park rangers and park office staff for their advice and assistance; Adrian Rigg for his help with the Ormiston map; and John Siseman (co-author of the Cradle Mountain guidebook) for permission to use information from that text. A special thank you to all our friends who accompanied us on many journeys into the Australian bush.

From the Publisher

This 2nd edition was edited by Jeff Williams at the Lonely Planet office in Melbourne. Vicki Beale corrected the maps, and Glenn Beanland did the cover design and layout. Sue Mitra, Kristin Odÿk and Louise Parsons proofed the final product and Tom Smallman, as usual, gave his good advice willingly.

Disclaimer

Although the author and publisher have done their utmost to ensure the accuracy of all information in this guide, they cannot accept any responsibility for any loss, injury or inconvenience sustained by people using this book. For example, they cannot guarantee that tracks and routes described have not been overgrown or otherwise become impassable in the interval between research and publication.

All walking times *exclude* rest stops, and

unless otherwise stated, assume that the path is not obstructed by snow. The fact that a trip or area is described in this guidebook does not necessarily mean that it is a safe one for you and your walking party. You are finally responsible for judging your own capabilities in light of the conditions that you encounter. Good walking!

Warning & Request

Things change – prices go up, schedules change, good places go bad and bad places go bankrupt – nothing stays the same. So if you find things better or worse, recently opened or long since closed, please write and tell us and help make the next edition better.

Your letters will be used to help update future editions and, where possible, important changes will also be included in a Stop Press section in reprints.

We greatly appreciate all information that is sent to us by travellers. Back at Lonely Planet we employ a hard-working readers' letters team to sort through the many letters we receive. The best ones will be rewarded with a free copy of the next edition or another Lonely Planet guide if you prefer. We give away lots of books, but, unfortunately, not every letter/postcard receives one.

Contents

MAP LEGEND

▬▬▬	Major Road
— —	Walking Track, Minor Road
- - - -	Walking Route only
┼─┼─	Railway Line
─⟋─⟋─	Fence Line
⌇	Streams
┼	Waterfall
▲	Mountain, Peak
■	Building
⊤⊤⊤⊤⊤	Cliff line, Scarp
⸜	Swamp
Λ	Campsite
Ⓢ	Start of Walk
Ⓕ	Finish of Walk (if not a circuit walk)

Introduction

One of the best ways to see Australia is by foot. Bushwalking, otherwise known as hiking, backpacking or tramping, is the recreation of walking in areas that are remote, unsettled or relatively unaffected by man. Australia with its diverse and beautiful wild areas is one of the best places in the world to enjoy this pastime and the self-sufficiency of bushwalkers enables them to do just this.

There are 24 walks in this guide, each of at least two days in length. The walks range from an easy two-day stroll along the coast of the Royal National Park near Sydney to an extended 11-day walk through Southwest Tasmania. There are walks in desert ranges, along rugged coastlines, through rainforests and across gentle alpine plateaus.

For most of the walks a large amount of experience is not necessary as they follow good tracks or well-used routes when possible. For the experienced, a few difficult walks following less defined tracks have been included.

The main features, track standard, possible variations, availability of campsites and water, climate, equipment needed and access to each walk are described in full. The track notes should be used in conjunction with the recommended maps. Where possible, circuit walks have been described to avoid the transport problems of arranging car shuffles.

With over 100 major national parks spread around the country there are hundreds of good bushwalks. It's up to you to decide which part of the country interests you and what style of walk will suit you best.

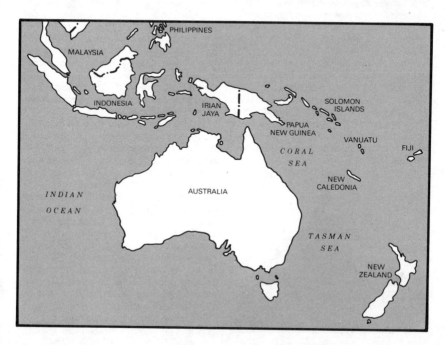

Facts about the Country

HISTORY

Australia is one of the oldest landmasses in the world and has been inhabited by the Aborigines for at least 40,000 years. The Aborigines lived in harmony with nature by hunting, fishing and gathering, sheltered in bark or leaf lean-tos and they went naked apart from a coating of grease and charcoal.

Aboriginal society is based on sharing and exchange – a concept the Europeans failed to come to terms with. Their art uses abstract symbols to represent the elements of nature and their religion involves a belief in a great supernatural being and a veneration of their ancestors.

Australia was the last great continent to be 'discovered' during the European period of exploration. Although Captain Cook is the name commonly connected with Australia's discovery, it was probably a Portuguese who first sighted the country, and the credit for its early coastal exploration must go to the Dutch.

The American Revolution led to the next phase of recent Australian history. With America cut off as a good place to ship Britain's convicts, a colony was established in Sydney in 1788. By 1792 the first difficult years had been endured and gradually more free settlers began to arrive and a new period of discovery started as the vast continent was explored.

George Bass charted the coast south of Sydney almost down to the present location of Melbourne in 1797-98 and, in 1798-99, with Matthew Flinders, sailed right round Tasmania thus establishing that it was an island. Flinders went on, in 1802-03, to circumnavigate Australia.

Colonial expansion often took place for one of two reasons: to find yet another place to keep the convicts, or to occupy land before anyone else arrived. In 1803 the first settlement in Tasmania was founded close to the present site of Hobart and in 1835 settlers from Tasmania, in search of more land, arrived at the present site of Melbourne.

Perth was settled in 1829, but as it was isolated from the rest of the country, growth there was very slow. The first settlement in Brisbane was made by a party of convicts and by the time it had been abandoned in 1839 free settlers had arrived in force. Adelaide was initially set up in 1837 as an experiment in free enterprise colonisation, but failed due to bad management and was then taken over by the British government.

Some of the early explorers, particularly the men who braved the hostile centre, suffered great hardships and, on more than one occasion, lost their lives.

In 1840 Edward John Eyre left Adelaide to try to reach the centre of Australia. He gave up at Mt Hopeless and then decided to attempt a crossing to Albany in Western Australia. Despite great difficulties Eyre managed to cross the continent.

Leaving Melbourne in 1860 the Burke & Wills expedition planned to cross the continent from south to north. It took them longer than anticipated to complete the leg of the journey between Coopers Creek in Queensland and the Gulf of Carpentaria and when Burke, Wills and King eventually struggled back to Coopers Creek they were nearly two months late. Both Burke and Wills died of starvation, not realising that food had been left for them buried beneath a tree.

After two attempts in 1860 and 1861 to

make the first south-north crossing, John Stuart managed to reach the north coast near Darwin in 1862. With the discovery of gold in Victoria in 1851 the population began to increase rapidly as a result of massive immigration. Similar discoveries in other states, in particular the WA gold rush of the 1890s, boosted populations and levels of economic activity. At the same time the Industrial Revolution in England created a demand for raw materials.

The 19th-century development of Australia, however, had a darker side. The Aborigines were looked upon as little more than animals and brutally forced off their tribal lands. In some places, Tasmania in particular, they were hunted down and destroyed like vermin.

By the end of the 19th century Australia had become more self-sufficient and independent from England but still followed the British lead on most matters of foreign policy and thus dutifully marched off to the Boer War and then to WW I. Australia, as a political entity, actually came into existence in 1901 when the separate states were federated and the decision to find a national capital was made.

Because of Australia's economic dependence on the rest of the world the Great Depression had an enormous effect on the economy. Then in WW II Australia once more went to war beside Britain. The war had two immediately obvious effects on the country: America's entry to the war and the defeat of the Germans made Australia aware of her dependence upon the US, and the threatened invasion by Japan made it clear that while Australia might be a European type of country, it is actually in Asia.

The prosperity and growth of the 1950s and 1960s was a period when Australia began to look more towards America than England. From the mid 1960s until 1972 Australia fought in the Vietnam war with the USA.

The 1970s was a period of economic, social and political upheaval. In the 1980s, conservation became a major issue and now in the 1990s, changes are still flowing on.

Bushwalking & Conservation

Since colonisation, Australians have had an affinity with the bush. Early explorers ventured out in search of greener pastures; miners dug for gold and other precious metals and minerals, and surveyors laid the foundations for the growth of towns and industry.

The mountains were explored first by the miners who pushed tracks up the large river valleys. Cattle owners seeking new pasture used these tracks to access the alpine plains for summer grazing. The cattle owners kept the tracks open, cut new routes and built an extensive chain of bush huts over the high country.

As the cities expanded, people began to visit the bush for recreation and pleasure and the first walking clubs began in the 1890s.

After WW I leading bushwalking figures began to realise that the native bush was

quickly disappearing in favour of farms, logging, mining and dam construction.

Myles Dunphy, a leading bushwalker and leader of the growing conservation movement around Sydney assisted the walking clubs in the purchase of the Blue Gum Forest (in the Blue Mountains) in the early 1930s and in the leasing of tracts of virgin bushland. He also produced many sketch maps and was instrumental in the formation of the Warrumbungle National Park and additions to Royal and Heathcote national parks. In 1932 the NSW Federation of Bushwalking Clubs was formed, creating the core of the conservation movement in that state.

Other states were slower to realise the threat of the vanishing bushland, probably because they were still exploring. Virtually all the long desert ranges of Central Australia were explored by William Bonython. Concurrently, a group of 'hard core' bushwalkers, including Jack Thwaites and John Bechervaise, were exploring the last major ridges in south-west Tasmania – the western and eastern Arthurs, including the first ascent of Federation Peak.

Through the 1950s there was steady destruction of the native bush with little or no opposition. Things remained quiet in NSW, except around Sydney, until the leading bushwalkers in the 1960s began to realise the native bush was dwindling.

The first major conservation confrontations developed in 1974 over the damming of Lake Pedder in south-west Tasmania. A dedicated band of bushwalkers and conservationists fought the mighty Hydro-Electric Commission (HEC), but lost the battle. However, they were better prepared for the next conflict in 1982-83 when the HEC proposed a series of dams to flood the spectacular gorges of the Franklin River.

The 'Tasmanian Wilderness Society' was formed by those opposed to this development and included many bushwalkers. It was a bitter, but successful, campaign that was instrumental in making conservation an important political issue. The focus given to the issue by the international media also brought the world's attention to the beauty of the Australian wilderness. Major successes of the conservation movement has resulted in World Heritage status being awarded to many of Australia's best areas. The conservation vote has become increasingly important to the government, opposition and smaller political parties.

After the Franklin River Dam campaign, the Society became a national concern and changed its name to 'The Wilderness Society'. Along with the Australian Conservation Foundation it is now actively challenging development of bushlands in all states in an effort to conserve one of Australia's major resources and attractions – the native bush (for more information see Useful Organisations in the Facts for the Bushwalker chapter).

GEOGRAPHY

Australia is an island continent whose landscape – much of it uncompromisingly bleak and inhospitable – is the result of gradual changes wrought over millions of years. Although there is still seismic activity in the eastern and western highland areas, Australia is one of the most stable land masses, and for about 100 million years has been free of the mountain-building forces that have given rise to huge mountain ranges elsewhere.

From the east coast a narrow, fertile strip merges into the greatly eroded, almost continent-long Great Dividing Range. The mountains are mere reminders of the mighty range that once stood here. Only in the section straddling the New South Wales border with Victoria and in Tasmania are they high enough to have winter snow.

West of the range the country becomes increasingly flat, dry and inhospitable. The endless flatness is broken only by salt lakes, occasional mysterious protuberances like Ayers Rock (Uluru) and the Olgas, and some starkly beautiful mountains like the MacDonnell Ranges near Alice Springs. In places, the scant vegetation is sufficient to allow some grazing, so long as each animal has a seemingly enormous area of land. However, much of the Australian outback is a barren land of harsh, stone deserts and dry lakes with evocative names such as Lake Disappointment.

The extreme north of Australia, the Top End, is a tropical area within the monsoon belt. Although the annual rainfall there looks adequate on paper, it comes in more or less one short, sharp burst. This has prevented the Top End from becoming seriously productive agriculturally.

The west of Australia consists mainly of a broad plateau. In the far west there is a mountain range and fertile coastal strip which heralds the Indian Ocean, but this is only to the south. In the north-central part of Western Australia, the dry country runs right to the sea.

Australia is the world's sixth largest country. Its area is 7,682,300 sq km, about the same size as the 48 mainland states of the USA and half as large again as Europe, excluding the former USSR. It is approximately 5% of the world's land surface. Lying between the Indian and Pacific oceans, Australia is about 4000 km from east to west and 3200 km from north to south, with a coastline 36,735 km long.

CLIMATE

Australian seasons are the antithesis of those in Europe and North America. It's hot in December and many Australians spend Christmas at the beach, while in July and August it's midwinter. Summer starts in December, autumn in March, winter in June and spring in September.

The climatic extremes aren't too severe in most parts of Australia. Even in Melbourne, the southernmost capital city on the mainland, it's a rare occasion when the mercury hits freezing point, although it's a different story in Canberra, the national capital. The poor Tasmanians, further to the south, have a good idea of what cold is.

As you head north the seasonal variations become fewer until, in the far north around Darwin, you are in the monsoon belt where there are just two seasons – hot and wet, and hot and dry. When the Wet hits Darwin, around November or December, it really does get wet. In the Snowy Mountains of southern New South Wales and the Alps of north-east Victoria there's a snow season with good skiing. The centre of the continent is arid – hot and dry during the day, but often bitterly cold at night.

Victoria and Tasmania are probably at their best at the height of summer, although spring and autumn are pretty good too. In the winter months of July and August, you might head south for the skiing but it's best to avoid Melbourne, which can be rather grey and miserable at this time.

By contrast, in the far north the best season is midwinter; Darwin is just right from July to August. In midsummer however it's often unbearably hot and humid; the sea is full of

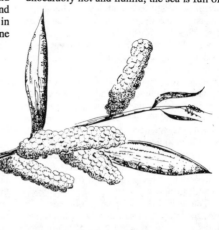

sea wasps (the deadly box jellyfish) and if there are cyclones about this is when they'll arrive. Similarly, in Alice Springs the midsummer temperatures can be far too high for comfort, while in midwinter the nights may be chilly but the days delightful.

FLORA & FAUNA
Native Plants

Despite vast tracts of dry and barren land, much of Australia is well vegetated. Forests cover 5%, or 410,000 sq km. Plants can be found even in the arid centre, though many of them grow and flower erratically. Human activities seriously threaten Australian flora but to date most species have survived.

Flowering gum

Origins Australia's distinctive vegetation began to take shape about 55 million years ago when Australia broke from the supercontinent of Gondwanaland, drifting away from Antarctica to warmer climes. At this time, Australia was completely covered by cool-climate rainforest, but due to its geographic isolation and the gradual drying of the continent, rainforests retreated, plants like eucalypts and wattles (acacias) took over and grasslands expanded. Eucalypts and wattles were able to adapt to warmer temperatures, the increased natural occurrence of fire and the later use of fire for hunting and other purposes by Aborigines. Now many species benefit from fire.

The arrival of Europeans 200 years ago saw the introduction of new flora, fauna and tools. Rainforests were logged, new crops and pasture grasses spread, hooved animals such as cows, sheep and goats damaged the soil, and watercourses were altered by dams. Irrigation, combined with excessive clearing of the land, gradually resulted in a serious increase in the salinity of the soil.

Wattle in flower

Distinctive Australian Plants The gum tree, or eucalypt, is ubiquitous in Australia except in the deepest rainforests and the most arid regions. Of the 700 species of the genus eucalyptus, 95% occur naturally in Australia, the rest in New Guinea, the Philippines and Indonesia.

Gum trees vary in form and height from the tall, straight hardwoods such as jarrah, karri, mountain ash and red river gum to the stunted, twisted snow gum with its colourful trunk striations. Other distinctive gums are the spotted variety of New South Wales's coast and the beautiful pink salmon gums of Katherine Gorge and elsewhere in the north. The gum tree features in Australian folklore, art and literature. Many varieties flower, the wood is prized and its oil is used for pharmaceuticals and perfumed products.

Fast-growing but short-lived wattles occur in many warm countries, but around 600 species are found in Australia, growing in a variety of conditions, from the arid inland to the rainforests of Tasmania. Many wattles have deep green leaves and bright yellow to orange flowers. Most species flower during late winter and spring. Then the country is ablaze with wattle and the reason for the choice of green and gold as our national colours is obvious. Wattle is Australia's floral emblem.

Many other species of Australian native plants flower but few are deciduous. Common natives include grevilleas, hakeas, banksias, waratahs, bottlebrushes (callistemons), paperbarks (melaleucas), teatrees, boronias, and bunya and hoop pines. An interesting book on the topic is *Field Guide to Native Plants of Australia* (Bay Books). You can see a wide range of Australian flora at the all-native National Botanic Gardens in Canberra. Brisbane's Mt Coot-tha Botanic Gardens features Australia's arid-zone plants.

Animals

Australia's most distinctive fauna are the marsupials and monotremes. Marsupials such as kangaroos and koalas give birth to partially developed young which they suckle in a pouch. Monotremes – platypuses and echidnas – lay eggs but also suckle their young on milk.

Since the arrival of Europeans in Australia 17 species of mammal have become extinct and 28 more are currently endangered. Many introduced non-native animals have been allowed to run wild and have caused a great deal of damage to native species and to Australian vegetation. Introduced animals include foxes, cats, pigs, goats, camels, donkeys, water buffalo, horses, starlings, blackbirds, cane toads and, best known of all, the notorious rabbit. Foxes and cats kill small native mammals and birds while rabbits denude vast areas of land, pigs carry disease and introduced birds take over the habitat of local species.

Kangaroos The extraordinary breeding cycle of the kangaroo is well adapted to Australia's harsh, often unpredictable environment.

The young kangaroo, or joey, just mm long at birth, claws its way unaided to the mother's pouch where it attaches itself to a nipple that expands inside its mouth. A day or two later the mother mates again, but the new embryo does not begin to develop until the first joey has left the pouch permanently.

At this point the mother produces two types of milk – one formula to feed the joey at heel, the other for the baby in her pouch. If environmental conditions are right, the mother will then mate again. If food or water is scarce, however, the breeding cycle will be interrupted until conditions improve.

Although kangaroos generally are not aggressive, males of the larger species, such as reds, can be dangerous when cornered. In the wild, boomers, as they are called, will grasp other males with their forearms, rear up on their muscular tails and pound their opponents with their hind feet, sometimes slashing them with their claws. Such behaviour can also be directed against dogs and, very rarely, people. It has also been said that kangaroos being pursued by dogs will sometimes hop into deep water and drown the dogs with their strong forearms.

There are now more kangaroos in Australia than there were when Europeans arrived, a result of the better availability of water and the creation of grasslands for sheep and cattle. Certain species are threatened, however, as their particular

Kangaroo

environments are being destroyed. In all there are about 45 species.

About three million kangaroos are culled legally each year, but probably as many more are killed for sport or by those farmers who believe the cull is insufficient to protect their paddocks from overgrazing by the animals.

Large kangaroos can be a hazard to people driving through the outback – hitting a two-metre kangaroo at 110 km/h is no joke.

Possums There is an enormous range of possums in Australia – they seem to have been able to adapt to all sorts of conditions, including those of the city, where you'll find them in parks, sometimes tame enough to eat from your hand. Look for them at dusk. Some large species are found in suburban roofs and will eat cultivated plants and food scraps.

Certain possums are small and extremely timid, such as the tiny honey possum, which is able to extract nectar from blossoms with its tube-like snout. Others are gliders, able to jump from treetop to treetop by extending flaps of membrane between their legs.

Wombats Wombats are slow, solid, powerfully built marsupials with broad heads and short, stumpy legs. These fairly placid and easily tamed creatures are also legally killed by farmers, who object to the damage done to paddocks by wombats digging large burrows and tunnelling under fences.

Koalas Koalas are distantly related to the wombat and are found along the eastern seaboard. Their cuddly appearance belies an irritable nature, and they will scratch and bite if sufficiently provoked.

Koalas initially carry their babies in pouches but later the larger young cling to their mothers' backs. They feed only on the leaves of certain types of eucalypt and are particularly sensitive to changes to their habitat. Today many koalas suffer from chlamydia, a sexually transmitted disease causing blindness and infertility.

Tasmanian Devils These carnivores are as ferocious as they look. Although it lives in groups, it gives a very good impression of detesting every other devil in sight, including its own offspring.

It's an ugly little creature found only in Tasmania, where the locals will gleefully torment visitors with morbid tales of its hideous habits. Its ability to chew through bone as easily as if it were cork is at the heart of its fearsome reputation. In fact, it only eats small mammals and birds.

Tasmanian Tigers The Tasmanian tiger, like the Tasmanian devil, was a carnivorous marsupial. At one time both the tiger *(thylacine)* and the devil were threatened with extinction. Efforts to avert this disaster ensured the survival of the latter, but the larger, dog-like tiger was unable to recover its numbers. The last known specimen died in Hobart Zoo in 1936, although there is still much speculation as to whether tigers still exist. Regular 'sightings' are reported, and these are often the cause for much excitement in the press, but as yet none of these sightings has been confirmed.

Platypuses & Echidnas The platypus and the echidna are the only living representatives of the most primitive group of mammals, the monotremes. Both lay eggs, as reptiles do, but suckle their young on milk secreted directly through the skin from mammary glands.

The amphibious platypus has a duck-like bill, webbed feet and a beaver-like body. Males have a poisonous spur on their hind feet. Recent research has shown that the platypus is able to sense electric currents in the water and uses this ability to track its prey.

Echidnas are spiny anteaters that hide from predators by digging vertically into the ground and covering themselves with dirt or rolling themselves into a ball and raising their sharp quills.

Dingoes Australia's native dog is the dingo, domesticated by the Aborigines and thought to have arrived with them 40,000 years ago.

Dingoes now prey on rabbits and sometimes livestock, and are considered vermin by many farmers.

Birds

The Royal Australasian Ornithologists Union runs bird observatories in New South Wales, Victoria and West Australia, which provide accommodation and guides. Contact the RAOU (☎ (03) 370 1422) at 21 Gladstone St, Moonee Ponds, Victoria 3039.

Emus & Cassowaries The only bird larger than the emu is the African ostrich, also flightless. It's a shaggy-feathered, often curious bird. After the female lays the eggs the male hatches them and raises the young.

Cassowaries are smaller than emus and more colourful. They are found in the rainforests of north Queensland.

Parrots & Cockatoos There is an amazing variety of these birds throughout Australia. The noisy pink and grey galahs are amongst the most common, although the sulphur-crested cockatoos have to be the noisiest. Rosellas have one of the most brilliant colour schemes and in some parks they're not at all backward about taking a free feed from visitors.

Rainbow lorikeets are more extravagantly colourful than you can imagine until you've seen one. They're quite common from northern New South Wales up. Budgerigars are mainly found towards the Centre; they often fly in flocks numbering 10,000 or more.

Kookaburras A member of the kingfisher family, the kookaburra is heard as much as it is seen – you can't miss its loud, cackling cry. Kookaburras can become quite tame and pay regular visits to friendly households, but only if the food is excellent. It's hard to impress a kookaburra with anything less than top-class steak.

Bower Birds The bower bird has a unique mating practice. The male builds a bower which he decorates with various coloured objects to attract females. In the wild, flowers or stones are used, but if artificial objects (clothes pegs, plastic pens, bottle tops – anything brightly coloured, but usually white, blue or green) are available, they'll certainly use them. The females are impressed by the males' neatly built bowers and attractively displayed treasures, but once they've mated all the hard work is left to her. He goes back to refurbishing the bower and attracting more females while she hops off to build a nest.

Snakes

Australian snakes are generally shy and try to avoid confrontations with humans. A few, however, are deadly. The most dangerous are the taipans and tiger snakes, although death adders, copperheads, brown snakes and red-bellied black snakes should also be avoided. Tiger snakes will actually attack. It's a good idea to stay right away from all snakes – and don't try stepping over them when they're asleep!

Crocodiles

There are two types of crocodile in Australia: the extremely dangerous saltwater crocodile, or saltie as it's known, and the less aggressive freshwater crocodile, or freshie.

Salties are not confined to salt water. They inhabit estuaries, and following floods may be found many km from the coast. They may even be found in permanent fresh water more than 100 km inland. It is important to be able to tell the difference between the saltie and its less dangerous relative, as both are prolific in northern Australia.

Freshies are smaller than salties – anything over four metres should be regarded as a saltie. Freshies are also more finely constructed and have much narrower snouts and smaller teeth. Salties, which can grow to seven metres, will attack and kill humans. Freshies, though unlikely to seek human prey, have been known to bite, and children in particular should be kept away from them.

Spiders

Most Australian spiders bite. In particular, two spiders to keep away from are the

Saltwater crocodile

Freshwater crocodile

redback, a relative of the American black widow, and the Sydney funnel-web. The redback is more widespread and has a legendary liking for toilet seats. Both are extremely poisonous and have been lethal. You should also beware of the white-tailed spider, commonly found in fields and gardens. It is slightly smaller than a 10c coin, with a distinct white spot on its grey-black back. Some people have extreme reactions to its bites and gangrene can result.

NATIONAL PARKS & RESERVES

Australia has more than 500 national parks – non-urban protected wilderness areas of environmental or natural importance. Each state defines and runs its own national parks, but the principle is the same throughout Australia. National parks include rainforests, vast tracts of empty outback, strips of coastal dune land and long, rugged mountain ranges.

Public access is encouraged if safety and conservation regulations are observed. In all parks you're asked to do nothing to damage or alter the natural environment. Approach roads, camping grounds (often with toilets and showers), walking tracks and information centres are often provided for visitors.

Some national parks are so isolated, rugged or uninviting that you wouldn't want to do much except look unless you were an experienced, well-prepared bushwalker or climber. Other parks, however, are among Australia's major attractions and some of the most beautiful have been included on the World Heritage List (a United Nations list of natural or cultural places of world significance that would be an irreplaceable loss to the planet if they were altered).

Internationally, the World Heritage List includes the Taj Mahal, the Pyramids, the Grand Canyon and, currently, eight Australian areas: the Great Barrier Reef; most of Kakadu National Park in the Northern Territory; the Willandra Lakes region of far west New South Wales, where human bones about 40,000 years old have been found; the Lord Howe Island group off New South Wales; the Tasmanian wilderness heritage area (South West, Lower Gordon Wild Rivers and Cradle

Mountain – Lake St Clair national parks); the east coast temperate and subtropical rainforest parks (15 national parks and reserves, covering 1000 sq km in the eastern highlands of New South Wales); and the wet tropics area of far north Queensland, which is in the Daintree-Cape Tribulation area. Further areas – Shark Bay on the Western Australian coast, and Fraser Island off the Queensland coast – are currently nominated for listing and will almost certainly be added.

Before a site or area is accepted for the World Heritage List it has first to be proposed by its country then must pass a series of tests at the UN culminating, if it is successful, in acceptance by the UN World Heritage Committee which meets late each year. Any country proposing one of its sites or areas for the list must agree to protect the selected area, keeping it for the enjoyment of future generations even if to do so requires help from other countries.

While state governments have authority over their own national parks, the federal government is responsible for ensuring that Australia meets its international treaty obligations, and in any dispute arising from a related conflict between a state and the federal government, the latter can override the former.

In this way the federal government can force a state to protect an area with World Heritage listing, as it did when the Tasmanian government wanted, in the early 1980s, to dam the Gordon River in the south-west of the state and thereby flood much of the wild Franklin River.

For National Park authority addresses see the Information section of the Facts for the Visitor chapter.

State Forests

Another form of nature reserve you may discover is the state forest. These are owned by state governments and have fewer regulations than national parks. In theory, the state forests can be logged, but often they are primarily recreational areas with campgrounds, walking trails and signposted forest drives. Some permit horses and dogs.

POPULATION & PEOPLE

Australia's population is about 17 million. The most populous states are New South Wales and Victoria, each with a capital city (Sydney and Melbourne) with a population of over three million. The population is concentrated along the east coast strip from Adelaide to Cairns and in the similar but smaller coastal region in Western Australia. The centre of the country is very sparsely populated. There are about 150,000 Aborigines, most heavily concentrated in central Australia and the far north.

Until WW II Australians were predominantly of British and Irish descent but that has changed dramatically since the war. First there was heavy migration from Europe creating major Greek and Italian populations but also adding Yugoslavs, Lebanese, Turks and other groups.

More recently Australia has had large influxes of Asians, particularly Vietnamese after the Vietnam war. In comparison to the country's population Australia probably took more Vietnamese refugees than any other Western nation. On the whole these 'new Australians' have been remarkably well accepted and 'multi-culturalism' is a popular concept in Australia.

If you come to Australia in search of a real Australian you will find one quite easily – they are not known to be a shy breed. He or she may be a Lebanese cafe owner, an English used-car salesperson, an Aboriginal artist, a Malaysian architect or a Greek greengrocer. And you will find them in pubs, on beaches, at barbecues, mustering yards and art galleries. And yes, you may meet a Mick (Crocodile) Dundee or two but he is strictly a country model – the real Paul Hogan was a Sydney Harbour Bridge painter, a job where after you finish at one end you just start again at the other.

The Aborigines

It is believed that the ancestors of the Aborigines journeyed from Indonesia to the Australian mainland more than 40,000 years ago. Archaeological evidence suggests that the descendants of these first settlers colonised the whole of the continent within a few thousand years. They were among the earliest people in the world to manufacture polished edge-ground stone tools, cremate their dead and engrave and paint representations of themselves and the animals they hunted.

Aborigines were traditionally tribal people living in extended family groups. Wisdom and skills obtained over millennia enabled Aborigines to use their environment to the maximum. An intimate knowledge of the behaviour of animals and the correct time to harvest the many plants they utilised ensured that food shortages were rare. They never hunted an animal species or harvested a plant species to the point where it was threatened with extinction. Like other hunter-gatherer peoples of the world, the Aborigines were true ecologists.

Although Aborigines in northern Australia had been in regular contact with the farming peoples of Indonesia for at least 1000 years, the farming of crops and domestication of livestock held no appeal.

The only major modification of the landscape practised by the Aborigines was the selective burning of undergrowth in forests and dead grass on the plains. This encouraged new growth, which in turn attracted game animals to the area, and prevented the build-up of combustible material in the forests, making hunting easier and reducing the possibility of major bush fires. Dingoes were domesticated to assist in the hunt and to guard the camp from intruders.

Similar technology – for example the boomerang and spear – was used throughout the continent, but techniques were adapted to the environment and the species being hunted. In the wetlands of northern Australia, fish traps hundreds of metres long made of bamboo and cord were built to catch fish at the end of the wet season. In the area now known as Victoria, permanent stone weirs many km long were used to trap migrating eels, while in the tablelands of Queensland finely woven nets were used to snare herds of wallabies and kangaroos.

Dwellings ranged from the beehive stone houses of Victoria's windswept western district to elevated platforms constructed by the peoples of the humid, mosquito-infested tropics.

The simplicity of the Aborigines' technology is in contrast with the sophistication of their cultural life. Religion, history, law and art are integrated in complex ceremonies which depict the activities of the ancestral beings who created the landscape and its people, and prescribe codes of behaviour and responsibilities for looking after the land and all living things.

Songs explain how the landscape contains these powerful creator ancestors, who can still exert either a benign or a malevolent influence. They also tell of the best places and the best times to hunt, where to find water in drought years, and specify kinship relations and correct marriage partners.

Ceremonies are still performed in many parts of Australia and the features of the landscape believed to be metamorphosed ancestral beings of the Dreamtime are commonly referrred to as 'sacred sites'. Many such sites are believed to be dangerous and entry is prohibited under traditional Aboriginal law. These restrictions may seem merely the result of superstition, but in many cases they have a pragmatic origin. One site in northern Australia was believed to cause sores to break out all over the body of anyone visiting the area. Subsequently, the area was found to have a dangerously high level of radiation from naturally occurring radon gas. In another instance, fishing from a certain reef was traditionally prohibited. This restriction was scoffed at by local Europeans until it was discovered that fish from this area had a high incidence of ciguatera, which renders fish poisonous if eaten by humans.

At the time of the settlement of Sydney Cove around 200 years ago, there were about 300,000 Aborigines in Australia and over 300 different languages. Many were as distinct from each other as English is from Chinese. Tasmania alone had five languages, and tribes living on opposite sides of present-day Sydney Harbour spoke mutually unintelligible languages.

In a society based on family groups with an egalitarian political structure, a co-ordinated response to the European colonisers was not possible. When Governor Phillip raised the flag at Sydney Cove in 1788, the laws of England became the law governing all Aborigines in the Australian continent. All land in Australia was from that moment the property of the English Crown.

If the Aborigines had had a readily recognisable political system and had resisted colonisation by organised force of arms, then the English might have been forced to recognise a prior title to the land and therefore legitimise their colonisation by entering into a treaty with the Aboriginal land owners.

Without any legal right to the lands they once lived on, Aborigines throughout the country became dispossessed; some were driven from their country by force, and some succumbed to exotic diseases. Others voluntarily left their lands to travel to the fringes of settled areas to obtain new commodities such as steel and cloth, and experience hitherto unknown drugs such as tea, tobacco, alcohol and narcotics.

At a local level, settlement was resisted. Warriors including Pemulwy, Yagan, Dundalli, Pigeon and Nemarluk were, for a time, feared by the colonists in their areas. But although some settlements had to be abandoned, the effect of such resistance only temporarily postponed the inevitable.

By the early 1900s legislation designed to segregate and 'protect' Aboriginal people was passed in all states. The legislation imposed restrictions on Aborigines' right to own property, to seek employment, and even allowed the state to remove children from Aboriginal mothers if it was suspected that the father was non-Aboriginal. Many Aborigines are still bitter about having been separated from their families and forced to grow up apart from their people.

The process of social change was accelerated by WW II – a number of Aborigines served with distinction in the Australian armed forces at this time. White Australians became increasingly aware of the inequity of their treatment of Aborigines and, in 1967 Australians voted to give the Commonwealth government power to legislate for Aborigines in all states.

One of the major tasks facing the government is responding to Aborigines' request that a proportion of the land owned by their ancestors be returned. Aborigines in the Northern Territory have been granted title to large areas of marginal land, formerly designated as Aboriginal reserves. The granting of land rights in other states has been delayed because most land is privately owned, and would have to be purchased by the government.

Aborigines form between 1% and 2% of the nation's population. Dozens of books have been written about them, yet they remain the least understood of Australia's minorities.

Facts for the Bushwalker

VISAS

Once upon a time, Australia was fairly free and easy about who was allowed to visit the country, particularly if you were from the UK or Canada. These days, only New Zealanders get any sort of preferential treatment and even they need at least a passport. Everybody else has to have a visa.

Tourist Visas

Tourist visas are issued by Australian consular offices abroad; they are free and valid for a stay of *up to* six months. That is, you can say you want to stay for six months and if they like the look of you the immigration official can give you six months. If they don't you might end up with two weeks.

As well as the visa, visitors are also required to have an onward or return ticket and 'sufficient funds' – the latter is obviously open to interpretation.

US citizens can now get visas from the Qantas offices in Los Angeles and San Francisco, if they are buying Qantas tickets.

Visa Extensions

Visa extensions are made through Department of Immigration offices in Australia and there's a $50 application fee. That's a fee simply for applying, and regardless of how long you want an extension for – *and* if they turn down your application they can still keep your 50 bucks! Some offices, like the one in Sydney, can be very thorough, requiring things like bank statements and interviews. Extending visas has always been a notoriously slow process and Australia's tourist boom has certainly not made it any easier. If you do end up overstaying your visa the fact that you did your damnedest to get the bureaucrats to extend it should stand in your favour.

MONEY
Currency

Australia's currency is good, old-fashioned dollars and cents. When they changed over from pounds, shillings and pence there was consideration of calling the new unit the 'royal'; however, that foolish idea soon got the chop. There are coins for 5c, 10c, 20c, 50c, $1 and $2, and notes for $5, $10, $20, $50 and $100.

There are no notable restrictions on importing or exporting currency or travellers' cheques except that you may not take out more than A$5000 except with prior approval.

Exchange Rates

In recent years the Australian dollar has fluctuated quite markedly against the US dollar, although these days it seems to have stabilised.

C$1   = A$1.15
DM 1   = A$0.90
HK$10 = A$1.75
NZ$1   = A$0.75
UK£1   = A$2.60
US$1   = A$1.35
Y100   = A$1.10

Changing Money

There is a variety of ways to carry your money around Australia with you. If your stay is limited then travellers' cheques are the most straightforward and they generally enjoy a better exchange rate than foreign cash in Australia.

Changing foreign currency or travellers' cheques is no problem at almost any bank. It's done quickly and efficiently and never involves the sort of headaches and grand production that changing foreign currency in the USA always entails. American Express, Thomas Cook and other well-known international brands of travellers' cheques are all widely used in Australia. A passport will usually be adequate for identification; it would be sensible to carry a driver's licence,

credit cards and a plane ticket in case of problems.

Commissions and fees for changing foreign currency travellers' cheques seem to vary from bank to bank and year to year. It's worth making a few phone calls to see which bank currently has the lowest charges. Some charge a flat fee for each transaction, while others take a percentage of the amount changed. The average fee to change a US$100 cheque is between A$2 and A$5. Australian dollar travellers' cheques can be exchanged immediately at the bank cashier's window without being converted from a foreign currency or incurring commissions, fees and exchange rate fluctuations.

WHEN TO GO

Any time! Australia is a large country covering many climatic zones and there is always an area providing excellent walking. Having said that there are preferred seasons for each region.

In general, the alpine regions of the southern states, Victoria and Tasmania are at their best during the mild summers from December to March. In winter, many of these good walking areas are covered with snow and more suited for cross country or nordic skiing. Of course, there are some exceptions as the coastline can provide some surprisingly enjoyable walking during the colder months.

As you travel further north into Queensland the weather patterns flip over with the unpleasant season being the wet summer months. In the far north of Australia the winter season from May to September is far more pleasant for walking. In between the two extremes, New South Wales has something to suit every season.

As the best season for walking varies so much, a table of walk standards and seasons has been included (see pages 38-39).

There are times best avoided; these are the local extended holiday periods when most Australians head into the bush somewhere. Places become booked out or overcrowded and inevitably prices are often more expensive. The Christmas break from late December until mid January is best avoided as is the Easter holiday which is held in March or April. Three-day weekends are also popular for getting away from it all but these holidays vary from state to state. In some places the school holiday break can be the most popular. Calendars showing the holidays for the next year are usually available each year from October on.

WHAT TO BRING
Clothing
Rainwear Up north it is usually far too hot to be covered in waterproof clothing. If you want to keep dry a simple cape or poncho is suitable and not too hot; or you could take an umbrella for wide tracks.

Down south a waterproof jacket is essential. Suitable jackets are made from Goretex, Japara or proofed nylon and should have a hood.

Most walkers carry a pair of waterproof overpants as well for colder conditions.

General Clothing In warmer regions a pair of shorts, long-sleeved light shirt and a light jumper or jacket will be sufficient for all needs. In cooler areas long pants are also needed and all clothing should be either of wool or synthetics that remain warm in wet conditions.

If snowfalls are a possibility take warm gloves and a hat. The notes for each walk will indicate what is needed.

Gaiters Canvas or nylon leggings, that extend from the ankle to just below the knee, are useful for protection against sharp or prickly grasses and bushes and for keeping mud out of boots. Use of gaiters is a matter of choice, with some bushwalkers always wearing them and others who rarely put them on.

Equipment
Australia covers wide geographical zones and large distances, and this creates its own problems for bushwalkers. Equipment and techniques designed for the cooler regions of the south do not perform adequately in the warmer climates of the north. Most walkers have their own set of equipment which works best for them and either make do or modify it when visiting a region with a markedly different climate.

The following suggested equipment is suitable for bushwalking in many areas of Australia. If anything special is needed for a particular walk or area it is described in the Equipment section for that particular walk.

It is sometimes possible to hire equipment in the capital city of each state, however, equipment for hire may be of poor quality or very well worn. Equipment in Australia is relatively expensive but some of it is unavailable elsewhere and worth buying.

Most New Zealand brands are well represented, including nylon tents designed for local conditions. Many of the well-known American and European brands of packs, tents and clothing can also be bought in bushwalking shops. Both Australian and imported brands of boots are available in bushwalking shops. The local boots have improved significantly and are almost as good as the European models. Canvas packs (they are almost waterproof, unlike nylon and cordura) are still in production in internal frame designs and should be considered if waterproofness is important.

Pack There is an amazing variety available, so you can easily buy a reasonably comfortable pack. Frame design is unimportant provided it is well made from strong materials and is comfortable for the individual to carry. The best place to buy a good quality pack is from a bushwalking shop.

Make sure the pack is going to be large enough for the biggest load you intend to carry. A 70-litre (a fairly standard size) is sufficient for most walkers with normal equipment and up to seven days food. For longer bushwalks an 80-litre or larger pack may be needed.

The very cheap packs available in the disposal and large retail stores are not recommended as they break easily and are capable of ruining your holiday! Most packs leak, so a waterproof pack liner of either nylon or plastic is a good idea.

Sleeping Bag With the broad temperature ranges from season to season in each state, there is no ideal sleeping bag. The most useful sleeping bags have long zippers which enable them to be used zipped up in cold weather and unzipped as a rug in warmer weather. For the southern half of Australia a sleeping bag containing 700 grams of super down is a good, general purpose bag.

If you intend visiting the alpine areas in the winter months then a warmer bag with 900 grams or more of super down is suggested. For the northern half of Australia a sleeping bag is often not needed. Around the coast a very light sleeping bag with 500 to 550 grams of super down will do for all seasons. Inland, in central Australia, it can fall below freezing at night and a warmer sleeping bag with at least 700 grams of super down is recommended.

For bushwalkers who are allergic to super down (or simply cannot afford it) synthetic filled bags are a realistic, cheaper alternative. These bags are heavier and bulkier to carry (make sure your pack is large enough). For short walks of only a few days they function well.

Sleeping bag liners are useful as they add some warmth and keep the sleeping bag much cleaner. Liners are usually made from light cotton or silk (expensive) and are available at most bushwalking shops.

Sleeping Mats Not essential but can dramatically improve the quality of sleep. Closed-cell foam and inflatable foam filled mats are the most popular. In the warmer areas air-filled 'lilos' are suitable.

Tent This can be a crucial item making the difference between an enjoyable holiday and a disaster. For many bushwalks a medium price tent with a tent fly is adequate. Such tents cost between $100 and $200. Up north many bushwalkers don't use a tent at all, but a large waterproof fly sheet for shelter. This works well in rainforests but allows insects to attack at night.

If walking in the alpine areas of Victoria and New South Wales or in Tasmania where severe storms can be expected, higher quality tents are needed. These tents are more waterproof (no tent is ever completely waterproof) and designed to withstand windy conditions. High quality tents can cost over $500 or more and while not cheap are worthwhile for the comfort and safety they can provide. If such a tent is needed it is indicated in the notes on equipment for each walk.

As most tent floors leak at times a useful extra is a groundsheet. This is simply a large piece of waterproof material which can be placed on top of the tent floor. You can also sit on it at lunch time (it has many uses!).

Footwear For most bushwalks, runners (also called sandshoes or tennis shoes) or light boots are suitable. Light boots are the best all round as they provide some ankle support and perform better on wet, slippery tracks. In areas which are extremely wet (notably Tasmania) medium to heavy boots are recommended. The most suitable type of footwear is given in the notes on equipment for each walk.

Water Containers For most bushwalking areas leakproof containers of one or two-litre capacity for carrying drinking water are sufficient. Screw-top aluminium bottles are popular and reliable. Plastic bottles can also be used but often leak. One exception to this is the range of laboratory-style bottles marketed by Nalgene – these also come with wide mouths.

Larger quantities of water can be carried in a winecask bladder, bought from a bushwalking shop; or buy a wine cask, enjoy the contents and then use the bladder.

Stove & Fuel All bushwalkers should carry a stove and know how to use it, because in some areas campfires are banned and in others dead wood has become difficult to find. Stoves vary greatly in price and style.

For short walks, methylated spirits and pressurised gas stoves work well and are easy to operate. For extended bushwalks, however, efficiency becomes more important and shellite or kerosene stoves are more practical.

Shellite is also known as white gas, camping gas and white spirits. In the event of unavailability, unleaded (standard) petrol can be used as a substitute. It can be bought at many bushwalking shops, in supermarkets and from some of the special bushwalking transport operators.

Compass Almost all bushwalkers use a compass for aid with navigation. The most popular and reliable styles are the liquid-filled 'Silva'and 'Suunto'. There are several brands now available and all seem to work well.

Magnetic deviation in Australia is not great and varies from 4° west (in Western Australia) to 12° east (in south-east Australia) and is clearly marked on most maps. Silva recognises five magnetic zones so you need to make sure that the compass you buy is balanced for magnetic south (suitable for use in Australia). If you use a compass from the northern hemisphere you will notice that the south end of the needle will dip toward the ground making it difficult to use accurately.

Suitable compasses cost about $25 to $40 in bushwalking shops and are definitely a worthwhile purchase.

Map Case Maps should be carried for all bushwalks in plastic bags or in a waterproof mapcase. Note that for each walk in this guide, topographic maps are recommended as the maps in this book are not intended to be used on their own.

Cooking Equipment Two aluminium billies are all you need for cooking most meals, although a lightweight frypan can be useful. Steel billies are not recommended as they rust quickly. Billy grips (or billy tongs)

are a good idea to prevent burnt fingers. Select cookware that can be stacked neatly inside each other.

Equipment Checklist

The following list is given as a general guide and is suitable for many areas of Australia. As experience is gained individual preferences will modify the following suggestions:

- Tent with pegs, poles, guy ropes and fly
- Groundsheet
- Spare nylon cord
- Pack with waterproof liner
- Sleeping bag and inner sheet
- Insulation mat (foam or air filled)
- Waterproof jacket and overpants
- Gaiters
- Warm hat (balaclava or beanie) and gloves
- Sun hat
- Long-sleeved Shirt
- Jumper or warm jacket
- Warm pants
- Spare underwear and socks
- Runners or boots
- Stove and fuel
- Billies and billy grips
- Pot scourer
- Eating utensils
- Water containers
- Trowel for toilet use
- Torch with spare batteries and globe
- Candles and matches
- First aid kit and toiletries
- Sunscreen
- Map, guides and compass
- Notebook and pencil
- Whistle
- Camera and film

Bushwalking Equipment Suppliers

There are specialist bushwalking shops in most of Australia's major cities. They are the best place to buy maps, guidebooks and equipment particular to that state. For a comprehensive list of shops refer to the current issue of *Wild* magazine.

Australian Capital Territory
Kathmandu (☎ (06) 257 5926), Shop 6, BMI Building, City Walk, Canberra 2600
Mountain Designs (☎ (06) 247 7488), 7 Lonsdale St, Braddon, 2601
Paddy Pallin (☎ (06) 257 3883), 11 Lonsdale St, Braddon 2601

New South Wales

Kathmandu (☎ (02) 261 8901), Shop 3A, Town Hall Arcade, cnr Kent & Bathurst Sts, Sydney 2000

Mountain Designs (☎ (02) 267 8238), 494 Kent St, Sydney 2000

Mountain Equipment (☎ (02) 264 3146), 291 Sussex St, Sydney 2000

Paddy Pallin (☎ (02) 264 2685), 507 Kent St, Sydney 2000

Southern Cross Equipment (☎ (02) 261 3435), 493 Kent St, Sydney 2000

Queensland

Kathmandu (☎ ((07) 252 8054), 144 Wickham St, Fortitude Valley 4006

Mountain Designs (☎ (07) 221 6756), 105 Albert St, Brisbane, 4000

Torre Mountain Craft (☎ (07) 870 2699), 40 High St, Toowong, 4066

South Australia

Mountain Designs (☎ (08) 232 0690), 76 Pirie St, Adelaide, 5000

Thor Paddy Pallin (☎ (08) 232 3155), 228 Rundle St, Adelaide 5000

Tasmania

Allgoods (☎ (003) 31 3644), 71 York St, Launceston 7250

Backpackers Barn (☎ (004) 24 3628), 12 Edward St, Devonport, 7310

Jolly Swagman (☎ (002) 34 3999), 107 Elizabeth St, Hobart 7000

Paddy Pallin (☎ (002) 31 0777), 76 Elizabeth St, Hobart 7000

Victoria

Bowyangs (Maps & Guides), (☎ (03) 862 3526), 259 High St, Kew 3101

Kathmandu (☎ (03) 642 1942), 78 Hardware St, Melbourne 3000

Mountain Designs (☎ (03) 670 3354), 377 Little Bourke St, Melbourne 3000

Outsports (☎ (03) 523 5727), 340B Hawthorn Rd, Caulfield South, 3162

Paddy Pallin (☎ (03) 670 4845), 360 Little Bourke St, Melbourne 3000

The Wilderness Shop (☎ (03) 898 3742), 1 Carrington Rd, Box Hill 3128

Western Australia

Mountain Designs (☎ (09) 322 4774), 862 Hay St, Perth 6000

Paddy Pallin (☎ (03) 321 2666), 1/891 Hay St, Perth, 6000

Wilderness Equipment (☎ (09) 335 2813), 29 Jewell Parade, North Fremantle 6159

TOURIST OFFICES

There are a number of information sources for visitors to Australia and, in common with a number of other tourist-conscious Western countries, you can easily drown yourself in brochures and booklets, maps and leaflets.

Local Tourist Offices

Within Australia, tourist information is handled by the various state and local offices. Each state and the ACT and Northern Territory have a tourist office of some form. Apart from a main office in the capital cities, they often have regional offices in main tourist centres and also in other states. Tourist information in Victoria is handled by the Royal Automobile Club of Victoria (RACV) organisation in Melbourne.

As well as supplying brochures, price lists, maps and other information, the state offices will often book transport, tours and accommodation for you. Unfortunately, very few of the state tourist offices maintain information desks at the airports and, furthermore, the opening hours of the city offices are very much of the 9-to-5 weekdays and Saturday-morning-only variety. Addresses of the state tourist offices are:

Australian Capital Territory

Canberra Tourist Bureau, Jolimont Centre, Northbourne Ave, Canberra City, ACT 2601 (☎ (06) 254 6464)

New South Wales

Travel Centre of NSW, 19 Castlereagh St, Sydney, NSW 2000 (☎ (02) 231 4444)

Northern Territory

Northern Territory Government Tourist Bureau, 31 Smith St, Darwin, NT 0800 (☎ (089) 81 6611)

Queensland

Queensland Government Travel Centre, corner Adelaide and Edward Sts, Brisbane, Qld 4000 (☎ (07) 221 6111)

South Australia

South Australian Government Travel Centre, 18 King William St, Adelaide, SA 5000 (☎ (08) 212 1505)

Tasmania

Tasmanian Travel Centre, 80 Elizabeth St, Hobart, Tas 7000 (☎ (002) 30 0250)

Victoria

RACV Travel Centre, 230 Collins St, Melbourne, Vic 3000 (☎ (03) 650 1522)

Western Australia

Western Australian Tourist Centre, Forrest Place, Perth, WA 6000 (☎ (09) 483 1111)

USEFUL ORGANISATIONS

If entering a national park it is usually necessary to inform the ranger of your presence. In most parks permission for bushwalking is automatically given and useful advice is often available.

There are a few parks which have no ranger station near the walking areas. In this case information about your proposed route can usually be left with the closest police station. As the police department in each state have an experienced search and rescue team this is usually the best body to leave details with anyway.

There are a few popular parks where limits are imposed on bushwalkers and in very small parks overnight camping is usually banned. For all the walks, the relevant permits needed are detailed in the notes about each walk.

National Park Organisations

Australia has an extensive collection of

national parks. In fact, the Royal National Park just outside Sydney is the second oldest national park in the world; only Yellowstone Park in the USA predates it.

The national park organisations in each state are state operated, not nationally run. They tend to be a little hidden away in their capital city locations, although if you search them out they often have excellent literature and maps on the parks. They are much more up-front in the actual parks where, in many cases, they have very good guides and leaflets to bushwalking, nature trails and other activities. The state offices are:

Australian Capital Territory
  Parks & Conservation, PO Box 158, Canberra, ACT 2601
  Australian National Parks & Wildlife Service, 3rd floor, Construction House, Turner, ACT 2601 (PO Box 636, Canberra City, ACT 2601)
New South Wales
  National Parks & Wildlife Service, 43 Bridge St, Hurstville, NSW 2220 (PO Box 1967, Hurstville, NSW 2220)
Northern Territory
  Conservation Commission of the Northern Territory, PO Box 1046, Alice Springs, NT 0800
  Australian National Parks & Wildlife Service, PO Box 1260, Darwin, NT 0800 (for Kakadu and Uluru National Parks)
Queensland
  National Parks & Wildlife Service, 160 Ann St, Brisbane, Qld 4000 (PO Box 155, North Quay, Qld 4002)
South Australia
  National Parks & Wildlife Service, Insurance Building, 55 Grenfell St, Adelaide, SA 5061 (GPO Box 667, Adelaide, SA 5001)
Tasmania
  Department of Parks, Wildlife & Heritage, 134 Macquarie St, Hobart, Tas 7000 (PO Box 44A, Hobart 7001)
Victoria
  Department of Conservation & Environment, 240 Victoria Parade, East Melbourne, Vic 3002 (PO Box 41)
Western Australia
  Department of Conservation & Land Management, 50 Hayman Rd, Como, Perth, WA 6152

Bushwalking Federations & Clubs

There are several hundred bushwalking clubs in Australia and most of them welcome visitors and new members. Most clubs are members of a state federation which can be contacted in advance by letter for a list of their current member clubs.

If you arrive in an area without any contacts or addresses and wish to join a club the best starting point is to visit the local bushwalking shops. Many of the staff will be members of one or more of the local clubs and should be able to advise you of the location of the next meeting.

Some clubs are also listed in the Yellow Pages telephone book under 'Clubs – Bushwalking'. Most clubs publish a walks program and usually allow visitors to participate on most walks. It is essential to contact the walk leader first before assuming that participation will be allowed.

South Australia, Western Australia and the Northern Territory do not have a federation and the major clubs are the best contact for bushwalking. Bushwalking shops will be able to help as well.

New South Wales
> NSW Federation of Bushwalking Clubs, GPO Box 2090, Sydney, 2001.

Northern Territory
> Darwin Bushwalking Club, PO Box 1938, Darwin, 5794.

Queensland
> Queensland Federation of Bushwalking Clubs, GPO Box 1573, Brisbane, 4001.

South Australia
> Adelaide Bushwalkers, 34 Strapsey Avenue, Hazelwood Park, 5066.

Tasmania
> There is a federation but its address has altered several times. There are three major walking clubs who welcome visitors and can direct bushwalkers to the other clubs.
> Hobart Walking Club, PO Box 753H, Hobart, 7001.
> Launceston Walking Club, PO Box 273C, Launceston, 7250.
> North-west Walking Club, PO Box 107, Ulverstone, 7315.

Victoria
> Federation of Victorian Walking Clubs, GPO Box 815F, Melbourne, 3001.

Western Australia
> Perth Bushwalkers, 2 Pearl Parade, Scarborough, 6091.
> Western Walking Club, 57 Alderbury St, Floreat Park, 6014.

Australian Conservation Foundation

The Australian Conservation Foundation (ACF) is the largest nongovernment organisation involved in.conservation. Only 9 to 10% of its income is from the government; the rest comes from memberships and subscriptions, and from donations (72%), which are mainly from individuals.

The ACF covers a wide range of issues, including the greenhouse effect and depletion of the ozone layer, the negative effects of logging, preservation of rainforests, the problems of land degradation, and protection of the Antarctic. They frequently work in conjunction with the Wilderness Society and other conservation groups.

Australian Conservation Foundation logo

Wilderness Society

The Tasmanian Wilderness Society was formed by conservationists who had been unsuccessful in preventing the damming of Lake Pedder in south-west Tasmania but who were determined to prevent the destruction of the Franklin River. The Franklin River campaign was one of Australia's first major conservation confrontations and it caught the attention of the international media. In 1983, after the High Court decided against the damming of the Franklin, the group changed its name to the Wilderness Society because of their Australia-wide focus on wilderness issues.

The Wilderness Society is involved in issues concerning protection of the Australian wilderness, such as forest management and logging. Like the ACF, government funding is only a small percentage of their income, the rest coming from memberships, donations, the shops and merchandising. There are Wilderness Society shops in all states (not in the Northern Territory) where you can buy books, T-shirts, posters, badges, etc.

Australian Trust for Conservation Volunteers

This nonpolitical, nonprofit group organises practical conservation projects (such as tree planting, track construction and flora & fauna surveys) for volunteers to take part in. Travellers are welcome and it's an excellent way to get involved with the conservation movement and, at the same time, visit some of the more interesting areas of the country. Past volunteers have found themselves working in places such as Tasmania, Kakadu and Fraser Island.

Most projects last for a week and all food, transport and accommodation is supplied in return for a small contribution to help cover costs. Most travellers who take part in ATCV join an Echidna Package, which lasts six weeks and includes six different projects. The cost is $460, and further weeks can be added for $63.

Guiding Companies

There are a few commercial companies who offer guided walking holidays in Australia. These vary from base camp-style to extended bushwalks where each person must carry all their own equipment. The list included here is not comprehensive and covers selected established operators. There are many others who can be located through the tourist offices and travel agencies. If you are considering a guided bushwalk further information may be obtained from the company or the tourist agencies in each state. Most companies are willing to arrange special trips for medium to large size groups,

Australian Hiking Adventures (☎ (03) 850 7997), 2 Edgevale Rd, Bulleen, Victoria, 3105. Runs bushwalks of varied lengths to alpine and coastal areas of Victoria.

Bogong Jack Adventures (☎ (057) 27 3382), PO Box 221, Oxley, Victoria, 3678. Run several bushwalks around the Bogong High Plains area of Victoria.

Craclair Tours (☎ (004) 24 3971), PO Box 516, Devonport, Tasmania, 7310. Run several extended trips in central Tasmania. This is the most experienced company for guided walks along the Overland Track in the Cradle Mountain-Lake St Clair National Park.

Peregrine Adventures (☎ (03) 663 8611), 2nd floor, 258 Lonsdale St, Melbourne, Victoria, 3000. Run rafting trips on the Franklin River and combined rafting, walking and cycling trips!

Rafting Tasmania (☎ (002) 27 8293), 63 Channel Highway, Taroona, Tasmania, 7053. Run rafting trips on various rivers including the Franklin.

Tasmanian Highland Tours (☎ (004) 26 9312), PO Box 168, Latrobe, Tasmania, 7307. Run extended walks along the Overland Track and to nearby areas.

Thor Adventure Travel (☎ (08) 232 3155), 228 Rundle St, Adelaide, South Australia, 5000. Run several extended guided walks to various parts of the Flinders Ranges.

Wilderness Expeditions (☎ (02) 956 8099), 3rd floor, 73 Walker St, North Sydney, 2060. Run several extended guided walks in southern New South Wales including the Budawangs and northern Kosciusko areas.

Wilderness Tours (☎ (002) 97 1384), Arve Rd, Geeveston, Tasmania, 7116. Run camps and short walks in the South West National Park in Tasmania. This is the most experienced company for guiding bushwalks into this national park.

Willis's Walkabouts (☎ (089) 85 2134), 12 Carrington St, Millner, Northern Territory, 0810. Run extended bushwalks in the Macdonnell Ranges, Kakadu and other places by arrangement.

BUSINESS HOURS

Although Australians aren't great believers in long opening hours, they are a long way ahead of the Kiwis, thank you! Most shops close at 5 or 5.30 pm weekdays. In some states shops are open all day Saturday, but in other places they close at noon. In some places Sunday trading is starting to catch on.

In most towns there are usually one or two late shopping nights each week, when the doors stay open until 9 or 9.30 pm. Usually it's Thursday and/or Friday night.

Banks are open from 9.30 am to 4 pm Monday to Thursday, and until 5 pm on Friday. Some large city branches are open 8 am to 6 pm Monday to Friday. Some are also open to 9 pm on Fridays. Of course there are some exceptions to Australia's unremarkable opening hours and all sorts of places stay open late and all weekend – particularly milk bars, delis and city bookshops.

POST & TELECOMMUNICATIONS
Post
Australia's postal services are relatively efficient but not too cheap. It costs 45c to send a standard letter or postcard within Australia, while aerogrammes cost 60c.

Air-mail letters/postcards cost 70/65c to New Zealand, Singapore and Malaysia, 90/80c to Hong Kong and India, $1.10/85c to the USA and Canada, and $1.20/90c to Europe and the UK.

Post offices are open from 9 am to 5 pm Monday to Friday, but you can often get stamps from local post offices operated from newsagencies or from Australia Post shops, found in large cities, on Saturday mornings.

All post offices will hold mail for visitors and some city GPOs have very busy poste restante facilities. Cairns GPO poste restante, for example, can get quite hectic. You can also have mail sent to you at the American Express offices in big cities if you have an Amex card or carry Amex travellers' cheques.

Telephone
From the year dot the Australian phone system was wholly owned and run by the government, but these days the market has been marginally deregulated with room for a second player. It is still unclear what this will mean for the end user in terms of prices and level of service. Currently the system (still run by the government-owned Telecom) is really remarkably efficient and, equally important, easy to use. Local phone calls all

cost 30c for an unlimited amount of time. You can make local calls from gold or blue phones – often found in shops, hotels, bars, etc – and from Payphone booths.

It's also possible to make long-distance (STD – Subscriber Trunk Dialling) calls from virtually any public phone. Many public phones now accept the Telecom Phonecards, which are very convenient. The cards come in $2, $5 and $10 denominations, and are available from retail outlets such as newsagents and pharmacies, and these places display the phonecard logo. You keep using the card until the value has been used in calls. Otherwise, have plenty of 20c, 50c and $1 coins, and be prepared to feed them through at a fair old rate.

Many businesses and some government departments operate a toll-free service, so no matter where you are ringing from around the country it's only the cost of a local call, or free from a public phone. These numbers have the prefix 008, and we've listed them wherever possible throughout the book.

From most STD phones you can also make ISD (International Subscriber Dialling) calls just like making STD calls. Dialling ISD you can get through to overseas numbers almost as quickly as you can locally and if your call is brief it needn't cost very much – 'Hi, I'll be on the flight to London next Tuesday' can cost no more than a postcard.

All you do is dial 0011 for overseas, the country code (44 for Britain, 1 for the USA or Canada, 64 for New Zealand), the city code (71 or 81 for London, 212 for New York, etc), and then the telephone number. And have a Phonecard or plenty of coins to hand. A call to the USA or Britain costs $1.60 a minute ($1.19 off peak), New Zealand is $1.30 a minute ($0.90 off peak). Off-peak times, if available, vary depending on the destination – see the front of the A-K phone book for more details. Saturdays are often the cheapest day to ring.

TIME
Australia is divided into three time zones: Western Time is plus eight hours from

Greenwich Mean Time (Western Australia), Central Time is plus 9½ hours (Northern Territory, South Australia), and Eastern Time is plus 10 (Tasmania, Victoria, New South Wales, Queensland). When it's noon in Western Australia it's 1.30 pm in the Northern Territory and South Australia and 2 pm in the rest of the country. During the summer things get slightly screwed up as daylight saving time (when clocks are put forward an hour) does not operate in Western Australia or Queensland.

ELECTRICITY

Voltage is 220-240 V and the plugs are three-pin, but not the same as British three-pin plugs. Users of electric shavers or hairdryers should note that, apart from in fancy hotels, it's difficult to find converters to take either US flat two-pin plugs or the European round two pin-plugs. Adapters for British plugs can be found in good hardware shops. You can easily bend the US plugs to a slight angle to make them fit.

WEIGHTS & MEASURES

Australia went metric in the early 1970s. Petrol and milk are sold by the litre, apples and potatoes by the kg, distance is measured by the metre or km, and speed limits are in km per hour. But there's still a degree of confusion; it's hard to think of a six-foot person as being 183 cm.

For those who need help with metric there's a conversion table at the back of this book.

BOOKS

There is a wide range of books available for bushwalkers at bookshops, bushwalking shops and specialist map and travel guide shops in most states. You'll also find sections devoted to Australiana and other books for every Australian subject. Guidebooks to specific areas can be hard to find and are usually only sold in shops close to the areas they describe.

General

Australia – a travel survival kit by Tony Wheeler (Lonely Planet, 1992). The guide book for travelling around Australia.

National Parks of New South Wales compiled by Graham Groves (Gregory's, 1980). A good coverage of walking areas in NSW.

Paddy Pallin's Bushwalking & Camping edited by Tim Lamble (Paddy Pallin Pty Ltd, 1988). A classic book about basic equipment, navigation and the bushcraft skills needed for walking in the Australian bush.

Bushwalking & Mountaincraft Leadership (Department of Youth Sport and Recreation, 1986). Covers leadership and planning skills for walking in Australia's bushlands. Available in Victoria only.

Map Reading Handbook (TASMAP, Tasmania, 1991). An excellent low priced publication on reading, interpreting and using topographic maps. Available in Tasmania and Victoria.

Australian Bushcraft by Richard Graves (National Book Distrubutors, 1991). A guide to survival and camping in Australia.

Wild – Australia's wilderness adventure magazine, (PO Box 415, Prahran, 3181). A quarterly publication containing articles, track notes and mini guidebooks to many areas of Australia. There are a number of useful tips on equipment modification in various issues.

Bushwalking Guide Books

New South Wales *Bushwalking in Kosciusko National Park* by Charles Warner (1989). Intended for experienced bushwalkers. Details all access routes and interesting features of this park. You will need to use your imagination to link the notes together when planning extended walks.

Fitzroy Falls & Beyond (Budawang Committee, 1988). A very comprehensive and pricey book on the northern half of the Budawang region. Most of the book details the history and natural resources and is interesting reading. While there is only a short section of bushwalking notes they are very useful for planning extended walks.

Pigeon House & Beyond (Budawang Committee, 1982). The companion book of the one above covering the southern section.

The 40 pages devoted to bushwalking routes are very useful for planning extended walks.

Bushwalking in the Budawangs by Ron Doughton (Envirobook, 1989) A useful guide covering bushwalks to most regions of this large park.

100 Walks in New South Wales by Tyrone Thomas (Hill of Content, 1991). This guide mainly outlines day walks spread across the state, but there are some overnight bushwalks.

Treks in New South Wales by Neil Paton (Kangaroo Press, 1991). A guide detailing 10 extended walks in the national parks close to Sydney.

Walks in the Blue Mountains by Neil Paton (Kangaroo Press, 1987). It covers mainly day walks but some useful overnight walk ideas are hidden in its pages.

Bushwalks in the Hunter Valley by Neil Paton (Macstyle, 1989). More day walks but with some ideas for visiting the Colo Wilderness Area.

The Great North Walk by Garry McDougall & Leigh Shearer-Heriot (Kangaroo Press, 1988). The guide to the 250-km walking track from Sydney to Newcastle.

A Guide to Northeastern New South Wales (University of New England Mountaineering Club, 1984). An excellent guide for both short and extended walks in northern New South Wales. Usually available in the Sydney bushwalking shops.

Bushwalking in North-East New South Wales by Bob Blanch & Vince Kean (Atrand, 1989). Mainly day walks with only four overnight walks described.

Northern Territory *Walks in the Northern Territory* by Neil Paton (Kangaroo Press, 1990) These are all day walks but as the only guide it is useful to gain an appreciation of what there is to explore.

Queensland *Exploring Queensland's Central Highlands* by Charles Warner (1987). Describes all access and interesting features of the inland parks 400 to 500 km north-west of Brisbane. It provides many

ideas without giving detailed track notes to this remote region.

100 Walks in South Queensland by Tony Groom & Trevor Gynther (Hill Of Content, 1987). Has only 10 overnight bushwalks but as the only guide it is of some use for bushwalkers.

100 Walks in North Queensland by Brian Mackness (Hill of Content, 1980). This book is virtually all one-day walks. The few overnight walks suggested are only variations of described day walks.

Discovering Fraser Island, by John Sinclair, (Australian Environmental Publications, 1987), is about the island's history and natural resources. The few pages devoted to bushwalking are very brief but do provide a few ideas of places to visit.

Bushwalking in South-East Queensland by Ross Buchanan (Bushpeople Publications, 1991). An excellent comprehensive book of walks of all lengths and difficulties for the region near Brisbane.

South Australia *Flinders Ranges Walks* (Conservation Council of South Australia, 1989). Mainly details short walks in the dry Flinders Ranges. Has a few ideas for creating extended walks around Wilpena Pound and in the Gammon Ranges.

The Heysen Trail – Encounter Bay to the Barossa Valley (Government Printing Division, 1988). Describes the track through the Lofty Ranges behind Adelaide. There is also *The Heysen Trail – Parachilna to Hawker* (Department of Recreation & Sport, 1987). Describes the track through the central part of the Flinders Ranges. Unfortunately no other guides exist to the rest of this long distance trail.

A Walking Guide to the Northern Flinders Ranges by Adrian Heard (State Publishing, 1990). An excellent guide to the Gammon Ranges and Arkaroola Sanctuary areas.

Tasmania *South West Tasmania* by John Chapman (1990). A comprehensive guide to extended bushwalks in a large national park.

Cradle Mountain Lake St Clair National Park by John Siseman & John Chapman

(Algona Guides, 1992). Describes both short and extended bushwalks in Tasmania's best known national park.

100 Walks in Tasmania by Tyrone Thomas (Hill of Content, 1991). Mainly describes one-day walks with some overnight walks.

Tasman Tracks by Shirley & Peter Storey (Koonya Press, 1990). Mainly day walks with one excellent extended walk to Cape Pillar.

The Tasmanian Tramp (Hobart Walking Club). An excellent club booklet that is published about every two years. Contains articles about Tasmania which are of interest to bushwalkers.

Victoria *Alpine Walking Track* by John Siseman (Pindari, 1988). The guide book to the Alpine Walking Track.

Bogong National Park by John Siseman (Pindari, 1990). Details both short and extended walks around the Bogong High Plains.

Wonnongatta Moroka National Park by John Siseman (Pindari, 1988). Includes both short and extended walks in an excellent bushwalking area.

Walking the Otways (Geelong Bushwalking Club, 1986). Mainly describes one-day walks, but includes a couple of excellent extended walks.

120 Walks in Victoria by Tyrone Thomas (Hill of Content, 1990). Contains a mixture of one-day and overnight bushwalks around Victoria.

Melbourne's Mountains by John Siseman (Pindari, 1992). Walking and touring the Great Dividing Range east of Melbourne.

50 Walks in the Grampians by Tyrone Thomas (Hill Of Content, 1986). Mainly day walks to this interesting area.

Car Touring & Bushwalking in East Gippsland by Grant Da Costa (Australian Conservation Foundation, 1988). A mixture of walks with some overnight gems hidden in its pages.

Head for the Hills by Andrew Mevisson (Macstyle, 1991). Mainly day walks with some overnight walks.

The Great South West Walk by Friends of the Great South West Walk. While only a thin 16-page booklet, it is invaluable if walking this track.

Western Australia *Guide to the Bibbulman Bushwalking Track* (CALM, 1988). The government's guide to the 500-km walking track that extends from Perth to the southern coast.

MAPS

There are reasonable maps to the more popular bushwalking areas, most produced by the government mapping agencies. Each state produces its own maps and it is usually necessary to buy maps in the capital city of that state.

Australian Capital Territory
NATMAP, Cameron Offices, Unit 3, Belconnen, 2616 (☎ (06) 252 6383). PO Box 31, Belconnen, 2616

New South Wales
Central Mapping Authority of New South Wales, Panorama Avenue, Bathurst, 2795 (☎ (063) 32 8200)

Queensland
SUNMAP, Anzac Square, Adelaide St, Brisbane, 4000 (☎ (07) 227 6892)

South Australia
South Australian Department of Lands, 12 Pirie St, Adelaide, 5000 (☎ (08) 226 3905)

Tasmania
Lands Department, 134 Macquarie St, Hobart, 7000 (☎ (002) 30 8011). TASMAP, GPO Box 44A, Hobart, 7000

Victoria
Map Sales, Information Centre Victoria, basement, 318 Little Bourke St, Melbourne, 3000 (☎ (03) 651 4130)

Western Australia
Department of Lands and Survey, Cathedral Avenue, Perth, 6000 (☎ (09) 323 1370).

Maps can be bought directly from government offices at the same price as in bushwalking shops, but it is better to buy from a bushwalking or map shop as they stock government maps, private maps and guidebooks. They can also give you advice about any new maps and the area you intend to visit.

The shops also have longer trading hours.

Top: Garie Beach, Royal National Park
Bottom: Blue Gum Forest, Grose Valley

Top: Mt Owen, Budawangs
Bottom: Budawangs, Pigeon House in the distance

Maps cost between $5 and $9. The maps in this book are designed to show only the general route of the suggested walk and are intended to be used in conjunction with the recommended maps. The map references in the text (when given) refer to the recommended topographic map sheet.

FILM & PHOTOGRAPHY

If you come to Australia via Hong Kong or Singapore it's worth buying film there but otherwise Australian film prices are not too far out of line with those of the rest of the Western world. Including developing, 36-exposure Kodachrome 64 or Fujichrome 100 slide films cost from around $20, but with a little shopping around you can find it for around $15 – even less if you buy it in quantity.

There are plenty of camera shops in all the big cities and standards of camera service are high. Developing standards are also high, with many places offering one-hour developing of print film. Melbourne is the main centre for developing Kodachrome slide film in the South-East Asian region.

Photography is no problem, but in the outback you have to allow for the exceptional intensity of the light. Best results in the outback regions are obtained early in the morning and late in the afternoon. As the sun gets higher, colours appear washed out. You must also allow for the intensity of reflected light when taking shots on the Barrier Reef or at other coastal locations. In the outback, especially in the summer, allow for temperature extremes and do your best to keep film as cool as possible, particularly after exposure. Other film and camera hazards are dust in the outback and humidity in the tropical regions of the far north.

As in any country, politeness goes a long way when taking photographs; ask before taking pictures of people. Note that many Aborigines do not like to have their photographs taken, even from a distance.

HEALTH

So long as you have not visited an infected country in the past 14 days (refuelling stops by aircraft do not count) no vaccinations are required for entry. Naturally, if you're going to be travelling around in outlandish places apart from Australia, a good collection of immunisations is highly advisable.

Medical care in Australia is first-class and only moderately expensive. A typical visit to the doctor costs around $25. Health insurance cover is available in Australia, but there is usually a waiting period after you sign up before any claims can be made. If you have an immediate health problem, contact the casualty section at the nearest public hospital.

Travel Insurance

Even if you normally carry health or hospitalisation insurance or live in a country where health care is provided by the government it's still a good idea to buy some inexpensive travellers' insurance that covers both health and loss of baggage.

Make sure the policy includes health care and medication in the countries you plan to visit and includes a flight home for you and anyone you're travelling with, should your condition warrant it.

Health Precautions

Travellers from the northern hemisphere need to be aware of the intensity of the sun in Australia. Those ultra-violet rays can have you burnt to a crisp even on an overcast day, so if in doubt wear protective cream, a wide-brimmed hat and a long-sleeved shirt with a collar. Australia has a high incidence of skin cancer, a fact directly connected to exposure to the sun. Be careful.

First Aid & Medicine

All bushwalkers should have a sound knowledge of general first aid practices. Special courses are run in most capital cities by the Red Cross and the St John Ambulance groups and these are recommended. What to include in the first aid kit has always been a much debated topic amongst experienced walkers. Ideally all general problems such as burns, cuts, gashes, blisters, sunburn and minor injuries should be provided for.

Personal Kit (each person)

- Triangular Bandage
- 10 cm- wide Elastic Bandage
- Notebook & Pencil
- Throat Lozenges
- UV Cream
- Insect Repellent
- Headache Tablets
- Lip Salve
- Assorted Bandaids
- Two large plastic bags

Group Kit (one per group)

- Antiseptic Powder
- Blister Treatments (paddings, adhesive tape)
- Wound Dressings
- Scissors
- Tweezers
- Sterile Eye Wash
- Laxative
- Oil of cloves
- Water Purifying Tablets
- Current first aid manual

Major injuries are rare and cannot be predicted so it is difficult to carry everything that might be needed. Usually the best kit has sufficient items in it to enable a patient to be looked after until outside help has been obtained.

Water

Australia is the driest continent in the world and water is often the most important natural resource for bushwalkers. There are some areas which have excessive quantities of it but much of the country suffers from a shortage of water. If a walk is in a particularly dry area it may be necessary to carry all water for the entire walk. This is detailed in the Permits section for each walk. It is worth talking to the local ranger and any other walkers about the current water situation.

Water needs vary for each individual but most adults require at least four to six litres a day. It is better to visit the dry areas in mild weather periods to avoid carrying heavy packs in hot weather. In many of the popular bushwalking areas water is available near most campsites but is rarely found while

walking. A water bottle of one-litre capacity per person is usually sufficient for drinking needs during the day. In hot weather you can expect to need more water and may need to carry up to three litres per person.

Rescues

Serious injury is rare in the bush if common sense is used. When an accident does occur the party must decide on the action to take. If anyone is seriously injured quickly seek help. The authority to contact is either the national park rangers or the police, whichever is closer. The police usually have an experienced search and rescue team and can also call upon a special list of experienced bushwalkers for further assistance if required.

Seriously injured walkers will be carried out by stretcher, or by helicopter if the weather permits. In the more remote areas of Australia it may take up to a week or more to obtain help and walkers should not rely on rescue teams helping them quickly if they have problems. With proper planning, equipment and common sense the need for external assistance should be very rare.

Heat (Hyperthermia)

Heatstroke (hyperthermia) can occur easily in the deserts and the tropics where day-time temperatures of 40°C (over 100°F) are common. A shady hat, an adequate supply of water and long, regular rests during the heat of the day are essential to avoid heatstroke.

Cold (Hypothermia)

The weather in even the preferred summer season can be very wet and miserable for weeks on end. Walking in such conditions for hours can lead to a drop in body temperature called hypothermia which is often fatal. The best method for treating exposure as its more commonly known is prevention.

Avoid walking for extended periods in cold, windy, wet-weather conditions. Good windproof and waterproof clothing can greatly reduce the risk of exposure. Many of the tragedies that have occured can be related to the use of poor inferior clothing. Sufficient warm dry clothing will also be needed around camp.

The easiest and best treatment for exposure conditions is to simply not walk in them. This is done by either altering plans to follow a more sheltered route or more commonly by staying put and waiting for improved weather conditions.

In Tasmania, this wait could require several days; earlier this year we waited five days for better weather and the small break allowed us to retreat to safety! Groups who plan strict walking timetables often get into dificulties with the cold and our advise is to allways allow some lee days into your trip plan. The suggested walking times given in this guide do allow for this.

EMERGENCY

For fire, police or ambulance, dial 000.

There is a telephone interpreter service available nationwide. Check the Community pages at the beginning of the White Pages phone book for the local number. Other telephone crisis services, such as Rape Crisis Centres, are also listed there.

DANGERS & ANNOYANCES
Animal Hazards

In Australia there are a few unique and sometimes dangerous creatures.

The best known danger in the Australian outback, and the one that captures visitors' imaginations, is snakes. Although there are many venomous snakes there are few that are aggressive, and unless you have the bad fortune to stand on one it's unlikely that you'll be bitten. Taipans and tiger snakes, however, will attack if alarmed. Sea snakes can also be dangerous.

To minimise your chances of being bitten always wear boots, socks and long trousers when walking through undergrowth where snakes may be present. Don't put your hands into holes and crevices, and be careful when collecting firewood or toileting.

Snake bites do not cause instantaneous death and antivenenes are usually available. Keep the victim calm and still, wrap the bitten limb firmly (to compress the tissues

but not constrict the flow of blood), as you would for a sprained ankle, and then attach a splint to immobilise it – do not remove splint or bandages once applied. Then seek medical help.

Never wash, cut, suck or use a constrictive bandage. Do *not* try and catch the snake.

We've got a couple of nasty spiders too, including the funnel-web, the redback and the white-tail, so it's best not to play with any spider. Funnel-web spiders are found in New South Wales and their bite is treated in the same way as snake bites. For redback bites apply a cold pack or compress and seek medical attention.

Among the splendid variety of biting insects the mosquito and march fly are the most common. The common bush tick (found in the forest and scrub country along the eastern coast of Australia) can be dangerous if left lodged in the skin, as the toxin the tick excretes can cause paralysis and sometimes death – check your body for lumps every night if you're walking in tick-infested areas. The tick should be removed by dousing it with stove fuel (shellite, methylated spirits and kerosene all work) and levering it out intact.

Leeches are common, and while they will suck your blood they are not dangerous and are easily removed by the application of salt or heat.

Up north the saltwater crocodile can be a real danger and has killed a number of people (travellers and locals). They are found in river estuaries and large rivers, sometimes a long way inland, so before diving into that inviting, cool water find out from the locals whether it's croc-free.

In the sea, the box jellyfish, or sea wasp as it's known, occurs north of Great Keppel Island during summer and can be fatal. It's responsible for more deaths than any other non-human creature in Australia (sharks, crocs and snakes included). The stinging tentacles spread several metres away from the sea wasp's body; by the time you see it you're likely to have been stung – and it's said you only get stung once in a lifetime! If someone is stung, they are likely to run out of the sea screaming and collapse on the beach, with weals on their body as though they've been whipped. They may stop breathing. Douse the stings with vinegar (available on many beaches or from nearby houses), do not try to remove the tentacles from the skin, and treat as for snake bite and monitor breathing closely.

If there's a first-aider present, they may have to apply artificial respiration until the ambulance gets there. Above all, stay out of the sea when the sea wasps are around – the locals are ignoring that lovely water for an excellent reason.

The blue-ringed octopus and Barrier Reef cone shells can also be fatal so don't pick them up. If someone is stung, apply a pressure bandage, immobilise, monitor breathing carefully and, if a first-aider is present, mouth-to-mouth resuscitation can be undertaken (if breathing stops).

When reef walking you must always wear shoes to protect your feet against coral. In tropical waters there are stonefish – venomous fish that look like a flat piece of rock on the sea bed. Also, watch out for the scorpion fish which has venomous spines.

On the Road

Cows and kangaroos can be a real hazard to the driver. A collision with one will badly damage your car and probably kill the animal. Unfortunately, other drivers are even more dangerous and particularly those who drink. Australia has an appalling road toll, particularly in the countryside, so don't drink and drive and please take care.

Bushfires & Blizzards

Bushfires happen every year in Australia. Don't be the mug who starts one. In hot, dry, windy weather, be extremely careful with any naked flame – no cigarette butts out of car windows, please. On a Total Fire Ban Day (listen to the radio or watch the billboards on country roads), it is forbidden even to use a camping stove in the open. The locals will not be amused if they catch you breaking this particular law.

If you're unfortunate enough to find yourself driving through a bushfire, stay inside your car and try to park off the road in an open space, away from trees, until the danger's past. Lie on the floor under the dashboard, covering yourself with a wool blanket if possible. The front of the fire should pass quickly, and you will be much safer than if you were out in the open.

Bushwalkers should take local advice before setting out. On a Total Fire Ban Day, don't go – delay your trip until the weather has changed. Chances are that it will be so unpleasantly hot and windy, you'll be better off anyway in an air-conditioned pub sipping a cool drink.

If you're out in the bush and you see smoke, even at a great distance, take it seriously. Go to the nearest open space, downhill if possible. A forested ridge is the most dangerous place to be. Bushfires move very quickly and change direction with the wind.

Having said all that, more bushwalkers die of cold than in bushfires! Even in summer, temperatures can drop below freezing at night in the mountains. The Tasmanian mountains can have blizzards at almost any time of year.

THE WALKS

The bushwalks described assume that the group has some experience of overnight walking and camping. Many of the walks are suitable for inexperienced bushwalkers provided there are some experienced walkers in the party. Taking into consideration that the standard of a walk can vary according to the weather and other local conditions, the walks

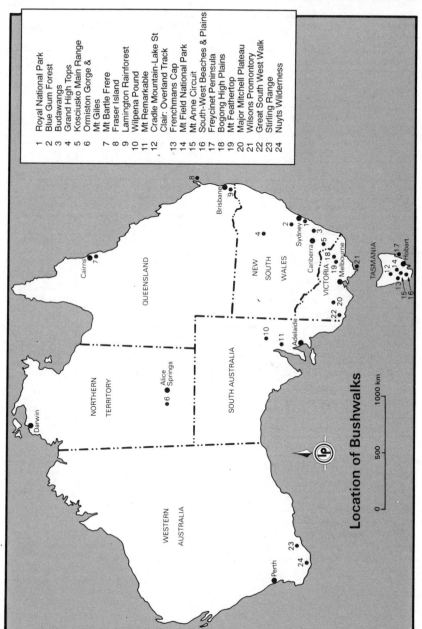

1 Royal National Park
2 Blue Gum Forest
3 Budawangs
4 Grand High Tops
5 Kosciusko Main Range
6 Ormiston Gorge &
   Mt Giles
7 Mt Bartle Frere
8 Fraser Island
9 Lamington Rainforest
10 Wilpena Pound
11 Mt Remarkable
12 Cradle Mountain-Lake St
   Clair: Overland Track
13 Frenchmans Cap
14 Mt Field National Park
15 Mt Anne Circuit
16 South-West Beaches & Plains
17 Freycinet Peninsula
18 Bogong High Plains
19 Mt Feathertop
20 Major Mitchell Plateau
21 Wilsons Promontory
22 Great South West Walk
23 Stirling Range
24 Nuyts Wilderness

Location of Bushwalks

0   500   1000 km

State	Walk Title	Standard	Number of Days	Transport
NSW	Royal National Park Coastal	Easy	2	Train
	The Blue Gum Forest	Easy	3(2)	Train/Taxi
	Corang Peak to The Castle	Medium-Hard	3(5)	Private
	Grand High Tops Circuit	Easy-Medium	2	Private
	Kosciusko Main Range	Easy	2(3)	Bus
NT	Ormiston Gorge & Mt Giles	Medium	3(4)	Private
QLD	Mt Bartle Frere	Medium	2	Bus
	Fraser Island Circuit	Medium	3(4)	Boat
	Lamington Rainforest Circuit	Easy	3(5)	Bus
SA	Wilpena Pound	Medium	2(3)	Bus
	Mt Remarkable Gorges	Medium	2(3)	Bus
TAS	The Overland Track	Easy-Medium	8(10)	Bus
	Frenchmans Cap	Medium	3(5)	Bus
	Mt Field National Park	Easy-Medium	2(3)	Bus*
	Mt Anne Circuit	Medium	3(4)	Bus*
	South-West Beaches & Plains	Medium	11(14)	Bus*
	Freycinet Peninsula	Easy-Medium	2	Bus
VIC	Bogong High Plains Circuit	Medium	5(6)	Bus/Taxi
	Mt Feathertop	Medium	2	Private
	Major Mitchell Plateau	Medium	2	Private
	Wilsons Promontory Circuit	Easy-Medium	2(3)	Private
	Great South West Walk	Easy-Medium	12(15)	Bus
WA	Stirling Range Circuit	Medium-Hard	2(4)	Private
	Nuyts Wilderness Area	Easy	2	Private

Number of Days: ( ) suggested alternative
Transport: * indicates summer only
Season: X ban applied to all bushwalking
R reasonable for bushwalking
E excellent season for bushwalking
S region normally under winter snows

Summer	Autumn	Winter	Spring	Features	Page Numbers
R	E	E	E	Rugged coastline	63-68
R	E	E	E	Gorges & forest	68-74
R	E	R	E	Sandstone peaks	74-81
	R	E	E	Volcanic landscape	81-86
E	E	S	E	Alpine plateau	86-91
	R	E	R	Desert gorge & peak	93-98
	R	E	R	Rainforest	100-104
R	E	E	E	Rainforest, lakes & beaches	105-110
R	E	E	E	Rainforest & waterfalls	110-115
	R	E	E	Desert mountains	117-121
X	R	E	E	Gorges	121-125
E	R	S	R	Lakes, peaks & moorlands	128-140
E	R	S	R	Spectacular quartzite cliffs	140-145
E	R	S	R	Glaciated landscape	145-149
E	R	S	R	Plateau & lakes	149-153
E	R		R	Coastline & plains	153-164
E	E	E	E	Beaches & peaks	164-168
E	R	S	R	Alpine plains	171-179
E	E	S	E	Alpine peaks	179-184
E	R	R	E	Sub-alpine plateau	184-188
E	E	E	E	Beaches & forests	188-192
R	E	R	E	Coastline & heathlands	192-204
	R	R	E	Craggy peaks	206-210
E	E	R	E	Coastline & heathlands	210-214

are graded easy, medium or hard according to the following criteria:

1 An *easy* bushwalk follows well-defined tracks and is capable of being completed by anyone of average fitness. Simple navigation may be needed. Previous experience of carrying a pack is not essential.
2 A *medium* bushwalk is intended for the bushwalker who is experienced at carrying a pack for a couple of days and is of average fitness. Prior navigational experience is essential as some careful navigation may be required, depending on the weather conditions.
3 A *hard* bushwalk requires extensive bushwalking and pack-carrying experience. Excellent navigational skills are usually required as well as a good level of fitness. Hard bushwalks do not necessarily cover extensive distances as they are often off tracks. Sometimes they enter areas of cliffs and gorges which can be dangerous to any inexperienced walker.

These grades are similar to those used by most Australian walking clubs. Intermediate grades of easy to medium and medium to hard are used as well as the three basic grades.

ACCOMMODATION

Australia is very well equipped with youth hostels, backpackers' hostels and camp sites – the cheapest shelter you can find. Furthermore, there are plenty of motels around the country and in holiday regions like the Queensland coast intense competition tends to keep the prices down.

A typical town of a few thousand people will have a basic motel at around $35/45 for singles/doubles, an old town centre hotel with rooms (shared bathrooms) at say $25/30, and a caravan park – probably with tent sites for around $8 and on-site vans or cabins for $21 to $25 for two. If the town is on anything like a main road or is bigger, it'll probably have several of each. You'll rarely have much trouble finding *somewhere* to lay your head in Oz, even when there are no hostels, although some surprisingly small and seemingly insignificant towns have backpackers' hostels these days. If there's a group of you, the rates for three or four people in a room are always worth checking.

Often there are larger 'family' rooms or units with two bedrooms.

There are a couple of give-away backpackers' newspapers available at hostels around the country, and these have fairly up-to-date listings of hostels, although they give neither prices nor details of each hostel.

For more comprehensive accommodation listings, the state automobile clubs produce directories listing hotels, motels, holiday flats, camp sites and even some backpackers' hostels, in almost every little town in the country. They're updated every year so the prices are generally fairly current. They're available from the clubs for a nominal charge if you're a member or a member of an affiliated club enjoying reciprocal rights. Alternatively, some state tourist offices (notably the Northern Territory and Western Australia) also put out frequently updated guides to local accommodation.

Camping & Caravanning

The camping story in Australia is partly excellent and partly rather annoying! The excellent side is that there is a great number of camp sites and you'll almost always find space available. If you want to get around Australia on the cheap then camping is the cheapest way of all, with nightly costs for two of around $8 to $15.

One of the drawbacks is that camp sites are often intended more for caravanners (house trailers for any North Americans out there) than for campers and the tent campers get little thought in these places. The fact that in Australia most of the sites are called 'caravan parks' indicates who gets most attention.

In many Australian campsites the top soil is scraped away to make the ground more suitable for caravans, so pitching a tent becomes very hard work.

Equally bad is that in most big cities sites are well away from the centre. This is not inconvenient in small towns, but in general if you're planning to camp around Australia you really need your own transport.

Still, it's not all gloom; in general Australian camp sites are well kept, conveniently located and excellent value. Many sites also have on-site vans which you can rent for the night. These give you the comfort of a caravan without the inconvenience of actually towing one.

On-site cabins are also widely available, and these are more like small, self-contained units. They usually have one bedroom, or at least an area which can be screened off from the rest of the unit – just the thing if you have small kids.

Cabins also have the advantage of having their own bathroom and toilet, although this is sometimes an optional extra. They are also much less cramped than a caravan, and the price difference is not always that great – say $25 to $30 for an on-site van, $30 to $40 for a cabin. In winter, if you're going to be using this sort of accommodation on a regular basis, it's worth investing in a small heater of some sort as many vans and cabins are unheated.

Youth Hostels

Australia has a very active Youth Hostel Association (YHA) and you'll find hostels all over the country, with more official hostels and backpackers' hostels popping up all the time.

YHA hostels provide basic accommodation, usually in small dormitories or bunk rooms although more and more of them are providing twin rooms for couples. The nightly charges are rock bottom – usually between $8 and $15 a night.

With the increased competition from the proliferation of backpackers' hostels, many YHA hostels have done away with the old fetishes for curfews and doing chores, but still retain segregated dorms. Many even take non-YHA members, although there may be a small 'temporary membership' charge. To become a full YHA member in Australia costs $22 a year (there's also a $16 joining fee). You can join at a state office or at any youth hostel.

Youth hostels are part of an international organisation, the International Youth Hostel Federation (IYHF), so if you're already a member of the YHA in your own country,

your membership entitles you to use the Australian hostels. Hostels are great places for meeting people and great travellers' centres, and in many busier hostels the visitors will outnumber the Australians. The annual *YHA Accommodation Guide* booklet, which is available from any YHA office in Australia and from some YHA offices overseas, lists all the YHA hostels around Australia with useful little maps showing how to find them. YHA members are eligible for discounts at various places and these facilities are also listed in the handbook.

You must have a regulation sleeping bag sheet or bed linen – for hygiene reasons a regular sleeping bag will not do. If you haven't got sheets they can be rented at many hostels (usually for $3), but it's cheaper, after a few nights' stay, to have your own. YHA offices and some larger hostels sell the official YHA sheet bag.

Most hostels have cooking facilities and some place where you can sit and talk. There are usually laundry facilities and often excellent notice boards. Many hostels have a maximum-stay period – because some hostels are permanently full it would hardly be fair for people to stay too long when others are being turned away.

The YHA defines its hostels as the simpler 'shelter' style and the larger 'standard' hostels. They range from tiny places to big modern buildings, with everything from historic convict buildings to a disused railway station in between. Most hostels have a manager who checks you in when you arrive, keeps the peace and maybe assigns chores. Because you have so much more contact with a hostel manager than the person in charge of other styles of accommodation he or she can really make or break the place. Good managers are often great characters and well worth getting to know.

Accommodation can usually be booked directly with the manager, through the YHA Central Reservations Bureau in Sydney (☎ (02) 267 3044) or with the state head office. The YHA handbook tells all.

The Australian head office is in Sydney, at the Australian Youth Hostels Association, 10

Hallett St, Camperdown, NSW 2050. If you can't get a YHA hostel booklist in your own country write to them but otherwise deal with the state offices:

New South Wales
   176 Day St, Sydney, NSW 2000 (☎ (02) 267 3044)
Northern Territory
   Darwin Hostel Complex, Beaton Rd via Hidden Valley Rd, Berrimah, NT 0828 (☎ (089) 84 3902)
Queensland
   154 Roma St, Brisbane, QLD 4000 (☎ (07) 236 1680)
South Australia
   38 Sturt St, Adelaide, SA 5000 (☎ (03) 231 5583)
Tasmania
   1st floor, 28 Criterion St, Hobart, Tas 7000 (☎ (002) 34 9617)
Victoria
   205 King St, Melbourne, Vic 3000 (☎ (03) 670 7991)
Western Australia
   65 Francis St, Northbridge, Perth, WA 6003 (☎ (09) 227 5122)

Not all of the approximately 130 hostels listed in the handbook are actually owned by the YHA. Some are 'associate hostels', which generally abide by hostel regulations but are owned by other organisations or individuals. You don't need to be a YHA member to stay at an associated hostel. Others are 'alternative accommodation' and do not totally fit the hostel blueprint. They might be motels which keep some hostel-style accommodation available for YHA members or camp sites with an on-site van or two kept aside, or even places just like hostels but where the operators don't want to abide by all the hostel regulations.

Backpackers' Hostels

In the last few years the number of backpackers' hostels has increased dramatically. This is partly a result of the recession in Australia; it seems that while tourist numbers are, in general, lower, the backpacker market continues to flourish. The standards of these hostels vary enormously. Some are rundown inner-city hotels where the owners have tried to fill empty rooms; unless renovations have been done, these

places are generally pretty gloomy and depressing. Others are former motels, so each unit, typically with four to six beds, will have fridge, TV and bathroom. When the climate allows, there's usually a pool too. The drawback with these places is that the communal areas and cooking facilities are often lacking, as motels were never originally designed for communal use. You may also find yourself sharing a room with someone who wants to watch TV all night – it happens!

Still other hostels are purpose built as backpackers' hostels; these are usually the best places in terms of facilities, although sometimes they are too big and lack any personalised service. As often as not the managers have backpackers running the places, and usually it's not too long before standards start to slip. Some of these places, particularly along the Queensland coast, actively promote themselves as 'party' hostels, so if you want a quiet time, they're often not the place to be. The best places are often the smaller, more intimate hostels where the owner is also the manager. These are usually the older hostels which were around long before the 'backpacker boom'.

With the proliferation of hostels has also come intense competition. Hop off a bus in any town on the Queensland coast and chances are there'll be at least three or four touts from the various hostels, all trying to lure you in. To this end many have introduced inducements, such as the first night free, and virtually all have courtesy buses. Even the YHA hostels have had to resort to this to stay in the race in some places.

Prices at backpackers' hostels are generally in line with YHA hostels, typically $10 to $12, although the $7 bed is still alive and well (in Cairns).

As with YHA hostels, the success of a hostel largely depends on the friendliness and willingness of the managers. One practice that many people find objectionable – in independent hostels only, since it never happens in YHAs – is the 'vetting' of Australians and sometimes New Zealanders, who may be asked to provide a passport or double ID which they may not carry. Virtually all city hostels ask everyone for some ID – usually a passport – but this can also be used as a way of keeping unwanted customers out.

Some places will actually only admit overseas backpackers. This happens mostly in cities and when it does it's because the hostel in question has had problems with some locals treating the place more as a doss house than a hostel – drinking too much, making too much noise, getting into fights and the like. Hostels which discourage or ban Aussies say it's only a rowdy minority that makes trouble, but they can't take the risk on who'll turn out bad. If you're an Aussie and encounter this kind of reception, the best you can do is persuade the desk people that you're genuinely travelling the country, and aren't just looking for a cheap place to crash for a while.

The Ys

In a number of places in Australia accommodation is provided by the YMCA or YWCA. There are variations from place to place – some are mainly intended for permanent accommodation, some are run like normal commercial guesthouses. They're generally excellent value and usually conveniently located. You don't have to be a YMCA or YWCA member to stay at them, although sometimes you get a discount if you are. Accommodation in the Ys is generally in fairly straightforward rooms, usually with shared bathroom facilities. Some Ys also have dormitory-style accommodation. Note, however, that not all YMCA or YWCA organisations around the country offer accommodation; it's mainly in the big cities.

Colleges

Although it is students who get first chance at these, nonstudents can also stay at many university colleges during the uni vacations. These places can be relatively cheap and comfortable and provide an opportunity for you to meet people. Bed & breakfast costs are typically from about $15 for students, twice that if you're not a student.

This type of accommodation is usually available only during the summer vacations (from November to February). Additionally, it must almost always be booked ahead; you can't just turn up. Many of Australia's new universities are way out in the suburbs and are inconvenient to get to unless you have wheels.

Hotels

For the budget traveller, hotels in Australia are generally older places – new accommodation will usually be motels. To understand why Australia's hotels are the way they are requires delving into the history books a little. When the powers that be decided Australia's drinking should only be at the most inconvenient hours, they also decided that drinking places should also be hotels. So every place which in Britain would be a 'pub' in Australia was a 'hotel', but often in name only.

The original idea of forcing pubs to provide accommodation for weary travellers has long faded into history and this ludicrous law has been rolled back. A 'private hotel', as opposed to a 'licensed hotel', really is a hotel and does not serve alcohol. A 'guesthouse' is much the same as a 'private hotel'.

New hotels being built today are mainly of the Hilton variety; smaller establishments will usually be motels. So, if you're staying in a hotel, it will normally mean an older place, often with rooms without private facilities. Unfortunately many older places are on the drab, grey and dreary side. You get a strong feeling that because they've got the rooms they try to turn a dollar on them, but without much enthusiasm. Others, fortunately, are colourful places with some real character. Although the word 'hotel' doesn't always mean they'll have rooms, the places that do have rooms usually make it pretty plain that they are available. If a hotel is listed in an accommodation directory you can be pretty sure it really will offer you a bed. If there's nothing that looks like a reception desk or counter, just ask in the bar.

A bright word about hotels (guesthouses

and private hotels, too) is that the breakfasts are usually excellent – big and 100% filling. A substantial breakfast is what this country was built on and if your hotel is still into serving a real breakfast you'll probably feel it could last you until breakfast comes around next morning. Generally, hotels will have rooms for around $20 to $30. When comparing prices, remember to check if it includes breakfast.

Motels, Serviced Apartments & Holiday Flats

If you've got wheels and want a more modern place with your own bathroom and other facilities, then you're moving in to the motel bracket. Motels cover the earth in Australia, just like in the USA, but they're usually located away from the city centres. Prices vary and with the motels, unlike hotels, singles are often not much cheaper than doubles. The reason is quite simple – in the old hotels many of the rooms really are singles, relics of the days when single men travelled the country looking for work. In motels, the rooms are almost always doubles. You'll sometimes find motel rooms for less than $30, and in most places will have no trouble finding something for $45 or less.

Holiday flats and serviced apartments are much the same thing and bear some relationship to motels. Basically holiday flats are found in holiday areas, serviced apartments in cities. A holiday flat is much like a motel room but usually has a kitchen or cooking facilities so you can fix your own food. Usually holiday flats are not serviced like motels – you don't get your bed made up every morning and the cups washed out. In some holiday flats you actually have to provide your own sheets and bedding but others are operated just like motel rooms with a kitchen. Most motels in Australia provide at least tea/coffee making facilities and a small fridge, but a holiday flat will also have cooking utensils, cutlery, crockery and so on.

Holiday flats are often rented on a weekly basis but even in these cases it's worth asking if daily rates are available. Paying for a week, even if you stay only for a few days, can still be cheaper than having those days at a higher daily rate. If there's more than just two of you, another advantage of holiday flats is that you can often find them with two or more bedrooms. A two-bedroom holiday flat is typically priced at about 1½ times the cost of a comparable single-bedroom unit.

In holiday areas like the Queensland coast, motels and holiday flats will often be virtually interchangeable terms – there's nothing really to distinguish one from the other. In big cities, on the other hand, the serviced apartments are often a little more obscure, although they may be advertised in the newspaper's classified ads.

Other Possibilities

That covers the usual conventional accommodation possibilities, but there are lots of less conventional ones. You don't have to camp in campsites, for example. There are plenty of parks where you can camp for free, or (in Queensland at least) roadside shelters where short-term camping is permitted. Australia has lots of bush where nobody is going to complain about you putting up a tent – or even notice you.

In the cities if you want to stay longer the first place to look for a share flat or a room is the classified ad section of the daily newspaper. Wednesday and Saturday are the best days for these ads. Notice boards in universities, hostel offices certain popular bookshops and other contact centres are good places to look for flats/houses to share or rooms to rent.

FOOD

A well-planned, balanced diet is essential when bushwalking for extended periods. Take food that is lightweight, high in energy, easy to prepare and good enough to look forward to each day. This is not as easy as it sounds and some thought needs to be put into planning a menu. The food must keep and also be suitable for the varying climatic conditions that will be encountered. For long walks it is best to plan on using foods that contain little or no water.

Obviously the needs and tastes of each bushwalker vary but a good supply would include: tea and coffee, sugar, powdered milk, egg powder, porridge, muesli, dry biscuits, rye bread, butter or margarine, cheese, salami, cabana, spreads (jam, peanut butter), nuts, dried fruit, lollies, chocolate, health food bars, fruit drink powders, pasta meals, freeze dried meals, bacon, packet soups, stock cubes, rice, flour, lentils, textured vegetable protein, dried vegetables, potato powder, dried tomato paste, instant puddings, instant custard, packet cheesecake, herbs and spices and salt.

Most of the food you will need can be purchased from any supermarket in city suburbs. Some items are also available from health food stores; although expensive they do stock special foods that can turn a dull menu into something interesting.

Bushwalking shops also stock some special foods such as freeze dried meals and are worth visiting for ideas. There are several books on food for the outdoors available from bushwalking shops.

FIRE, CONSERVATION & HUTS
Rubbish

In every text on bushwalking, tramping or backpacking it is emphasised that *all* rubbish must be carried out, yet wherever you go there is always someone who left it behind. Please carry out with you all your rubbish including aluminium packets and plastics.

Camping

In most national parks there are few rules about where to camp. Generally camping is freely allowed once you are away from the roads. To preserve the environment it is recommended that old campsites and fireplaces be used. Fire regulations require that any campfires be at least three metres clear of any flammable material such as long grass, stumps and logs. Fires must be attended at all times as all too often the result of unattended fires can be seen in the bush.

The risk of bushfires is great so *all* fires should be drowned with water before before being left. One park, Royal National Park near Sydney, has completely banned campfires and this ban will probably extend, in the next few years, to other parks. The best advice is to carry a stove and use it.

Permits There are a few parks which are extremely popular and permits are required to control the number of bushwalkers. Often this permit will detail the allowed camping areas and it should be obeyed as the regulations are made to help preserve the park. Wilsons Promontory is one such example.

Huts & Hut Etiquette In some alpine areas in New South Wales, Victoria and Tasmania there are open huts for the use of bushwalkers. These can be very welcome in cold, wet weather. Most of these huts are owned or maintained by people for others to use and some basic courtesy is required if using them. Upon arrival the hut is not automatically owned by the first party to occupy it, but is to be shared by all regardless of when they arrive. If the hut is full, preference should be given to any weaker walkers who would benefit from its shelter.

Be very careful with open fires and stoves inside huts; several huts have burnt down and people have been injured due to carelessness. This has resulted in the irreplaceable loss of part of our built heritage, and for an indication of how wealthy this is read *Huts of the High Country* by Klaus Hueneke (ANU Press, Canberra, 1982).

When leaving a hut it should always be left clean, firewood replaced and all rubbish carried out. The huts should not be relied upon as the only shelter because they are sometimes difficult to find in poor weather conditions. All parties should be fully equipped for camping in the expected weather conditions.

When sharing a campsite or hut with other groups there are some simple guidelines that should be followed to reduce friction between groups. The most basic rule is that all walkers have an equal right to all amenities regardless of whether they were first or last to arrive. Naturally, the first will have camped in the most comfortable places but everyone has an equal right to any facilities like bunks, tables, chairs and water supplies. Those arriving late are often appreciative of a little help and many friendships have often resulted from communal sharing.

If your camping patterns are in conflict with others then you should consider camping away from other groups to remove the possibility of any conflict. Very early risers or those who sit up late drinking should consider their fellow walkers and at least warn others as to their intentions. Groups that make excessive amounts of noise, such as singing early in the morning, should keep away from quieter groups. When conflicts do occur, discuss the matter with the other groups.

The usual best solution is to mutually decide to camp well apart. Remember that each person has come for a different reason and wants a different experience. All experiences are valid provided that they don't interfere with the intended experiences of others.

Getting There & Away

Basically getting to Australia means flying. Once upon a time the traditional transport between Europe and Australia was by ship, but those days are long gone. Infrequent and expensive cruise ships apart, there are no regular shipping services to Australia. It is, however, sometimes possible to hitch a ride on a yacht to or from Australia. See the Getting Around chapter for more details.

The basic problem with getting to Australia is that it's a long way from anywhere. Coming from Asia, Europe or North America there are lots of competing airlines and a wide variety of airfares, but there's no way you can avoid those great distances. Australia's current international popularity adds another problem – flights are often heavily booked. If you want to fly to Australia at a particularly popular time of year (the middle of summer, ie Christmas time, is notoriously difficult) or on a particularly popular route (like Hong Kong-Sydney or Singapore-Sydney) then plan well ahead.

Australia has a large number of international gateways. Sydney and Melbourne are the two busiest international airports with flights from everywhere. Perth also gets many flights from Asia and Europe and has direct flights to New Zealand and Africa. Other international airports include Hobart in Tasmania (New Zealand only), Adelaide, Port Hedland (Bali only), Darwin, Cairns and Brisbane. One place you can't arrive at directly from overseas is Canberra, the national capital.

Although Sydney is the busiest gateway it makes a lot of sense to avoid arriving or departing there. Sydney's airport is stretched way beyond its capacity and flights are frequently delayed on arrival and departure. Furthermore the Customs and Immigration facilities are cramped, crowded and too small for the current visitor flow so even after you've finally landed you may face further long delays. If you can organise your flights to avoid Sydney it's a wise idea but

unfortunately many flights to or from other cities (Melbourne in particular) still go via Sydney. If you're planning to explore Australia seriously then starting at a quieter entry port like Cairns in far north Queensland or Perth in Western Australia can make a lot of sense.

Discount Tickets

Buying airline tickets these days is like shopping for a car, a stereo or a camera – five different travel agents will quote you five different prices. Rule number one if you're looking for a cheap ticket is to go to an agent, not directly to the airline. The airline can usually only quote you the absolutely straight-up-and-down, by-the-rule-book regular fare. An agent, on the other hand, can offer all sorts of special deals particularly on competitive routes.

Ideally an airline would like to fly all their flights with every seat in use and every passenger paying the highest fare possible. Fortunately life usually isn't like that and airlines would rather have a half-price passenger than an empty seat. When faced with the problem of too many seats, they will either let agents sell them at cut prices, or occasionally make one-off special offers on particular routes – watch the travel ads in the press.

Of course, what's available and what it costs depends on what time of year it is, what route you're flying and who you're flying with. If you're flying on a popular route (as from Hong Kong) or one where the choice of flights is very limited (South America or from Africa) then the fare is likely to be higher or there may be nothing available but the official fare.

Similarly the dirt cheap fares are likely to be less conveniently scheduled, go by a less convenient route or with a less popular airline. Flying London/Sydney, for example, is most convenient with airlines like Qantas, British Airways, Singapore Airlines or Thai

International. They have flights every day, they operate the same flight straight through to Australia and they're good, reliable, comfortable, safe airlines. At the other extreme you could fly from London to an Eastern European or Middle East city on one flight, switch to another flight from there to Asia, change to another airline from there to Australia. It takes longer, there are delays and changes of aircraft along the way, the airlines may not be so good and furthermore the connection only works once a week and that means leaving London at 1.30 on a Wednesday morning. The flip side is it's cheaper.

TO/FROM UK

The cheapest tickets in London are from the numerous 'bucket shops' (discount ticket agencies) which advertise in magazines and papers like *Time Out, City Limits, Southern Cross* and *TNT*. Pick up one or two of these publications and ring round a few bucket shops to find the best deal. The magazine *Business Traveller* also has a great deal of good advice on airfare bargains. Most bucket shops are trustworthy and reliable but the occasional sharp operator appears – *Time Out* and *Business Traveller* give some useful advice on precautions to take.

Trailfinders (☎ (071) 938 3366) at 46 Earls Court Rd, London W8, STA Travel (☎ (071) 581 4132) at 74 Old Brompton Rd, London SW7 and 117 Euston Rd, London NW1 (☎ (071) 465 0484) are good, reliable agents for cheap tickets.

The cheapest London to Sydney or Melbourne bucket shop tickets are about £300 one-way or £550 return. Such prices are usually only available if you leave London in the low season – March to June. In September and mid-December fares go up about 30% while the rest of the year they're somewhere in between. Perth is usually about £20 cheaper than Sydney or Melbourne one-way, £30 to £50 cheaper return. Average fares are around £480 one-way and £860 return.

Many cheap tickets allow stopovers on the way to or from Australia. Rules regarding how many stopovers you can take, how long you can stay away, how far in advance you

have to decide your return date and so on, vary from time to time and ticket to ticket, but recently most return tickets have allowed you to stay away for any period between 14 days and one year, with stopovers permitted anywhere along your route. As usual with heavily discounted tickets the less you pay the less you get. Nice direct flights, leaving at convenient times and flying with popular airlines, are going to be more expensive than flying from London to Singapore or Bangkok with some Eastern European or Middle East airline and then changing to another airline for the last leg.

From Australia you can expect to pay around A$800 one-way and A$1550 return to London and other European capitals, with stops in Asia on the way.

TO/FROM NORTH AMERICA

There are a variety of connections across the Pacific from Los Angeles, San Francisco and Vancouver to Australia including direct flights, flights via New Zealand, island-hopping routes or more circuitous Pacific rim routes via nations in Asia. Qantas, Air New Zealand, United and Continental all fly USA/Australia; Qantas, Air New Zealand and Canadian Airlines International fly Canada/Australia.

One advantage of flying Qantas or Air New Zealand rather than Continental or United is that on the US airlines, if your flight goes via Hawaii, the west coast to Hawaii sector is treated as a domestic flight. This means that you have to pay for drinks and headsets; goodies that are free on international sectors. Furthermore, when coming in through Hawaii from Australasia it's not unknown for passengers who take a long time clearing Customs to be left behind by the US airline.

To find good fares to Australia check the travel ads in the Sunday travel sections of papers like the *Los Angeles Times, San Francisco Chronicle-Examiner, New York Times* or *Toronto Globe & Mail*. The straightforward return excursion fare from the USA west coast is around US$1000 to US$1500 depending on the season but plenty of deals

Top: Bluff Mountain, Warrumbungles
Left: Belougery Spire, Warrumbungles
Right: Volcanic formation, Crater Bluff, Warrumbungles (JW)

Top: Alpine plains, Kosciusco National Park
Bottom: Summer daisies, near Mt Townsend, Kosciusco National Park

are available. You can typically get a one-way ticket from US$500 west coast or US$550 east coast, returns from US$800 west coast or US$900 east coast. At peak seasons – particularly the Australia summer/Christmas time – seats will be harder to get and the price will probably be higher. In the US good agents for discounted tickets are the two student travel operators, Council Travel and STA Travel, both of which have lots of offices around the country. Canadian west coast fares out of Vancouver will be similar to the US west coast. From Toronto fares go from around C$1500 return.

The French airline UTA have an interesting island-hopping route between the US west coast and Australia which includes the French colonies of New Caledonia and French Polynesia (Tahiti, etc). The UTA flight is often discounted and its multiple Pacific stopover possibilities makes it very popular with travellers. The UTA ticket typically costs about US$760 Los Angeles/Sydney one-way.

If Pacific island-hopping is your aim, several other airlines offer interesting opportunities. One is Hawaiian Airlines who fly Honolulu/Sydney via Pago Pago in American Samoa once a week. Qantas can give you Fiji or Tahiti along the way, Air New Zealand can offer both and the Cook Islands as well. See the Circle Pacific section for more details.

One-way/return fares available from Australia include: San Francisco A$750/1100, New York A$900/1460 and Vancouver $900/1449.

TO/FROM NEW ZEALAND
Air New Zealand and Qantas operate a network of trans-Tasman flights linking Auckland, Wellington and Christchurch in New Zealand with most major Australian gateway cities. You can fly directly between a lot of places in New Zealand and a lot of places in Australia.

Fares vary depending on which cities you fly between and when you do it but from New Zealand to Sydney you're looking at around NZ$540 one-way and NZ$699

return, to Melbourne NZ$605 one-way and NZ$799 return. There is a lot of competition on this route – with United, Continental and British Airways all flying as well as Qantas and Air New Zealand, so there is bound to be some good discounting going on.

Cheap fares to New Zealand from Europe will usually be for flights via the USA. A straightforward London/Auckland one-way bucket shop ticket costs from £350, or you could make that London/Auckland/Sydney or Melbourne from £510. Coming via Australia you can continue right around on a Round-the-World (RTW) ticket which will cost from around £1000 for a ticket with a comprehensive choice of stopovers.

TO/FROM ASIA
Ticket discounting is widespread in Asia, particularly in Singapore, Hong Kong, Bangkok and Penang. There are a lot of fly-by-nights in the Asian ticketing scene so a little care is required. Also the Asian routes have been particularly caught up in the capacity shortages on flights to Australia. Flights between Hong Kong and Australia are notoriously heavily booked while flights to or from Bangkok and Singapore are often part of the longer Europe-Australia route so they are also sometimes very full. Plan ahead. For much more information on South-East Asian travel and on to Australia see Lonely Planet's *South-East Asia on a shoestring*.

Typical one-way fares to Australia from Asia include from Hong Kong for around HK$2750 (US$370) or from Singapore for around S$600 (US$300). These fares are to the east coast capitals. Brisbane, Perth or Darwin are sometimes a bit cheaper.

You can also pick up some interesting tickets in Asia to include Australia on the way across the Pacific. UTA were first in this market but Qantas and Air New Zealand are also offering discounted trans-Pacific tickets. On the UTA ticket you can stop over in Jakarta, Sydney, Noumea, Auckland and Tahiti.

From Australia some typical return fares from the east coast include Singapore $865,

Kuala Lumpur $869, Bangkok $695, Hong Kong $990 and Delhi $1325.

The cheapest way out of Australia is to take one of the flights operating between Darwin and Kupang (Timor, Indonesia). Current one-way/return fares are $198/330. See the Darwin Getting There & Away section for full details.

TO/FROM AFRICA & SOUTH AMERICA
The flight possibilities from these continents are not so varied and you're much more likely to have to pay the full fare. There is only one direct flight between Africa and Australia and that is from Zimbabwe – the weekly Qantas Harare/Perth/Sydney route. A much cheaper alternative from East Africa is to fly from Nairobi to India or Pakistan and on to South-East Asia, then connect from there to Australia.

Two routes now operate between South America and Australia. The long-running Chile connection involves a Lan Chile flight Santiago/Easter Island/Tahiti from where you fly Qantas or another airline to Australia. Alternatively there is a route which skirts the Antarctic circle, flying Buenos Aires/Auckland/Sydney, operated by Aerolineas Argentinas in conjunction with Qantas.

ROUND-THE-WORLD TICKETS
Round-the-World tickets have become very popular in the last few years and many of these will take you through Australia. The airline RTW tickets are often real bargains and since Australia is pretty much at the other side of the world from Europe or North America it can work out no more expensive, or even cheaper, to keep going in the same direction right round the world rather than U-turn when you return.

The official airline RTW tickets are usually put together by a combination of two airlines, and permit you to fly anywhere you want on their route systems so long as you do not backtrack. Other restrictions are that you (usually) must book the first sector in advance and cancellation penalties then apply. There may be restrictions on how many stops you are permitted and usually the tickets are valid from 90 days up to a year. Typical prices for these South Pacific RTW tickets are from £760 to £1000 or US$2500 to US$3000.

An alternative type of RTW ticket is one put together by a travel agent using a combination of discounted tickets from a number of airlines. A UK agent like Trailfinders can put together interesting London-to-London RTW combinations including Australia for £1500 to £2000.

CIRCLE PACIFIC TICKETS
Circle Pacific fares are a similar idea to RTW tickets which use a combination of airlines to circle the Pacific – combining Australia, New Zealand, North America and Asia.

Examples would be Continental-Thai International, Qantas-Northwest Orient, Canadian Airlines International-Cathay Pacific and so on. As with RTW tickets there are advance purchase restrictions and limits to how many stopovers you can take.

Typically fares range between US$1200 and US$2000. A possible Circle Pacific route is Los Angeles/Hawaii/Auckland/Sydney/Singapore/Bangkok/Hong Kong/Tokyo/Los Angeles.

ARRIVING & DEPARTING
Arriving in Australia
Australia's dramatic increase in visitor arrivals has caused some severe bottlenecks at the entry points, particularly at Sydney where the airport is often operating at more than full capacity and delays on arrival or departure are frequent. Even when you're on the ground it can take ages to get through Immigration and Customs. One answer to this problem is to try not to arrive in Australia at Sydney. Sure, you'll have to go there sometime – but you can save yourself a lot of time and trouble by making Brisbane, Cairns, Melbourne or another gateway city your arrival point.

First-time travellers to Australia may be alarmed to find themselves being sprayed with insecticide by the airline stewards. It happens to everyone.

Leaving Australia

When you finally go remember to keep $20 aside for the departure tax.

Warning

This chapter is particularly vulnerable to change – prices for international travel are volatile, routes are introduced and cancelled, schedules change, rules are amended, special deals come and go, borders open and close. Airlines and governments seem to take a perverse pleasure in making price structures and regulations as complicated as possible and you should check directly with the airline or travel agent to make sure you understand how a fare (and ticket you may buy) works.

In addition, the travel industry is highly competitive and there are many lurks and perks. The upshot of this is that you should get opinions, quotes and advice from as many airlines and travel agents as possible before you part with your hard-earned cash. The details given in this chapter should be regarded only as pointers and cannot be any substitute for your own careful, up-to-date research.

Getting Around

GETTING TO BUSHWALKING AREAS

Most of the good bushwalking areas are well away from the large towns and major highways. As a result access to many areas by public transport is non-existent. Local bushwalkers generally use private cars. If you join a local bushwalking club then transport will be less of a problem.

There are a few regions which have reasonable access by public transport. The area around Sydney has a regular electric train service along the coast and up into the mountains and these trains provide access to some excellent bushwalks.

In contrast, Victoria has no public transport at all to the better bushwalking areas and this is true for most of Australia. The walks detailed have been chosen to make use of public transport if available and notes on transport are given for each walk.

Tasmania is the exception as it has regular, special bushwalkers bus services to the more popular walking areas. These buses only operate in the summer months. In other seasons the buses can be chartered (worthwhile for four or more people) to take you to any bushwalking access point. The operators of these special buses provide an excellent service and are highly recommended.

For those who want to walk in the more remote areas hiring a car is a good idea. Cars should be hired in a major city where more than one firm operates and rates are competitive. Hitchhiking to the bushwalking areas is not a good idea as some of the roads receive very few cars (only a couple a day), so you could be in for a very long walk along hard roads. As well it is officially not allowed in most states.

When arriving at the start of a walk late at night most bushwalkers camp beside their vehicle at the car park. Although in most states it is illegal to camp beside a road, in practice it is tolerated provided that you are not camped in a town and you pack up your equipment *very* early in the morning.

Information regarding any special problems with a late arrival is included in the Access notes for each walk.

The information which follows is provided for foreign bushwalkers who need to know transport details for those times in between forays into the bush.

AIR

Australia is so vast (and at times so empty) that unless your time is unlimited you will probably have to take to the air sometime. It has been calculated that something like 80% of long-distance trips by public transport are made by air.

The big news on the air travel front in Australia has been the deregulation of the domestic airline industry. For 40-odd years Australia had the 'two-airline policy'; just two airlines, Australian and Ansett, had a duopoly on domestic flights. With this cosy cohabitation the airlines could charge virtually what they liked, and operate virtually identical schedules. This meant that for the traveller, domestic airline travel within Australia was expensive and the choices of flights limited, particularly on low-volume routes.

With deregulation, which arrived in late 1990, came a new player on the scene, Compass Airlines. With just two wide-bodied aircraft it took on the two big operators, offering drastically reduced fares on the major runs. In just a short time it had captured a creditable 6% of the market – a huge achievement given the size of its fleet. Virtually overnight prices tumbled as the big airlines scrambled to keep up with their new fleet-footed opposition.

In December 1991, however, Compass went bust, and as we go to press its fate is still uncertain. If it does survive in any form, it may be a very different outfit. There are still quite a few bargain airfares on the domestic market, however, so shop around before you buy.

Note that all domestic flights in Australia are nonsmoking.

Cheap Fares
Random Discounting A major feature of the deregulated air travel industry seems to be random discounting. As the airlines try harder to fill planes, they are offering discounts of up to 70% on selected routes. Although this seems to apply mainly to the heavy volume routes, that's not always the case – at one stage Ansett were offering $100 seats from Alice Springs to Melbourne (normally $411), just for one flight.

To make the most of the discounted fares, you need to keep in touch with what's currently on offer, mainly because there are usually conditions attached to cheap fares – such as booking 14 or so days in advance, only flying on weekends, or between certain dates and so on. Also the number of seats available is usually fairly limited. The further ahead you can plan the better.

The places which this sort of discounting applies to are the main centres – Melbourne, Sydney, Brisbane, Cairns, Adelaide and Perth. For example, the full economy return fare from Melbourne to Perth is $1016; but the airlines are also currently offering special return flights for around $280.

Stand-by Stand-by fares are still the only discount offered on many routes. Basically they save you around 20% of the regular economy fare – Melbourne/Sydney, for example, is $229 one-way economy but only $175 stand-by (but specials of $80 one-way were on offer for much of 1991).

You have no guarantee of a seat when travelling stand-by. You buy your ticket at the airport, register at the stand-by desk and then wait for the flight to board. If at that time there is sufficient room for the stand-by passengers, on you go. If there's room for 10 additional passengers and 20 are on stand-by then the first 10 to have registered get on. If you miss the flight you can stand-by for the next one (you'll be that much further up the line if some stand-by passengers have got on) or you can try the other airline.

A catch with stand-by fares is that they only work on a sector basis. If you want to fly Melbourne/Perth and the flight goes via Adelaide you may have to stand-by on the Melbourne/Adelaide sector and then for the Adelaide/Perth sector. Furthermore the fares will be a combination of the two sectors, not a reduction from the direct Melbourne/Perth fare. Fortunately there are a lot more direct flights these days.

If you intend to stand-by the most likely flights will be, of course, the ones at the most inconvenient times. Very early in the morning, late at night or in the middle of the day are your best bets. Many inter-capital flights in Australia are really commuter services – Mr/Ms Businessperson zipping up from Sydney to Brisbane for a day's dealings – so the flights that fit in with the 9 to 5 life are the most crowded. 'Up for the weekend' flights – leaving Friday evening, coming back Sunday afternoon – also tend to be crowded. At other times you've got a pretty good chance of getting aboard.

Other Possibilities If you're planning a return trip and you have 21 days up your sleeve then you can save 40% by travelling Apex. You have to book and pay for your tickets 21 days in advance and once you're inside that 21-day period you cannot alter your booking in either direction. If you cancel you lose 50% of the fare.

Excursion fares, called Excursion 45 by Australian Airlines and Flexi-Fares by Ansett, give a 45% reduction on a round-trip ticket, can only be booked between four and 14 days prior to travel and the maximum stay away is 21 days. You book a flight for a nominated day and contact the airline before 12 noon on the day prior to departure to be advised of which flight you will be on. Your travel arrangements need to be flexible.

University or other higher education students under the age of 26 can get a 25% discount off the regular economy fare. An airline tertiary concession card is required for Australian students. Overseas students can use their International Student Identity Card, a New Zealand student card or an overseas airline ticket issued at the 25% student reduction. The latter sounds a good bet!

All international travellers can get a 25% discount on internal flights to connect with their arriving or departing international flight – so if you're flying in to Sydney from Los Angeles but intend to go on to the Black Stump you get 25% off the Sydney/Black Stump flight.

Non-Australian travellers coming to Australia by any inbound international flight, or even by ship, can get 25% off all regular fares so long as you buy the tickets before you arrive or within 30 days of arriving and complete all travel within 60 days of arriving. Whew!

International visitors can also get a good deal on domestic flights with Qantas. Normally Qantas isn't allowed to carry domestic passengers but if you're a visitor to Australia with an international ticket you can fly Qantas at 50% of the standard economy fare. The catch is that these flights are often just the finishing or starting sectors of longer international flights and often operate at less convenient times. Also, although domestic passengers are spared a great deal of the international rigmarole the departure and arrival formalities still take rather longer than with a regular domestic flight.

There are also some worthwhile cheaper deals with regional airlines such as East-West or a number of Queensland operators. On some lesser routes these operators undercut the big two. Keep your eyes open for special deals at certain times of the year.

Air Passes

Ansett and Australian Airlines both have special round the country fares – Australian Airlines' is called an Explorer Airpass, Ansett's is a Kangaroo Airpass. Both have two tickets available – 6000 km for $949 and 10,000 km for $1499. There are a number of restrictions applied to these tickets, despite which they can be a good deal if you want to see a lot of country in a short period of time. You do not need to start and finish at the same

place; you could start in Sydney and end in Darwin for example.

Restrictions include a minimum travel time (10 days) and a maximum (45 days). On the 6000-km pass you must stop at least twice but at most three times. On the 10,000-km pass you must stop at least three times but at most seven. One of the stops must be at a non-capital-city destination and be for at least four days. There are requirements about changing reservations although generally there is no charge unless the ticket needs to be rewritten.

On a 6000-km airpass you could, for example, fly Sydney/Alice Springs/Cairns/Brisbane/Sydney. That gives you three stops and two of them are in non-capital cities. The regular fare for that circuit would be $1378, so you save $429. A one-way route might be Adelaide/Melbourne/Sydney/Alice Springs/Perth. There are three stops of which one is a non-capital city. Regular cost for that route would also be $1378, so again you save $429.

Other Airline Options

There are a number of secondary airlines apart from the two major domestic carriers. In Western Australia there's Ansett WA with an extensive network of flights to the mining towns of the north-west and to Darwin in the Northern Territory. Ansett NT operate from Darwin down to Alice Springs and Ayers Rock and also across to the Queensland and Western Australian coasts. East-West Airlines operate along the east coast, and across to Ayers Rock and Alice Springs from Sydney.

There are numerous other smaller operators. Sunstate operate services in Queensland including out to a number of islands. They also have a couple of routes in the south to Mildura and Broken Hill. Skywest have a number of services to remote parts of Western Australia. Eastern Airlines operate up and down the New South Wales coast and also inland from Sydney as far as Bourke and Cobar. Air NSW have services all over New South Wales, up to Brisbane, down to Melbourne and in to Alice Springs.

Airport Transport

There are private or public bus services at almost every major town in Australia. In one or two places you may have to depend on taxis but in general you can get between airport and city reasonably economically and conveniently by bus. Quite often a taxi shared between three or more people can be cheaper than the bus.

BUS

Bus travel is generally the cheapest way from A to B, other than hitching of course, but the main problem is to find the best deal.

There are only two truly *national* bus networks – Greyhound/Pioneer and Bus Australia. Greyhound and Pioneer were once separate companies, and although they still operate their own buses, tickets on either company are interchangeable. Bus Australia is the cheaper of the two networks, with fares up to 10% lower, but this is offset against a smaller network of services. Students under 26 years of age can get a discount on some routes, usually 10%; ditto for YHA and backpacker card holders. YHA travel offices sometimes offer discounts on buses.

There are also many smaller bus companies operating locally or specialising in one or two main intercity routes. These often offer the best deals – Firefly costs \$40 for Sydney to Melbourne, for example. In South Australia Stateliner operate around the state including the Flinders Ranges. Westrail in Western Australia and V/Line in Victoria operate bus services to places the trains no longer go.

A great many travellers see Australia by bus because it's one of the best ways to come to grips with the country's size and variety of terrain, and because the bus companies have such comprehensive route networks – far more comprehensive than the railway system. The buses all look pretty similar and are similarly equipped with air-conditioning, toilets and videos.

In many places there is now one bus terminal shared by all the operators. Big city terminals are generally well equipped – they usually have toilets, showers and facilities.

Routes & Stopovers

The bus companies do not operate identical routes and it's the small print on the tickets which can make the big differences between one company and another when it comes to stopovers and other important considerations. Always check the stopover deals if you want to make stops en route to your final destination, as you can save quite a few dollars on supposedly similar fares.

Bus Passes

Set Period Version Bus Australia and Greyhound both have bus passes which offer unlimited travel for a set period, but you should think very carefully before getting one. It *sounds* good but many travellers find that the passes are too restrictive and that to make proper use of them they have to travel faster than they would wish. This particularly seems to apply to people who buy their passes before they arrive in Australia. Often there are cheap deals making it attractive to buy a pass in advance. So think carefully about exactly which, if any, pass is best for you and whether you really can't wait till you get to Oz before laying out the cash.

Bus passes generally go from 15 to 90 days although there are some shorter seven or 10-day passes. The very short passes really don't make sense. If you started in Adelaide, travelled to Melbourne, spent four days there, travelled to Canberra, spent two days there, travelled to Sydney, spent four days there and then travelled to Brisbane you'd have run through a 15-day pass (around \$450) and only got around \$175 of bus travel out of it. Even if you'd started in Perth, and only spent a couple of days in each place the sector fare would still have cost you only \$335 on Greyhound, generally the most expensive bus line.

A 15-day pass typically costs about \$450, a 21-day pass about \$630, a 30-day pass \$850, a 60-day pass \$1250, and a 90-day pass \$1700. Greyhound/Pioneer, with the most extensive route network and the most frequent services, is more expensive than Bus Australia. Your bus pass also gives you discounts on accommodation, local sightseeing tours, rental cars and so on. Neither of the big two operate in Tasmania but there are usually tie ins with the local operators.

Set Route Version Better value is the set route pass, which gives you six or 12 months to cover a set route. You haven't got the go-anywhere flexibility of the unlimited travel bus pass but nor do you have the time constraints. Greyhound and Bus Australia both have numerous set-route passes, so it's a matter of deciding which one suits your needs. The main limitation is that you can't backtrack, except on 'dead-end' short sectors such as Darwin to Kakadu, Townsville to Cairns and Ayers Rock (Yulara) to the Stuart Highway.

Greyhound's 'Aussie Highlights' allows you to loop around the eastern half of Australia from Sydney taking in Melbourne, Adelaide, Coober Pedy, Ayers Rock, Alice Springs, Darwin (& Kakadu), Cairns, Townsville, Whitsundays, Brisbane and Surfers Paradise for A\$584. Or there are one-way passes, such as the 'Go West' pass from Sydney to Cairns via Melbourne, Adelaide, Ayers Rock, Alice Springs, Katherine, Darwin (& Kakadu), and Townsville for \$535; or 'Trans Aussie', which goes from Cairns to Perth via the Top End and down the centre, for \$477. There's even an 'All Australian' pass which takes you right around the country, including up or down through the centre, for \$916. This would be far better value than a 90-day bus pass since you'd be utterly wrecked trying to cover all that ground in a mere two or three months!

Distance Version The most recent variety of bus pass offers six to 12 months' travel to any combination of destinations, priced according to the distance you expect to travel: a minimum 2000 km from Greyhound/ Pioneer for \$110 (1500 km for \$85 from Bus Australia), plus \$50 for every subsequent 1000 km. The trip from Sydney through Melbourne, Adelaide, Ayers Rock, Alice, Darwin, Kakadu, Darwin again,

Cairns, Brisbane and back to Sydney would amount to 11,500 km and cost \$600. You would have the option of changing your mind halfway through at Darwin and zooming off to Perth via Broome instead, leaving you with enough unused ticket to get you to Monkey Mia and back.

TRAIN

Rail travel in Australia today is basically something you do because you really want to – not because it's cheaper, especially now with the reduced airfares, and certainly not because it's fast. Rail travel is generally the slowest way to get from anywhere to anywhere in Australia. On the other hand the trains are comfortable and you certainly see Australia at ground level in a way no other means of travel permits.

Austrail passes, allowing unlimited travel on all Australian rail systems, are available, but only for overseas residents. The Australian dollar costs are 14 days \$415 (\$690 1st class), 21 days \$535 (\$850), 30 days \$650 (\$1050), 60 days \$930 (\$1460) and 90 days \$1070 (\$1680). The economy pass does not cover meals and berth charges on trips where these are charged for as additional costs. The passes can be bought in Australia (as long as you don't live here) or in the UK through Compass Travel and in the USA through Tour Pacific.

Australian students can get a 50% discount on regular fares but they need to have a railways student concession card from their college or university. Caper fares are an advance purchase deal which gives a saving of up to 30% and on some major routes there are stand-by tickets. On interstate rail journeys you can usually break your journey at no extra cost provided you complete the trip within two months on a one-way ticket, or six months with a return ticket.

On some routes you can take your car with you by train.

For timetables and fares for the major interstate routes, contact the Railways of Australia, 85 Queen St, Melbourne (☎ (03) 608 0811).

CAR

Australia is a big, sprawling country with large cities where public transport is not always very comprehensive or convenient. Like America the car is the accepted means of getting from A to B and many visitors will consider getting wheels to explore the country – either by buying a car or renting one.

Driving in Australia holds few real surprises. Australians drive on the left-hand side of the road just like in the UK, Japan and most countries in south and east Asia and the Pacific. There are a few local variations from the rules of the road as applied elsewhere in the West. The main one is the 'give way to the right' rule. This means that if you're driving along a main road and somebody appears on a minor road on your right, you must give way to them – unless they are facing a give-way or stop sign. This rule caused so much confusion over the years – with cars zooming out of tiny tracks onto main highways and expecting everything to screech to a stop for them – that most intersections are now signposted to indicate which is the priority road. It's wise to be careful because while almost every intersection is signposted in southern capitals, when you get up to towns in the north of Queensland, stop signs are few and far between and the old give-way rules will apply.

The general speed limit in built-up areas in Australia is 60 km/h and out on the open highway it's usually 100 or 110 km/h depending on where you are, although in the Northern Territory there is no speed limit outside of built-up areas.

Australia was one of the first countries in the world to make the wearing of seat belts compulsory. All new cars in Australia are required to have seat belts back and front and if your seat has a belt then you're required to wear it. You're liable to be fined if you don't. Small children must be belted into an approved safety seat.

Although overseas licences are acceptable in Australia for genuine overseas visitors, an International Driving Permit is even more acceptable.

On the Road

Australia is not crisscrossed by multi-lane highways. There simply is not enough traffic and the distances are too great to justify them. You'll certainly find stretches of divided road, particularly on busy roads like the Sydney-to-Melbourne Hume Highway or close to the state capital cities – the last stretch into Adelaide from Melbourne, the Pacific Highway from Sydney to Newcastle, the Surfers Paradise-Brisbane road, for example. Elsewhere, Australian roads are only two-lane, but well-surfaced on all the main routes.

You don't have to get very far off the beaten track, however, to find yourself on dirt roads, and anybody who sets out to see the country in reasonable detail will have to expect to do some dirt-road travelling. If you really want to explore outlandish places, then you'd better plan on having four-wheel drive (4WD) and a winch. A few useful spare parts are worth carrying if you're travelling on highways in the Northern Territory or the north of Western Australia. A broken fan belt can be a damn nuisance if the next service station is 200 km away.

Buying a Car

If you want to explore Australia by car and haven't got one or can't borrow one, then you've either got to buy one or rent one. Australian cars are not cheap – another product of the small population. Locally manufactured cars are made in small, uneconomic numbers and imported cars are heavily taxed so they won't undercut the local products. If you're buying a second-hand vehicle reliability is all important. Mechanical breakdowns way out in the outback can be very inconvenient – the nearest mechanic can be a hell of a long way down the road.

Shopping around for a used car involves much the same rules as anywhere in the Western world but with a few local variations. First of all, used car dealers in Australia are just like used car dealers from Los Angeles to London – they'd sell their mother into slavery if it turned a dollar. For any given car you'll probably get it cheaper by buying privately through newspaper small ads rather than through a car dealer. Buying through a dealer does give the advantage of some sort of guarantee, but a guarantee is not much use if you're buying a car in Sydney and intend setting off for Perth next week. Used-car guarantee requirements vary from state to state – check with the local automobile organisation.

There's much discussion amongst travellers about where is the best place to buy used cars. Popular theories exist that you can buy a car in Sydney or Melbourne, drive it to Darwin and sell it there for a profit. Or was it vice versa? It's quite possible that prices do vary but don't count on turning it to your advantage.

What is rather more certain is that the further you get from civilisation, the better it is to be in a Holden or a Ford. New cars can be a whole different ball game of course, but if you're in an older vehicle, something that's likely to have the odd hiccup from time to time, then life is much simpler if it's a car for which you can get spare parts anywhere from Bourke to Bulamakanka. When your fancy Japanese car goes kaput somewhere back of Bourke it's likely to be a two-week wait while the new bit arrives fresh from Fukuoka. On the other hand, when your rusty old Holden goes bang there's probably another old Holden sitting in the ditch with a perfectly good widget waiting to be removed. Every scrap yard in Australia is full of good ole Holdens.

Note that in Australia third-party personal injury insurance is always included in the vehicle registration cost. This ensures that every vehicle (as long as it's currently registered) carries at least minimum insurance. You're wise to extend that minimum to at least third-party property insurance as well – minor collisions with Rolls Royces can be surprisingly expensive.

When you come to buy or sell a car there are usually some local regulations with which to comply. In Victoria, for example, a car has to have a compulsory safety check (Road Worthiness Certificate – RWC) before

it can be registered in the new owner's name – usually the seller will indicate if the car already has a RWC. In New South Wales, on the other hand, safety checks are compulsory every year when you come to renew the registration. Stamp duty has to be paid when you buy a car and, as this is based on the purchase price, it's not unknown for buyer and seller to agree privately to understate the price! It's much easier to sell a car in the same state that it's registered in, otherwise it has to be re-registered in the new state. It may be possible to sell a car without re-registering it, but you're likely to get a lower price.

Renting a Car

For bushwalkers this isn't a great option as you will be walking on days you are paying for rental, but for days in-between walks it is an option. If you've got the cash there are plenty of car rental companies ready and willing to put you behind the wheel. Competition in the Australian car rental business is pretty fierce so rates tend to be variable and lots of special deals pop up and disappear again. Whatever your mode of travel on the long stretches, it can be very useful to have a car for some local travel. Between a group it can even be reasonably economical. There are some places – like around Alice Springs – where if you haven't got your own wheels you really have to choose between a tour and a rented vehicle since there is no public transport and the distances are too great for walking or even bicycles.

The three major companies were Budget, Hertz and Avis with offices in almost every town that has more than one pub and a general store. Budget went into liquidation in 1992 but franchise holders continued to operate, and have taken over the airport desks. The second-string companies which are also represented almost everywhere in the country are Thrifty and National. Then there is a vast number of local firms or firms with outlets in a limited number of locations. You can take it as read that the big operators will generally have higher rates than the local firms but it ain't necessarily so, so don't jump to conclusions.

The major companies all offer unlimited km rates in the city, but in country and 'remote' areas it's a flat charge plus so many cents per km. On straightforward off-the-card city rentals they're all pretty much the same price. It's on special deals, odd rentals or longer periods that you find the differences. Weekend specials – usually three days for the price of two – are usually good value. If you just need a car for three days around Sydney make it the weekend rather than midweek. Budget offer 'stand-by' rates and you may see other special deals available.

Daily metropolitan rates are typically about $60 a day for a small car (Ford Laser, Toyota Corolla, Nissan Pulsar), about $75 a day for a medium car (Holden Camira, Toyota Camry, Nissan Pintara) or about $80 to $90 a day for a big car (Holden Commodore, Ford Falcon). Add another $12 a day for insurance. Typically country rates will be metropolitan plus $5 a day plus 30c a km beyond 200 km a day. Remote rates will be metropolitan plus $10 a day plus 30c a km beyond 100 km a day. It soon gets expensive!

MOTORCYCLE

Motorcycles are a very popular way of getting around. The climate is just about ideal for biking most of the year, and the many small trails from the road into the bush often lead to perfect spots to spend the night in the world's largest camping ground.

The long, open roads are really made for large-capacity machines above 750 cc, which Australians prefer once they outgrow their 250 cc learner restrictions. But that doesn't stop enterprising individuals – many of them Japanese – from tackling the length and breadth of the continent on 250 cc trail bikes. Doing it on a small bike is not impossible, just tedious at times.

BICYCLE

Whether you're hiring a bike to ride around a city or wearing out your Bio-Ace chainwheels on a Melbourne-Darwin marathon, you'll find that Australia is a great place for cycling. There are bike tracks in most cities, and in the country you'll find thousands of km of good roads which carry so little traffic that the biggest hassle is waving back to the drivers. Especially appealing is that in many areas you'll ride a very long way without encountering a hill.

Bicycle helmets are compulsory wear in Victoria and Queensland, and other states are thinking about legislation.

It's possible to plan rides of any duration and through almost any terrain. A day or two cycling around South Australia's wineries is popular, or you could meander along beside the Murrumbidgee for weeks. Tasmania is very popular for touring, and mountain bikes would love Australia's deserts – or its mountains, for that matter.

HITCHING

Travel by thumb may be frowned upon by the boys and girls in blue in some places but it can be a good way of getting around and it is certainly interesting. Sometimes it can even be fast, but it's usually foolish to try and set yourself deadlines when travelling this way – you need luck. Successful hitching depends on several factors, all of them just plain good sense.

The most important is your numbers – two people are really the ideal, any more make things very difficult. Ideally those two should comprise one male and one female – two guys hitching together can expect long waits. It is probably not advisable for women to hitch alone, or even in pairs. Queensland in particular is notorious for attacks on women travellers. Factor two is position – look for a place where vehicles will be going slowly and where they can stop easily. A junction or freeway slip road are good places if there is stopping room. Position goes beyond just where you stand. The ideal location is on the outskirts of a town – hitching from way out in the country is as hopeless as from the centre of a city. Take a bus out to the edge of town.

Factor three is appearance. The ideal appearance for hitching is a sort of genteel poverty – threadbare but clean. Looking too good can be as much of a bummer as looking too bad! Don't carry too much gear – if it looks like it's going to take half an hour to pack your bags aboard you'll be left on the roadside.

Factor four is knowing when to say no. Saying no to a car-load of drunks or your friendly rapist may be pretty obvious, but it can be time-saving to say no to a short ride that might take you from a good hitching point to a lousy one. Wait for the right, long ride to come along. On a long haul, it's pointless to start walking as it's not likely to increase the likelihood of you getting a lift and it's often an awfully long way to the next town.

Trucks are often the best lifts but they will only stop if they are going slowly and can get started easily again. Thus the ideal place is at the top of a hill where they have a downhill run. Truckies often say they are going to the next town and if they don't like you, will drop you anywhere. As they often pick up hitchers for company, the quickest way to create a bad impression is to jump in and fall asleep. It's also worth remembering that while you're in someone else's vehicle, you are their guest and should act accordingly – many drivers no longer pick up people because they have suffered from thoughtless hikers in the past. It's the hitcher's duty to provide entertainment!

Hitching in Australia is reasonably safe if you travel in pairs and take care with your rides. Of course people do get stuck in outlandish places but that is the name of the game. If you're visiting from abroad a nice prominent flag on your pack will help, and a sign announcing your destination can also be useful. Uni and hostel notice boards are good places to look for hitching partners. The main law against hitching is 'thou shalt not stand in the road' – so when you see the law coming, step back.

New South Wales

This is Australia's oldest state and provides some ideal bushwalking country. Most of the walking is in the Great Dividing Range which runs parallel to the eastern coast for 1000 km. Parts of this range are still heavily timbered and dissected with many deep gorges. In such an ideal walking area there is a large range of bushwalks for both the beginner and the experienced.

Most of the popular areas are close to Sydney, Australia's largest city. Royal National Park, established in 1879 and the second oldest park in the world, is on the southern edge of Sydney and is very popular with bushwalkers. It provides easy walking along a relatively natural coastline. There are a few holiday houses and surf clubs within this park yet the natural beauty has still been retained. Regular public transport provides easy access to each end of the park. For a relaxing two-day walk the traverse along the coastline of this park is highly recommended.

On the western side of Sydney are the Blue Mountains, an uplifted sandstone plateau whose name comes from the characteristic blue haze created by the forests of gum (eucalyptus) trees. The Blue Mountains are only 1000 metres above sea level but are impressive as every valley is rimmed with sandstone cliffs. There are many narrow canyons, waterfalls and unspoilt valleys

within these ranges for bushwalkers to explore.

Between the cliffs and canyons is the Blue Gum Forest, an unusual forest composed almost entirely of a single species of gum tree. An interesting walk based on this forest, the surrounding cliffs, canyons and waterfalls, gives bushwalkers a chance to see the Blue Mountains at their best. Potential for extensive bushwalking in the region is unlimited as there are large national parks that protect the ranges north and south of Katoomba.

Extending north from the Blue Mountains the Great Dividing Range dips then rises to become the New England Tablelands. Good bushwalking exists in the area although only part of the region is protected by national parks.

Inland from the Great Dividing Range there is a small spectacular group of volcanic peaks called the Warrumbungles which tower above the flat plains. The range lies in a rain shadow and receives very little rainfall and often water must be carried, however, the clear dry air compensates with fine views almost every day of the year. It is worth walking and camping high on the range to watch the dramatic sunsets and sunrises. An easy circuit using the track system is described. Experienced bushwalkers can extend the walk south to Tonduron Spire as listed in the suggestions.

To the south of Sydney, the sandstone and granite ranges of the Great Dividing Range are protected by a series of national parks. In particular the Morton National Park contains some of the most spectacular scenery in the state. In the north of this park are Fitzroy Falls which are very popular for short walks. The southern half of this park is more remote and protects the northern Budawang Range.

This range has the highest and most impressive cliffs in the area and many hidden features which are only accessible to bushwalkers. The Castle and Monolith Valley provide the best bushwalking in the state and are well worth the effort required to visit them. The approach walk from the western side of the park to the major features is described in the section on the Budawang Ranges. The area is very rugged and there is so much to see it can be visited several times and still be interesting.

West of the Budawangs is Canberra, the capital city of Australia, 250 km south-west of Sydney. Extending south from Canberra to the Victorian border is a high mountain range which contains all of Australia's highest peaks. A huge reserve, the Snowy Mountains National Park, protects most of this region.

The most popular walking areas are the high plateaus where the low alpine vegetation allows very easy scenic walking in fine weather. The southern half of this park contains the three highest peaks in the country. The circuit walk visiting these peaks and lakes remaining from the last glacial period is very popular and included in this guide.

Inland from the Great Dividing Range much of New South Wales is a broad featureless plain covered with farmlands of little interest to bushwalkers. Most of the national parks here are for the protection of swamplands and river systems and not ideal for bushwalking.

The walks described for NSW visit some of the best bushwalking country but are just a few of the many excellent walks that can be done. Experienced bushwalkers who are looking for more unusual walks should read the guidebooks for NSW. Following are a few suggestions to provide a starting point:

Other Suggested Bushwalks
Sydney Area
Great North Walk This links Sydney to Newcastle with a 250-km walking track through suburbs, farms and extensive forest sections. Allow 14 days for this easy walk.

Hume & Hovell Track A 372-km walking track following a historic trail from Yass to Woomargama (near Albury). It passes through some farmlands and extensive forest sections in undulating country.

The Three Peaks This famous walk is from Kanangra Walls to Mts Cloudmaker, Strongleg, Konangaroo, Guouogang, Paralyser, and Thurat, and back to Kanangra Walls. It is a classic three to four-day medium to hard circuit in the Blue Mountains south of Katoomba.

Katoomba to Kanangra Walls Follow Narrowneck to Mt Dingo and down to Cox's River; head up to Kanangra Walls via Mt Cloudmaker or the Gingra Ridge. This popular three to four-day medium walk requires a long car shuffle. It is located in the Blue Mountains south of Katoomba.

Kowmung River From Kanangra Walls, follow the Uni Rover Trail south to the river then east down the river and up Hughes Ridge onto Gingra Ridge and back to the start. A two to three-day circuit in the Blue Mountains.

Wollangambe Crater From Bell, descend into the valley and up to the Wollangambe Crater and return via Mt Wilson. A two-day walk requiring a short car shuffle north of Katoomba.

Grose River From Blackheath, follow tracks to the Blue Gum Forest, then follow the Grose River downstream to the Nepean River. A three to five-day medium to hard bushwalk north of Katoomba. It requires a car shuffle but can be done with public transport.

Southern Area
Shoalhaven River & Bungonia Gorge From Long Point descend to the river and walk two km upstream to Bungonia Creek. Explore the gorge and return by the same route. A popular, easy two-day walk near Goulburn, 90 km north-east of Canberra.

Ettrema Creek From Quiera Clearing follow Myall Creek into the gorge, downstream to Tullyangela Creek then west to Tullyangela Clearing. A medium to hard three-day walk.

Budawangs Circuit From Newhaven Gap descend via Folly Point then past Angel Falls to Mt Cole. Explore Monolith Valley and The Castle and return via Mt Tarn and Quilty's Mountain to Newhaven Gap. A medium to hard four to five-day circuit in the Budawangs.

Northern Kosciusko Circuit From Round Mountain walk south via Valentine Falls to Schlink Pass. Then climb up onto Gungartan and north past Mawson's Hut to Mt Jagungal. From here, follow Farm Ridge back to Round Mountain. This is an easy five-day circuit walk in the alpine country north of Mt Kosciusko.

Guthega Circuit From Guthega climb through Schlink Pass to Valentines Falls then west to Grey Mare Mountain and south to Olsen's Lookout. Descend south into the valley and climb up to Lake Albina. Visit Mt Kosciusko and Mt Townsend as a day trip. Continue east over Mt Twynham and Mt Tate to Guthega. This is a five to seven-day medium to hard circuit walk in the Kosciusko National Park.

Northern Area

Warrumbungles Southern Circuit From Camp Pincham climb to Ogma Saddle then south through the bush past Bluff Mountain to Gale's Bore. Climb Tonduron Spire as a day trip and return via Twin Pools and Dagda Saddle back to Camp Pincham. This bushwalk is a three to four-day medium circuit.

Kaputar Southern Gorges From Governor Mountain walk south past Joker Spring and down to Scutts Hut and Kurrawonga Falls. Follow the ridge north to Bundabulla Cliffs and Dawsons Spring. This is a medium two-day circuit, 50 km east of Narrabri.

New England Circuit From the park entrance follow Robinson's Knob Trail, then Comara Trail and Postmans Trail to Five Day Creek. Follow the trails north to Diamond Flat Trail then Cliffs Trail back to the start. This is a medium four to five-day circuit, 70 km east of Armidale.

ROYAL NATIONAL PARK COASTAL WALK

Royal National Park is the second oldest national park in the world. Close to Sydney it is easily accessible by public transport. Bushwalking in this park is easy and very enjoyable. Although well used the park does not give the impression of being badly overcrowded, a result of the large number of access points. The bushwalker has a variety of tracks to walk; the classic walk is to traverse the length of the park along its impressive coastline, passing through two main tourist recreation beaches where aid can be obtained if needed. The circuit is completed with the use of public transport.

Features

Royal National Park is a coastal park with low sandstone ridges, deeply cut by several streams and a magnificent, varied coastline. The coast has sandy beaches between rocky headlands and sheer cliffs up to 100 metres high. The cliff tops and inland ridges are covered with heath which is a blaze of colour in spring and around the sheltered coves and bays are banksia and ti-tree forests. Further inland patches of subtropical forest fill the gullies. The wide variety of trees and plants support a large range of birds and animals, unusual for a park this close to a major city.

Standard

The walk follows well worn tracks along the coast. These are easy to follow, but some care is required at junctions as not all tracks are signposted. The walk is graded easy.

Days Required

The walk along the coast takes two easy days to complete. There is little scope for extending the length of the walk, but a pleasant extra day could be spent swimming or watching the birds and wildlife at one of the bays or beaches.

Seasons

Any season is suitable for walking in this park. In summer water may need to be carried as the creeks are often dry. The containers can be refilled at taps in the picnic areas at Garie and Wattamolla Beaches.

During very hot summer weather the park may be closed because of the risk of bushfires. The Sutherland Park Office (☎ (02) 542 0648) can be contacted for the current fire danger level. Autumn or spring is an ideal time to go as it is usually fine and mild during the day. In winter a jumper or wool shirt is needed because of the cold winds, but walking is still very pleasant.

Equipment

No special equipment is needed apart from a stove. All fires are totally banned in the park and stoves must be carried for cooking. Runners/trainers or very light boots are ideal footwear. In summer, sunscreen and a wide-brimmed hat are advised. Water containers may also be required if the creeks are dry.

Maps

The 1:30,000 special topographic map, *Royal National Park*, is very good and the only map needed. This map shows all the regular camping areas, tracks and access points and also has many facts and points of interest marked on it. It is published by the Central Mapping Authority of New South Wales. In Sydney you can get it in bushwalking shops.

The 1:25,000 topographic maps, *Port Hacking* and *Otford*, are also useful. These can be bought from the Central Mapping Authority and bushwalking shops.

Permits

You need to get a Bush Camping permit for each member of the party, available from the park's Visitor Centre at Audley (the parks main entrance), any ranger, or from the National Parks & Wildlife Service Office (☎ (02) 585 6444), in Sydney or the local park office (☎ (02) 542 0648). There is no fee for the permit (a rarity these days) and it is valid for one year (July 1st to June 30th). The permit details the regulations which are: no camping within one km of any road or picnic area, no wood fires allowed (stove cooking only) and all rubbish must be carried to a garbage bin or out of the park.

There is a series of established campsites and the park service prohibits camping at one of these locations in order to allow regeneration. This is done on a rotational basis and causes no problem as camping areas are fairly close.

Before starting this walk the Sutherland Park Office (☎ (02) 542 0648) should be contacted about possible closure of Curracurong and Curracurang camping areas. This could save some unnecessary walking.

Access

Royal National Park is 32 km south of Sydney on the southern edge of the suburbs.

It actually separates the cities of Sydney and Wollongong. The train line from Sydney to Wollongong forms the western border of the park making the park accessible by train. If coming by car to do this walk, park the car near Sutherland or Cronulla railway stations as the walk is not a circuit and the trains and a ferry are used to complete it.

The suburban electric train service is the best access for this walk. Contact the State Rail Authority (☎ (02) 954 4422 or (008) 044037) for the current timetable. Take a train from Sydney to Sutherland where it is sometimes necessary to change trains. Continue by train to Otford which is a small station on the Sutherland to Wollongong line. Check the timetable as very few trains stop at Otford station in the morning. Allow about 30 minutes from Sydney to Sutherland and a further 30 minutes to Otford.

Returning from the walk the northern end of the park is recommended as it has a very regular public transport service. The walk ends at Bundeena and a ferry leaves there for Cronulla on the hour, at every hour between 9 am and 6 pm. This meets a connecting train service at Cronulla returning to Sutherland (where trains may need to be changed) and then to Sydney Central.

Stage 1: Otford to Curracurrang
(17 km, 4-5 hours)

Leave the train at Otford railway station, in thick bushlands. From the east platform climb up the steps and along 20 metres to the right-hand end of the station. Two tracks join here, turn left to climb up the steep hill on a badly eroded track. This soon joins with an old road and climbs to meet a good gravel road.

Turn left and follow this major gravel road for 500 metres around the top of the hill to meet the sealed road. Turn left (north) onto the road and walk 100 metres to a car park. Above the car park is a lookout. Follow the track to it for the first good views of the coast. This takes about 15 minutes from the station.

The track continues north-east and soon there is a turnoff on the right which leads to Werrong Beach. Take the left track, as

Top: Ormiston Pound
Bottom: Ormiston Gorge

Top: Ocean Beach, Fraser Island
Left: Strangler Fig, Fraser Island
Right: Basin Lake, Fraser Island

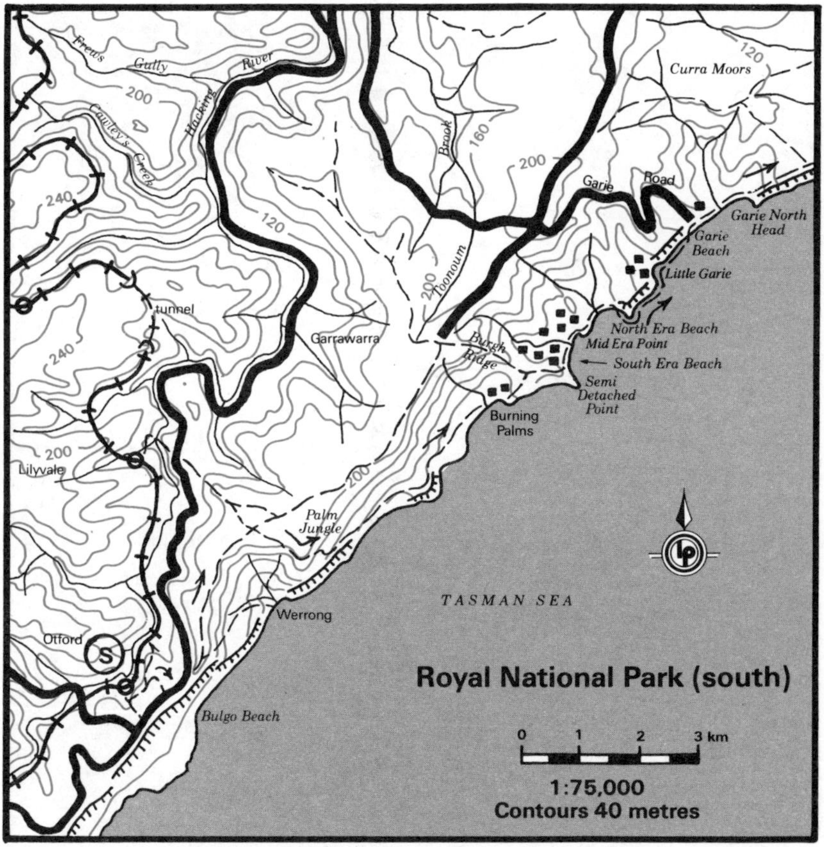

Royal National Park (south)

0   1   2   3 km

1:75,000
Contours 40 metres

Werrong is a dead end. The track continues along the ridge and becomes an old, sandy vehicle track and, 20 minutes after the Werrong junction, you get to another track junction. Turn right (east) and follow the well-trodden, but slightly overgrown, track towards the coast.

The track skirts under small cliffs, where there are patches of interesting rainforest, and follows the coast north-east for two km to descend to the sand at Burning Palms Beach. The track passes a rangers' hut just before the beach.

Walk north-east along the beach to its end.

Several tracks leave the beach and climb steeply up past the shacks. Climb past the last shack on the right to the ridge top. The coastal track veers right across the steep hillside for 500 metres to the grassy flats above Semi-Detached Point. If you have climbed onto a long flat ridge (called Burgh Ridge) turn north-east and descend steeply to the obvious grassy flats above the point.

From the grassy area the track enters some light scrub and descends to the South Era Beach, past several more shacks. Many tracks exist and you can take any that lead down to the sand.

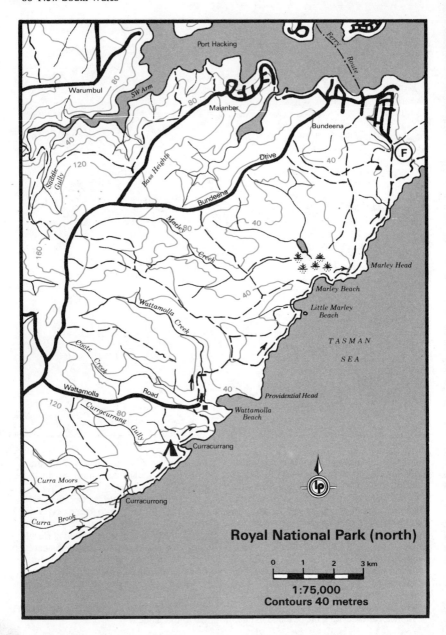

Port Hacking

Warumbul

SW Arm

Malanbar

Bundeena

Bass Heights

Drive

Bundeena

Marley Creek

Marley Head

Marley Beach

Little Marley Beach

Wattamolla Creek

TASMAN SEA

Coote Creek

Wattamolla Road

Providential Head

Wattamolla Beach

Curracurrang Gully

Curracurrang

Curra Moors

Curracurrong

Curra Brook

Saddle Gully

Royal National Park (north)

0   1   2   3 km

1:75,000
Contours 40 metres

Follow the beach north-east and walk around Mid Era Point on the rock platform. If it is covered by a very high tide you can follow a track along the cliff edge to the sand. Walk east along the North Era Beach. At the end of the beach a high cliff towers over the ocean. Follow the base of the cliff for one km to Little Garie then along the rocks to Garie Beach. The rock platform at the cliff base is above the high-tide level and can always be traversed except when there is a very heavy sea running.

Garie Beach is accessible by a road and has a surf life saving club, toilets and a kiosk. The kiosk is open on the weekends all year from mid-morning until mid-afternoon.

Leaving the kiosk walk north-east along the sand for one km to the end of the beach. From here the track climbs over Garie North Head and begins at the open grassy area near the start of the rocks. The rocks cannot be traversed to the next beach which is five km away. The track zigzags its way onto the top of the ridge with good views to the south. The track then follows the cliff edge closely through dense heath and ti-tree shrubs for three km.

There are very few views along this section due to the thickness of the bush. The well-defined track then descends to Curracurrong with good views of the rock walled bay below. It crosses a small creek, Curra Brook, then 300 metres further on it crosses the larger Curracurrong Creek. Camp can be made here if time is short as Curracurrang (don't get the two places confused!) is a further 40-minute walk. If Curracurrang is closed for regeneration then the overnight stop must be made at Curracurrong.

From Curracurrong the track continues to follow the cliff edge for another two km to the lovely little bay at Curracurrang. There are campsites all along the creek valley as it is a popular camping area.

Alternative Campsites

Burning Palms There are plenty of tent sites at the southern end of the bay. This is only 1½ to two hours from Otford railway station.

Stage 2: Curracurrang to Bundeena
(12 km, 3-4 hours)

From the creek the track rises up into the bush. It does not continue along the beach. The track turns right almost immediately to follow the edge of the low cliff line and then climbs gradually for one km through the bush to meet a 4WD track at some watertanks.

Turn left onto the rough road and follow it for 200 metres then turn right onto an unmarked walking track. This leads downhill past the edge of some car parks to the kiosk at Wattamolla. This is the other road access to the coast and has the same facilities as Garie, with the kiosk open from mid-morning to mid-afternoon at weekends only.

From here the coast track goes inland, so don't carry your packs down to Wattamolla Beach. Instead, cross the creek just above the waterfall and walk up onto the grassy flat on the north side of the creek. The start of the track is not obvious but you'll find it leading

up the hill in the centre of the flat. It passes through the bush to cross Wattamolla Creek just above an old dam, a lovely swimming hole in warm weather.

Just past the creek turn right at an unmarked track junction. You climb slowly east through the heathlands and follow the track for one km to meet the coastal cliff top again. The track swings north-east along the coast with some good views and descends to Little Marley Beach. Cross the tiny beach and either traverse the rock platform or use the track just above it to the larger, Marley Beach. Swimming is not recommended at this beach as it has a steep slope and rough surf.

At the east end of the beach you cross a tiny creek. The track is 20 metres back from the edge of the rocks near the lagoon. Climb up the track onto a low bluff and continue east over the open rock slabs about 50 metres from the cliff edge. Soon you'll see old bricks and pipes which are the remains of an old road. Follow this road for 200 metres to where it divides and take the right hand track. After 20 metres turn sharp right on an unmarked track and within another 10 metres this track turns sharp left and from there it is easily followed.

There are no markers in this area; if you end up walking along a well-defined vehicle track in thick low heathlands then you have missed the walking track. To find it simply return towards Marley Beach and turn sharp left onto another vehicle track. This connects with the Coast Track within 150 metres.

Continue north-east along the coast track which keeps close to the cliff edge and passes through very low scrub and heath giving commanding views of the coast and the suburbs of Sydney to the north. After one km the track approaches a large gully and descends to the right on the rocky cliff edge where there are good views of the waterfall and huge fallen blocks at the foot of the gully. After the gully, follow the main track which leaves the coast (there are some very minor side tracks, ignore them) for one km to the suburbs of Bundeena and the locked gate near the end of the walk.

The final one km is a pleasant walk on the paved streets of Bundeena. There are several streets that can be taken. Firstly, head north to the main road above the sea, then walk west along this to the short jetty from where the ferry leaves for Cronulla. This is opposite the general store on a sharp left-hand corner. The ferry leaves on the hour until 6 pm each day. Fares are paid on board the ferry. This connects with the train back to Sutherland railway station.

THE BLUE GUM FOREST

The Blue Gum Forest is a rare stand of one species of gum tree and is particularly beautiful to walk through and well worth visiting. Gum forest, however, is not the only feature of this walk. Narrow canyons, deep cliff-lined valleys and the waterfalls of the Upper Grose River all make this a memorable walk. Access is good from Sydney and the tracks are easy to follow. This walk is a *must* for all bushwalkers.

Features

The Blue Mountains is an elevated and fairly flat sandstone plateau. This plateau is deeply dissected by numerous streams and rivers leaving a series of flat topped ridges and deep valleys. The rivers have cut deeply into the sandstone exposing spectacular vertical cliffs that rim every valley and form the most dominant feature of the area.

The plateau is still being eroded as can be seen in the narrow confines of the Grand Canyon where a small stream is cutting very deeply into the soft rock. Hidden in these valleys are many small streams which cascade over many beautiful waterfalls.

The park is extensively vegetated. There are forests and heaths growing in the thin soil on the ridges, while down in the valleys the deeper, richer soils support rainforests and tall mixed eucalypts. Many native animals are found in the park but, as most are nocturnal, sightings while walking will be rare. Birds are more common and wild brumbies may be seen in the Grose Valley.

Standard

Most of the walk is along well-maintained tracks. A less used scrubby track is followed down the Grose Valley, but there are no navigational problems and the walk is graded easy. The walk can be done in either direction, but transport is easier to arrange for the suggested route.

Days Required

The walk through the Upper Grose Valley takes two easy days to complete. The suggested route includes an excellent circular day walk and this increases the walk to three days. There is little scope for extending the route because of restrictions placed on overnight camping.

Seasons

This valley can be walked at any time of the year. Autumn and spring are the most pleasant with mild days and a reasonable flow of water in the streams. Winter is also pleasant with cool days and plenty of water flowing over the falls. In summer the heat can be oppressive and the streams are at a very low level and more polluted than in other seasons. No fires are allowed during periods of high fire danger.

Equipment

No special hiking equipment is needed. Light boots or runners are suitable footwear. Carrying stoves is a good idea as wood is scarce due to the valley's popularity. You can get water from the streams, but it should be boiled before drinking because of pollution. The best suggestion is to carry all drinking water.

Maps

The 1:150,000 topographic map, *Blue Mountains – Burragorang Tourist Map*, gives an excellent indication of all the tracks and permitted campsites in and around the Blue Mountains National Park. This map is sufficient for the walk.

For more detail the 1:31,680 *Mount Wilson* and the 1:25,000 *Katoomba* topographic maps are recommended. All three maps are published by and available from the Central Mapping Authority of New South Wales, or you can get them in most bushwalking shops in Sydney.

The National Parks Authority produce many free leaflets to this park. These are available personally from the Blue Mountains Heritage Centre (☎ (047) 87 8877), Govetts Leap Road, Blackheath, or by writing to National Parks & Wildlife Service, PO Box 43, Blackheath, 2785.

Permits

No permits are required for walking or camping overnight within the park. All walkers are asked to fill out the intended route and expected date of return in the book kept at the police station (☎ (047) 87 8444), 119 Wentworth St, Blackheath. As the Grose Valley has been very popular with walkers, camping within the valley is restricted to only two locations: Burra Korain Flat and Acacia Flat. Both are good, well-located sites.

Access

The Blue Mountains National Park is 100 km due west of Sydney. It has good road and public transport access, as both the Great Western Highway and railway line to Bathurst pass through the centre of the park.

Blackheath is the start of this walk and has several shops and petrol stations. This small town is 115 km west from Sydney on the Great Western Highway and 11 km north of Katoomba. There is a regular electric train service from Sydney to Blackheath station. Consult the current timetable or ring the State Rail Authority (☎ (02) 954 4422 or (008) 044037) for details of current timetables. The train journey from Sydney to Blackheath takes about 2¼ hours each way.

Before starting the walk, visit the police station first to fill out the overnight walkers' registration book. The station is at 119 Wentworth St, near the post office. Victoria Falls Lookout, the start of the walk, is about 10 km away by road.

The best way to get there is to hire a taxi in Blackheath (☎ (047) 87 8356) from the

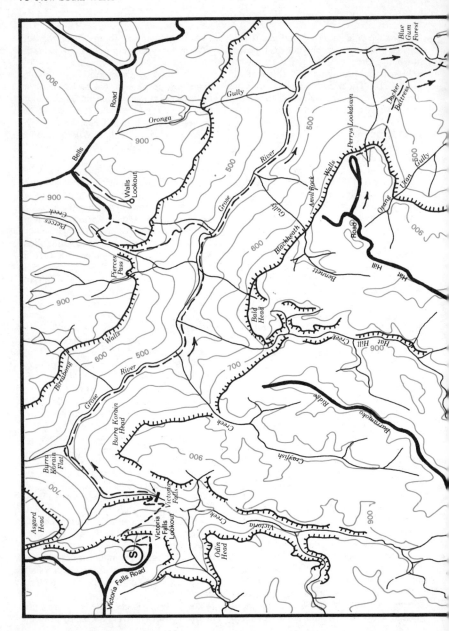

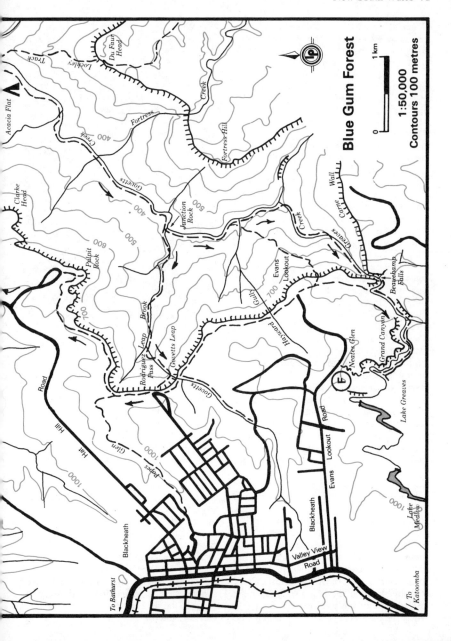

Blue Gum Forest

1:50,000
Contours 100 metres

0 1 km

General Store, 20 Govetts Leap Rd. You can also book the taxi to pick you up at Neates Glen upon completion of the walk. This is about five km from Blackheath.

If the party has two or more cars, a car shuffle to leave one car at Neates Glen and Victoria Falls should be done before beginning the walk.

Stage 1: Victoria Falls Lookout to Acacia Flat

(11 km, 5-7 hours)

From Blackheath use either private transport or a taxi to get to the Victoria Falls Road, five km north away on the Great Western Highway, towards Bathurst. The signposted Victoria Falls Road is on the right. It is a further five km to the turntable and shelter at its end.

From the car park at the end of the Victoria Falls Road follow the wide track east for 100 metres to the lookout. This gives a good view over the Upper Grose Valley. Turn left and follow the well used track as it descends a small cliffline then through light forest to Victoria Creek and a track junction. To the right is a cascade which is well worth a look. Turn left and continue descending the steep zigzag track to the base of the Victoria Falls (you'll get glimpses of the falls as you go).

The falls have a 30-metre drop and are spectacular when the creek is flowing. The track crosses the creek on slippery rock slabs 100 metres downstream of the falls and continues downstream along the east bank. You climb up and down over several small ridges and cross the creek again, 30 minutes from the falls. Walk east 200 metres to the open campsite at Burra Korain Flat. This river flat is situated between the junction of the Grose River and the Victoria Creek.

From Burra Korain Flat to the Blue Gum Forest the track is partly overgrown, but is reasonably defined and can be followed with care. From the campsite at the flat, walk east to the river junction. Cross Victoria Creek (the stream on the right) and walk along the eroded edge of the river for 200 metres to where the track begins. This will vary a little

Victoria Falls, Blue Mountains

at times depending on the extent of the last flood damage.

The indistinct track now follows the right bank downstream (looking down river) for 3½ km to the junction with the Pierces Pass walking track. Continue down the river on the west bank for another 4½ km to the Blue Gum Forest. Several tracks branch off as you approach the Blue Gum Forest and most of these are created by the wild brumbies (horses). Most tracks can be taken, but do not cross any major streams or climb away from the river flat.

The Blue Gum Forest is an almost pure stand of tall, thin blue gums and is quite unusual and beautiful. Wild brumbies live here and camping is totally banned within the forest. Cross the open forest floor to meet a signposted track junction on its southern edge. To the right the track climbs steeply to Perrys Lookdown.

Follow the track straight ahead for five minutes to the extensive camping area called Acacia Flat. This flat extends for over 500 metres through several clearings and has two toilets. Water is available from Govetts Brook (100 metres south-east) but boil it before drinking.

Stage 2: Acacia Flat to Govetts Leap Falls & Pulpit Rock, return

(17 km, 7-9 hours)

This is an excellent circular one-day walk from Acacia Flat which climbs up to the rim of the valley for spectacular views before returning to camp. While the route can be walked in either direction the direction described is preferred as it presents the major attractions at the best time of day for lighting.

From Acacia Flat several tracks lead south-west along the valley floor. Follow any track as they quickly join together (within five minutes) and climb onto a low ridge. Below, to the left, the creek can be seen. The main track here is not obvious and leaves the ridge to the left, descending steeply to the creek bank. Be careful not to continue climbing up the false track that follows the ridge crest.

The track continues upstream on the north-west bank of Govetts Creek for three km (about 50 minutes) to a track junction at Junction Rock. The left turn crosses the side-stream of Govetts Leap Brook and will be followed tomorrow. Follow the right-hand track beside Govetts Leap Brook upstream through interesting rainforest. Initially this climbs gently for one km passing some cascades then ascends steeply across the rocks below Govetts Leap Falls. At this point it is worthwhile looking up at the cliffs above to see where the track amazingly ascends!

Steel ladders and handrails assist on the narrow track as it climbs the cliff to the north of Govetts Leap Falls. There are many excellent vantage points on the very steep climb. Approaching the rim of the valley ignore a minor track to the right and continue upwards to a major track junction. Turn right and follow the main track north along the rim of the valley. This leads down towards Popes

Glen Creek and you should turn right at the junction. The track crosses the creek then passes through steep cliffs to the narrow ridge of Pulpit Rock. This is worth visiting so turn right and descend to the very end of the ridge. Bridges lead out onto Pulpit Rock which is a spectacular isolated tower jutting out over the valley. This provides grandstand views of Govetts Leap Falls and the cliffs. The lookout is exposed and not suitable for anyone scared of heights and care is required with the rickety wire and railing fence.

Return back up the spur and continue up it past a small hut to the car park. Follow the road north for one km then turn right onto Hat Hill Road and follow the gravel for 2½ km. Turn right towards Perrys Lookdown and a further km leads to the car park. Follow the walking track out to the lookout. This provides good views of Banks Wall on the opposite side of the valley and is particularly attractive around sunset.

The walking track continues south from the lookout across a small gully then descends steeply south-east down Docker Buttress. A fast descent leads down to the track junction in the valley beside the Blue Gum Forest. Turn right and a short walk leads into Acacia Flat.

Stage 3: Acacia Flat to Neates Glen

(10 km, 3½-5 hours)

From Acacia Flat follow the same track beside the river for three km as for yesterday to Govetts Leap Brook. Turn left to cross the stream and the track continues to follow the valley of Govetts Creek upstream for another two km (40 minutes) to cross Greaves Creek. The track now turns west and follows this creek upstream climbing steadily for one km (20 minutes) to cross the creek again at a lovely set of rock slabs and cascades.

The track continues climbing up mossy rocks and between large boulders to the base of the Beauchamp Falls. Some care is needed on the way up as the rocks are slippery. The falls are 20 metres left of the track and worth a visit. The track zigzags above with some good views over the valley before entering the entrance of the Grand Canyon.

About 15 minutes from the falls there is a turnoff on the right to Evans Lookout, follow the left track into the Grand Canyon. The track follows the stream bed upstream for 15 minutes, turns left, climbs onto a ridge and then continues upstream through the cliffs of the Grand Canyon. The canyon is only two metres wide in places and over 50 metres deep forming a thin ravine beside the track. The canyon has been misleadingly named as it is not huge but it is an interesting narrow ravine well worth exploring.

After 40 minutes from the Evans Lookout track, the track passes under a waterfall and through a short tunnel formed by the collapse of some of the cliff.

At the flat area, about 100 metres past the tunnel, the track climbs steeply left and continues upstream for another 15 minutes to a creek and track junction.

The track turns right (the left branch leads nowhere) and climbs steeply up the fern-filled creek bed of Neates Glen. This narrow valley is overhung with cliffs and the track is usually wet underfoot. The last part of the track is up a well-formed zigzag trail to the car park.

Here transport can be met or you can walk five km through the town streets back to Blackheath. To do this turn left along the road and follow it for three km then turn right onto Valley View Road. A further two km leads to the police station and post office. Remember to record your return in the walkers' registration book at the police station before leaving Blackheath.

CORANG PEAK TO THE CASTLE

The northern Budawang Ranges offer some of the most spectacular walking found near Canberra. Massive cliffs of layered sandstone form the valley walls, while the ridges are gentle plateaus which provide easy walking. No roads or maintained walking tracks enter the core of these ranges so the main features of the area are accessible to bushwalkers only. The Castle is spectacular and Monolith Valley so unusual that this walk is a must for every bushwalker.

Features

The northern Budawangs are tabletop mountains that overlook deep valleys, formed when an uplifted sandstone plateau was eroded by rivers. The process also created narrow canyons such as Monolith Valley and long continuous cliffs that tower above the valleys.

On the plateaus and sandstone blocks the soil is poor, supporting only shrubs and grasses. Heaths, sedge grasses and prickly shrubs are common and the majority of the walk passes through this type of flora. Below the cliff lines, the damper, deeper soils support forests of tall trees; the forest floors remain fairly open except in the shady gullies.

The diverse landscape and flora support most of the native Australian animals – kangaroos, wallabies, koalas and dingos are all here along with the smaller animals. The average walker, however, will see only a few of these animals as most are nocturnal while others feed at dusk and are inactive during the heat of the day. Birdlife is equally varied and many species are usually seen.

Standard

This excellent walk follows rough bushwalkers' tracks formed by the passage of many walkers. The route is well defined, but involves scrambling up and down rocks and climbing over logs in places. The walking route involves three full walking days; the first and third days are of medium standard along a well-defined pad and the suggested day trip is a long hard day. The walk overall is graded medium to hard.

Days Required

A minimum of three days is needed to reach The Castle and return. It is an interesting area so some extra days can be well spent exploring in the range. Five days would make the walk more leisurely. Mt Tarn, Mt Bibbenluke, Crooked Falls and the Corang River are all easily visited from the Mt Bibbenluke camping area as day trips.

Seasons

The Budawangs can be visited at any time of the year. Autumn and spring are the best seasons as the streams have water and the temperatures are mild. Summer is a popular time but water is scarce and during any hot dry spells visits are not recommended because of the high fire danger. In winter the area has heavy frosts and occasionally snow so parties should be well equipped for cold conditions.

Equipment

Normal walking clothing and equipment is adequate for these ranges. There are numerous caves in the area which can be camped in if your tent fails during very wet weather. It is still a good idea to carry a tent as caves may be occupied and with a tent the party has more campsites to choose from. For footwear, light boots or runners are adequate.

Maps

The sketch map, *The Northern Budawang Range*, is very useful as it shows the approximate location of all the regularly used routes in the northern Budawang Ranges. It is produced by a club called The Budawang Committee at 40 Alexandra Avenue, Eastwood, 2122, and is sold in most walking shops in Sydney, Canberra and Melbourne.

The 1:25,000 topographic map, *Corang*, is excellent to use and shows most of the tracks the walk uses. If taking only one map then this is the one to have. The map references indicated relate to this map. It is published by the Central Mapping Authority of New South Wales. You can get it from most bushwalking shops in Sydney and Canberra.

The Budawang Committee also produce a very informative book, *Pigeon House & Beyond*. It includes walking notes and it details all facets of the park. It is essential if you wish to visit other areas of the Budawangs; it can usually be bought in Sydney shops.

Permits

No permits are required for bushwalking in the Budawangs. Camping is freely permitted in the area except in Monolith Valley and its surrounds. Restriction signs are erected on all the entrances into the valley defining the restricted area.

Elsewhere, the National Parks Service request that walkers use existing fireplaces for wood fires. On Total Fire Ban days no fires or stoves may be lit at all. For current information contact the national park rangers at the Nowra/Goulburn District Office (☎ (044) 21 9969), 24 Berry St, Nowra, 2541.

Access

The northern Budawang Range is in the southern half of the Morton National Park, 200 km south-west of Sydney between Canberra and the coast. Access points to the northern Budawangs are few and often on poor roads. The approach used on this walk utilises all-weather roads on the western side of the park around Braidwood, 90 km east of Canberra. Private transport (or hired cars) is essential as there is no public transport service available.

From Sydney follow the Princes Highway south for 164 km to Nowra. One km past the centre of the town, turn right to the naval base HMAS Albatross, and continue along this sealed road for seven km to a road junction just before the naval base. Turn right for Braidwood down the gravel road and after 14 rough km you reach another gravel road. Turn right and drive along the gravel road 45 km over Mt Sassafras to the tiny town Nerriga.

Follow the road from Nerriga to Braidwood for 17 km then turn left onto the road to Mongarlowe. There is a cattle grid at the junction. Be careful not to take the sharp left turn as this is a private road. Follow the Mongarlowe road for 2½ km to a ford over Wog Wog Creek. Drive across the creek and 2½ km from the ford there is a national park sign on the left, near a fenceline.

Cars can be parked in the open area behind the sign (easily missed). If you reach the Wog Wog Station gate go back for 1½ km and the

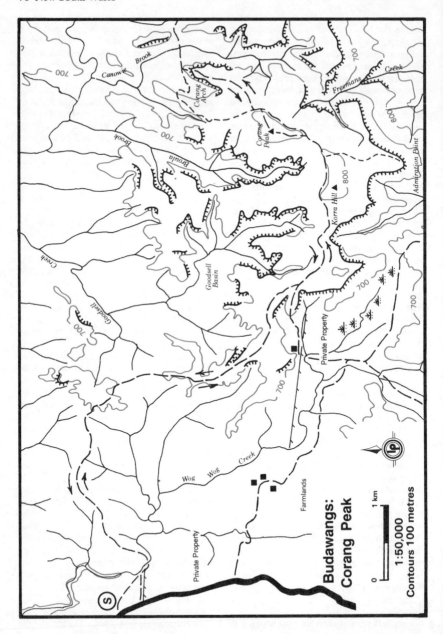

Budawangs:
Corang Peak

1:50,000
Contours 100 metres

sign will be next to the property boundary on the right.

From Canberra drive for 90 km to Braidwood. Just before entering the town turn left onto the Nerriga and Nowra road. The first 12 km are sealed then the road becomes gravel. About 37 km from the Braidwood junction, turn right onto the Mongarlowe road. From the cattle grid to the start of the walk continue as for the directions from Sydney.

If coming from the southern coast of New South Wales, follow the highway from Batemans Bay to Braidwood and, one km past the town, turn right onto the Nerriga and Nowra road and continue as for the directions from Canberra.

If arriving at the start at night the car parking area is suitable for camping, but has no water nearby. The closest town for food and petrol supplies is Braidwood, 43 km away.

Sulphur-Crested Cockatoo

Stage 1: Mongarlowe Road to Bibbenluke Camp
(18 km, 5-7 hours)

From the car parking area follow the track downhill parallel to the fence line for five minutes to Wog Wog Creek. A national park signpost gives distances to Bibbenluke as well as a reminder of the camping ban in Monolith Valley. The track follows the creek upstream 100 metres then crosses it to the north-east bank. The track is reasonably well defined and marked from here by well-spaced markers on poles and trees.

Leave the creek and follow the track gradually up a gentle spur for two km (30 to 40-minute walk). A rock shelter is passed and five minutes later past it, the track winds around the top of a hill and descends south-east to an open saddle (map ref 332931). Cross the saddle and climb gently south-east, then south, through light forest. Following the track you descend a gully passing between two large rocks and then climb to the ridge crest which has good views.

The track swings south-east along a series of rock slabs in light forest to the next open ridge. Walk east along the rock slabs 500

metres then descend briefly to an unmarked track junction (map ref 3449089) about two hours (seven km) from the start. The right-hand track is the old bridle track to Bibbenluke which started from Wog Wog Station and walkers had to cross private property to gain access, whereas the track described is all within the national park and is a more pleasant walk.

From the track junction turn left and follow the clearly defined track south-east. This track gradually swings east and passes along the north side of Korra Hill to another unmarked track junction in the flat area before Corang Peak (map ref 363908). The major track to the right continues along the eastern side of Corang Peak. The left track climbs directly onto the cone-shaped summit of Corang Peak.

From the top all the major mountains of the Budawangs are clearly visible provided the weather is fine. The track continues over the top and down the north-east ridge to meet the other track that bypassed the peak.

From Corang Peak follow the main track north-east for one km along the top of a flat ridge to Corang Arch. This natural rock arch, 50 metres west of the track, is worth visiting. The track is not clearly marked from here and continues north to descend the rocky crest of the ridge on a steep conglomerate slope.

From the foot of the rock band the track is better defined and descends east to the grassy plain of Canowie Brook. This is three to four hours (12 km) from the start. The track continues east over a low ridge to a track junction. Either track can be followed but the right track is better as it uses a bridge to cross the creek. Both tracks join again and continue south-east up the valley of Burrumbeet Brook.

Several campsites are passed and there are three camping caves under the cliff line to the south. The track divides several times along the valley and sidetracks lead to the campsites and camping caves. Follow the valley south-east – all the routes join together as the valley swings east. The track then climbs north-east to a ridge crest and turns sharp right at a cairn in a tiny clearing.

The ridge crest is followed towards Mt Bibbenluke for one km before the track swings north around a hill and crosses a small creek. About 100 metres east of the creek a side track on the left leads to a camping cave. Continue east for 300 metres on the main track and the open camping area can be seen down near the creek.

Several tracks lead down to the campsite which is signposted as the 'Bibbenluke Mountain Camping Area' but referred to here as Bibbenluke Camp. This campsite has room for very large parties and water is available from the creek 10 metres away, except in very hot, dry summer weather.

Alternative Campsites
Canowie Brook Good camping is found on the western edge of the plain near the track. Water is available from the creek 300 metres to the east. This is three to four hours from the road.

Burrumbeet Brook There are many campsites near the creek and camping caves under the southern cliffs. Fetch water from the creek. This campsite is 20 minutes past Canowie Brook.

Stage 2: Bibbenluke Camp to Monolith Valley and The Castle, return
(16 km, 6-9 hours)
This is a long return day trip from the Bibbenluke campsite so an early start is advised. The route passes Mt Cole to the north, winds through to Monolith Valley then leads to The Castle, returning to Monolith Valley along the same track then returning to the campsite via Mt Owen. No camping is allowed in Monolith Valley and once you visit this unique area you'll understand why.

From the campsite cross the creek and climb north-east through light scrub to the ridge crest. A track from Mt Tarn is met. Turn right and follow this south-east for 400 metres to a track junction. An alternative route from the campsite is to climb south to meet the track from Corang Peak, turn east and follow this to the junction. However, as well as being more difficult than the route using the Mt Tarn ridge, this track deteriorates in the forest to become a maze.

From the track junction follow the well-worn pad south into the forest. For one km you have to climb over logs and skirt obstacles in open forest, until the track descends briefly to a broad saddle. You need to follow the track carefully as it is poorly marked. From the saddle the track climbs steeply south-east towards the cliffs above. Halfway up the track divides. Take the left turn (the return will be on the other track) and continue climbing to the base of the cliffs of Mt Cole.

Follow the base of the cliffs north-east for one km passing through three camping caves and up into the pass between Donjon Mountain and Mt Cole. A sign here marks the start of the Monolith Valley Protected Area. No camping or fires are permitted from here to Nibelung Pass.

From the sign descend the gully east for 200 metres. The track from here is not obvious. It winds across the rock slabs on the southern side, above the gully, for a further

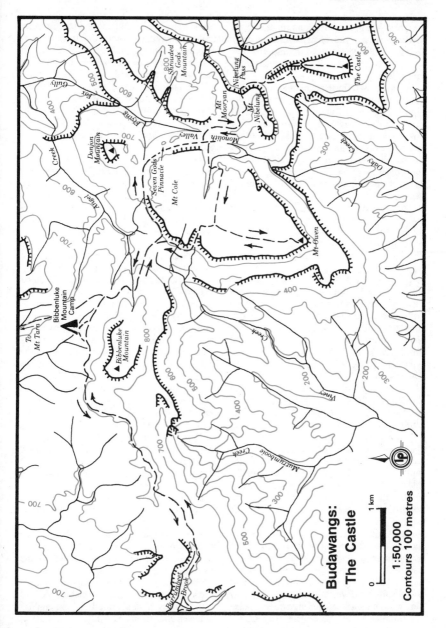

Budawangs:
The Castle

1:50,000
Contours 100 metres

0   1 km

300 metres to the end of a long rib of rock on Mt Cole which you cross. The track now swings south-east to climb into the flat saddle between Mt Cole and Seven Gods Pinnacle.

From the saddle descend south into the gully following the creek bed between the high rocky walls. There is a good view of Seven Gods Pinnacle on the way and further down you'll see a natural rock arch above you on the right. This canyon is called Monolith Valley and 700 metres from the saddle the old camping flat is reached. Large overhangs tower on both sides and there are many tree ferns.

The creek has water except in dry summer weather. Bibbenluke Camp to Monolith Valley will take 1½ to 2½ hours. If you want to climb The Castle from here allow a further two to four hours, returning to Monolith Valley.

To climb The Castle walk back upstream for 30 metres from the old camping flat, then turn right and climb a short slope. Follow a well used track east beside a gully for 300 metres (ignoring minor sidetracks) until the track curves south into the grass covered gully between Mt Nibelung and Mt Mooryan winding past a pinnacle into Nibelung Pass. The track then descends into a very narrow chasm on the right. This can be squeezed through, but the easier route is to walk to the left along the rock slabs for 150 metres and climb down a steep ramp to the gully floor.

The valley is easily followed south-east then east past some old campsites, where camping is not allowed; it then descends under a waterfall. A sign here indicates the end of the Monolith Valley Protected Area.

To continue to The Castle follow the track south for 300 metres keeping close to the base of the cliffs of Mt Nibelung and then descend south-east into a saddle signposted the 'Cooyoyo Camping Area'. Another signpost points to The Castle and this track climbs a short way before following the eastern base of the cliffs for 400 metres past some camping caves to the tunnel, a narrow slot marked by a scratched sign on the rocks. Continue along the eastern base of the

cliffs for another 200 metres past another camping cave to where the track climbs steeply onto the tail of The Castle. This climb is marked by an arrow on a tree, followed by well-worn arrows on the rocks. Near the top of the tail the track climbs up and down between large boulders and continues south along the ridge to a tower. This is easily passed on its eastern side and 30 metres further on is the foot of the final chimney-gully.

The easiest route up is to traverse out to the right for seven metres, then up the two short chimneys above, to the plateau of The Castle. There are good views from all edges of the plateau and you can record your comments in the log book stored in a container on the very southern tip of the plateau.

To return to Monolith Valley follow the same tracks back to the old camping flat under the overhangs.

The return route to Bibbenluke Camp is via Mt Owen and starts at the northern edge of the old campsite in Monolith Valley. A rough track climbs steeply west for five minutes through a rocky slot and down into a small valley. Cross the floor of the valley and walk west for 150 metres following the cairns. The track then climbs very steeply up ledges to a long final gully to reach the east end of the Mt Owen plateau. Follow the cairns carefully west over the plateau for one km to some larger cairns near the saddle between Mt Owen and Mt Cole.

If you have enough time it is worthwhile making a sidetrip to visit the summit and lookout on Mt Owen. This will take one to 1½ hours extra to return. From the large cairns, a cairned route (not obvious for the first 200 metres) is followed south-west, then south, across the plateau for 1½ km to the separated tower on the southern tip of Mt Owen. The views from Mt Owen of The Castle are spectacular; a logbook is kept there. Return to the large cairns by the same cairned route.

From the large cairns follow the cairned track north to the edge of the plateau. A short gully is then descended to the saddle between Mt Owen and Mt Cole.

Scramble down the main gully to the west following the cairns. The descent is very steep in places with the most awkward obstacle being a large wide rock slab on the left side of the gully. The track descends down the slab and requires care. Further down the gully a signpost indicates the end of the Monolith Valley Protected Area.

From the foot of the gully follow the base of the cliffs to the right for 400 metres past two camping caves and a waterfall (often dry). The track leaves the cliff and descends north-west to meet the other track which was used in the morning. Follow this down to the saddle. If you traverse around the cliffs too far you will come to the first camping cave met in the morning. Turn sharply left and descend to the saddle along the tracks.

From the saddle carefully follow the track through the forest for one km to the track junction 500 metres south-east of the Bibbenluke Camp. Return to the camp by the same route used in the morning.

Stage 3: Bibbenluke Camp to Mongarlowe Road

(18 km, 5-7 hours)

The same track that was used on the approach is used for the return journey. From the campsite walk south to meet the track. Follow the track westwards along the same route to Corang Peak. About 2½ km past Corang Peak you'll meet an unmarked track junction which is not obvious on the walk out.

The left track heads downhill to cross the private property of Wog Wog Station. The correct track to follow is to the right and this climbs briefly onto the open rocky ridge top. The track from here is easily followed (from the first day's notes) back to the car park beside the road where the walk started.

GRAND HIGH TOPS CIRCUIT

The Warrumbungle National Park is a spectacular group of rocky peaks and spires rising above the flat plains of New South Wales. This park is very popular and has a network of well-marked and constructed walking tracks. These visit many of the major features along the high ridge that is known as the Grand High Tops. This ridge has many fine views and is the one of the most scenic walks in the state.

Features

The obvious barren spires that dominate the landscape of this park are the remnants of an active volcanic period of about 13 million years ago. A series of large volcanoes formed and have since been eroded. The softer ashes and pumice were easily broken down and worn away and have left behind the harder volcanic trachyte rocks. This rock formed as plugs in the volcano vents and filled cracks in the walls of the cones which are known as dykes. The obvious towers of Crater Bluff and Belougery Spire are old plugs and the spectacular Breadknife is a perfect example of a large elongated dyke.

The area has a semi-arid climate; fine and hot for much of the year with very low rainfall. The soils are shallow and rocky supporting scrubby bushes and dry woodlands. In the gullies native pines stand beside the usually dry watercourses.

Kangaroos, wallabies and koalas are often seen grazing on the open plains and in the dry forests. Birdlife is abundant – in particular, the parrot family is well represented and readily seen.

Standard

This circuit walk follows well defined and maintained walking tracks. Signposts exist at all major track junctions. Because water has to be carried for most of the walk it has been graded easy to medium.

Days Required

In two days the circuit covers most of the major walking tracks and easily visited features in the park. An extra half day can be used to walk the short circuit to Belougery Split Rock. Without leaving the tracks, there is little scope for varying the walk.

Seasons

This national park is dry for most of the year. The very hot dry summer season from November to March is unsuitable for bushwalking. April through to October is the best time to visit this park. Water is variable and depends on when the last major rainfall occurred, sometimes several years before.

Equipment

No special hiking equipment is needed. Light boots or runners are ideal footwear for the tracks. Stoves must be carried as fires are only allowed in constructed fireplaces. Under normal conditions water must also be carried and this means a sufficient number of containers for two days water. For shelter, any simple tent or fly sheet will do except in rare, wet weather.

Maps

There is a 1:30,000 topographic map, *Warrumbungle National Park*, which accurately covers the entire park in excellent detail. It is available from the Central Mapping Authority of New South Wales. You can also buy it at bushwalking shops in Sydney and from the rangers' station at Canyon Camp in the park.

Also available from the rangers' station are a series of information sheets which provide interesting reading about the park.

If you can obtain a copy, *A Complete Guide to The Warrumbungle National Park*, by Alan Fairley (Murray Child, 1977), has stacks of information on walking in the 'Bungles, physical geography and flora & fauna.

Permits

Permits for bushwalking are required. You can get a pack-camping permit from the rangers' station at Canyon Camp and an additional charge is made for each car brought into the park.

Walking is generally allowed unless there is a dangerous fire situation (occurs occasionally during the summer). In such conditions even the use of fuel stoves is banned.

The park rangers can also advise on the availability of water within the park. For advance bookings and information on road and water conditions contact the Senior Ranger (☎ (068) 25 4364) at PO Box 39, Coonabarabran, 2357.

Access

The Warrumbungle National Park is in northern New South Wales, 360 km northwest of Sydney. It lies close to the Newell Highway, the major road route between Melbourne and Brisbane. There is no public transport to the park and access is by private (or hired) cars only.

From Sydney follow the Great Western Highway through Katoomba to Lithgow where there is a choice of routes. One is via Bathurst and Dubbo to Gilgandra. The other route is via Mudgee and Dunedoo to Coonabarabran. Both routes are about 500 km by road from Sydney. There are many other approaches possible to the nearby towns of Gilgandra and Coonabarabran.

From Coonabarabran follow a sealed road west past the Siding Springs Observatory (worth visiting if you have time) to the park border. The last 12 km is on a gravel road inside the park. Turn sharp right onto the sealed road to the rangers' office at Canyon Camp. The closest petrol and food supplies are at Coonabarabran.

From Gilgandra follow the Castlereagh Highway north for 22 km towards Coonamble. Turn right and follow the signposts, pointing to the Warrumbungle National Park, along a series of quiet country roads. Most of this approach is on sealed roads.

Within the park all roads are gravel except for the short section around Camp Blackman which is the main area for car camping. If you arrive late in the day it is best to set up

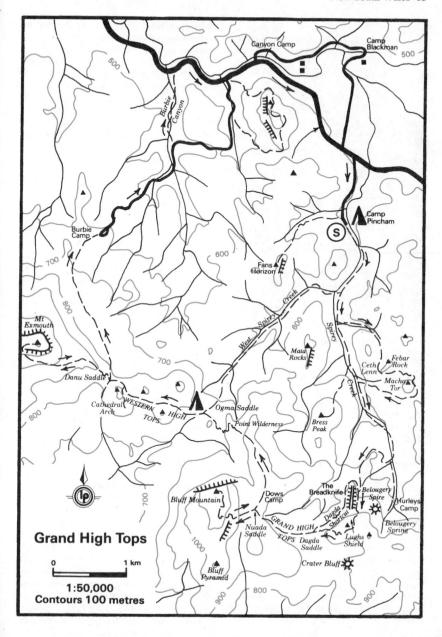

Grand High Tops

0   1 km

1:50,000
Contours 100 metres

Crater Bluff from the Grand High Tops

camp at Camp Blackman and visit the ranger next morning for the appropriate permit.

If the party has more than one vehicle a short car shuffle can be made to leave one car near Burbie Canyon before commencing walking.

Stage 1: Camp Pincham to Ogma Camp
(18 km, 5-7 hours)

For this walk the cars can be left at either Camp Pincham or near the rangers' office at Canyon Camp. From the rangers' office at Canyon Camp walk south to cross the creek and climb up to the main road. Walk southeast along the road for 1½ km and turn right onto the Camp Pincham road. Follow this south for 15 minutes to the car park and the end of the road.

From the car park follow the closed road south for 200 metres to Camp Pincham. A shelter with a table, water tank and toilets nearby are the only facilities. If necessary the water containers should be filled here.

From the camp follow the main walking track south for 20 minutes to a well signposted track junction. Follow the left track (right leads up West Spirey Creek to Ogma Camp) and within 10 minutes, you'll meet the next track junction, where you turn left onto the Gould Circuit. This track climbs steadily for 20 minutes to a saddle. A short walk to the right gives a view from Ceth Lenn (a minor peak) that is well worth the effort.

Continue left along the main track as it swings east under Febar Rock and up to the base of Macha Tor. Leave your pack at the signpost for a short scramble to the right, up a steep gully, where there are excellent views from the summit of Macha Tor.

Return to the signpost and your packs and follow the track as it descends west into the valley. You pass a lookout and five minutes later meet the track along Spirey Creek. Turn left onto this track and follow it south for 30 minutes along the valley to the Hurleys Camp track junction. If there is water at this camp (inquire first with the ranger) drop the packs and follow the poor track south along the creek valley to the campsite at a creek junction (the campsite was named after the famous Australian photographer, Frank Hurley). Belougery Spring is five minutes further up the western branch and the water containers should be filled for the nights camp. Return to the main track.

From the junction the track begins to climb steadily up to another track junction at the base of the Breadknife. Turn left for the Grand High Tops. The track follows the base of the cliffs of the Breadknife south. The Breadknife is a spectacular 90-metre-high volcanic dyke which is only a few metres wide at its base. The track leaves the Breadknife at its southern end and after five minutes there is an unmarked track on the right. The short 10 metres scramble up this unmarked track will give you a superb view of the Breadknife from another dyke, Lughs Shield. From here the main track continues onto the Grand High Tops. These rocky slabs are well named giving good views of Belougery Spire, Crater Bluff and Bluff Mountain. Most of the peaks in the park can be seen from this vantage area.

From the high tops the track swings west and descends down the rocks into Dagda Saddle to meet the other track around the Breadknife, then climbs gently west into Nuada Saddle. From here a track to the left leads to Bluff Mountain. This is a return sidetrip taking about 1½ hours. Drop the packs and follow the left track leading southwest. This track climbs steadily for 20 to 30 minutes to the plateau then swings north for the final gentler climb to the summit. Bluff Mountain has magnificent views of the entire park and the surrounding plains and should not be missed if the weather is fine.

Return to collect the packs and follow the Dows High Top track north for five minutes to the rough stony camping area named Dows Camp. This is not a great place to put tents up so follow the Dows High Tops track north for 30 to 40 minutes to the campsites at Ogma Saddle near the track junction. Remember there is no water on any of the High Tops and it must be carried to the camps.

Stage 2: Ogma Camp to Burbie Camp
(13 km, 3½-5 hours)

From Ogma Saddle follow the track west along the Western High Tops for 40 minutes to the Cathedral Arch track junction. Drop packs and follow the sidetrack for 10 minutes to the arch. The track is not clearly marked where it crosses some rocky slabs and the continuation is 40 metres further on and uphill slightly. From here it descends to the arch, an interesting large rock formation where there is an excellent view of the massive northern cliff face of Bluff Mountain. Return to the main track.

Collect the packs and continue north from the track junction descending for 10 minutes to the multiple track junction at Danu Saddle. The last sidetrip is to Mt Exmouth, 2½ km away. Leave the packs at the saddle and follow the signposted track west to Mt Exmouth. The track passes under the summit

on the southern side using some rock ledges. It then climbs to the ridge crest before doubling back east along the plateau to the summit. There are good views from the summit plateau.

Return to the packs and follow the vehicle track north descending for two km to Burbie Camp. There is a water tank 100 metres to the right fed from the Burbie Spring. Toilets are found on the edge of the large clearing.

As this camp is accessible to 4WD vehicles only, most parties will need to walk to the main road at Canyon Camp. From the large clearing follow the sandy vehicle track north-east for two km to a signposted walking track on the left leading to Burbie Canyon. Follow the walking track through the short but interesting canyon for one km to meet the road and your vehicle if a car shuffle was made.

Koala

Turn right and walk one km east along the major gravel road to the road junction that leads left to Canyon Camp. Follow the gravel road on the right a further two km then turn right (south) and walk to the car park near Camp Pincham at the end of the walk.

KOSCIUSKO MAIN RANGE

The Kosciusko National Park is one of the largest and most important parks in Australia, in fact it is the rooftop of the country containing the highest mountains and the headwaters of the greatest river system. The section known as the Main Range is a series of high rolling plains and includes Mt Kosciusko, at 2228 metres, Australia's highest peak. The area is bounded by deep river valleys and provides easy pleasant walking with extensive views in fine weather.

Features

The Kosciusko National Park is 160 km in length and 40 km wide. It covers a range of landscapes and habitats. The best known areas are the higher regions of rolling hills and plains which have been cut deeply by river gorges. Mt Kosciusko is more like a hill than a peak and is rather unspectacular.

Nearby, however, are Mts Townsend and Twynham, Australia's second and third highest peaks, which are more rugged and impressive. and which provide fine views. Tucked close to the highest peaks are a series of shallow glacial lakes and cirque-shaped valleys. These are remnants of the last ice age. Moraines (ridges and mounds of glacial debris) and some U-shaped valleys are found on the southern slopes of most of the peaks.

The area is fairly bare and open with most of the walk being above the treeline. Grasses, herbs, heaths, buttercups and daisies cover the slopes in summer.

Another major feature of the area is the Snowy Mountains Hydroelectric Scheme, a series of dams, power stations and tunnels to provide electricity to south-eastern Australia. This scheme has been highly beneficial for the country but has left its mark on the park with old roads, tracks and huts remaining throughout the area. Many of these are gradually being removed and while the park is not a true wilderness area it still provides very enjoyable walking.

Standard

This easy walk follows the crest of the Main Range and is generally above the treeline. Because of this, the walking route is exposed to poor weather, so you need to take full wet weather equipment and be prepared for cold windy weather. The suggested two-day walk is of an easy standard.

Days Required

The walk takes two days and can be extended to three days to allow more time to enjoy the views or to explore the lakes and their surrounds. If doing so, please observe the restriction of camping away from the alpine lakes.

Seasons

The most popular season to visit the Main Range is summer. The warm, and occasionally hot, weather provides ideal walking conditions. As it is an alpine area, parties should still be well equipped as severe storms can occur even during the summer and rainfalls are fairly common.

Autumn is the next best season as the weather is usually stable and, while being cool, walking is still pleasant. Fogs and mists are more common and sometimes last all day, never clearing.

In winter the range is under a heavy cover of snow and best left to skiers. In spring the thaw begins and the park is particularly beautiful, because of the profusion of wildflowers. Walkers need to be prepared, however, to walk through large patches of snow. Strong winds and storms are still common.

Equipment

This area is deceptive as it is usually very easy to walk across, but can also be very cold and windy. Tents should be capable of standing up in strong winds and keeping out heavy rain. Light leather boots are ideal footwear, suitable in snow, yet light enough on hot days. Most walking in summer is in shorts and a light shirt. Parties should also carry full wet weather clothing and some warm clothing, just in case.

A water bottle is necessary for use during the day. Because the lakes may be polluted, water should only be collected from running streams, preferably upstream from the camping areas. Stoves and fuel must be carried as fires are banned above the treeline and there is no wood to burn here anyway.

Maps

The entire walk is covered by the 1:50,000 topographic map, *Mt Kosciusko*, published by the Central Mapping Authority of NSW. In Sydney and Canberra it can be bought at bushwalking shops.

The other map used by bushwalkers is the 1:100,000 topographic map, *Kosciusko*, published by NATMAP. This is also generally on sale in most bushwalking shops in south-eastern Australia. There is also the extremely detailed 1:25,000 *Thredbo Ski Touring Map* (NSW Ski Association).

For those interested in more walks in this park there are two guidebooks: *Snowy Mountains Walks*, published by the Geehi Bushwalking Club, which gives detailed track notes to many other routes in the park, and *Bushwalking in Kosciusko National Park* by Charles Warner, which is very detailed about access and general descriptions of features, but does not provide track notes and is more suited to walkers familiar with the area.

Both of the abovementioned books can be bought from most bushwalking shops in south-eastern Australia.

Permits

No permits are required for bushwalking. All walkers are asked to register their walk, however, by filling out a bushwalking and touring form before commencing. You can get these at the visitor centres and ranger stations. There are ranger stations in the Thredbo village (☎ (064) 57 6255) and at Sawpit Creek (☎ (064) 56 1700). Camping

is not allowed near any of the alpine villages or near the alpine lakes.

If you are arriving by private transport late at night you are allowed to camp for one night at the rest areas beside the Alpine Way which is the main road to Thredbo. Otherwise, camping is not allowed within two km of any road.

Access

The Kosciusko National Park is mid-way between Melbourne and Sydney and about 150 km from the coast. The park covers a large area just south of Canberra. The walk begins at the Thredbo alpine village.

From Sydney, follow the Hume then Federal Highway for 242 km to Canberra. From there, follow the Monaro Highway south for 118 km to Cooma, then turn west and follow minor roads for 65 km through Berridale to Jindabyne. The Alpine Way is then followed for the final 36 km to the Thredbo alpine village. There is plenty of car parking near the chair lift and the village has several shops and a petrol station.

From Melbourne follow the Hume Highway for 300 km to Wodonga. Turn east and follow the Murray Valley Highway for 177 km towards Corryong. Just before Corryong turn left and a further 16 km leads to Khancoban. From there drive along the Alpine Way for 75 km to Thredbo. There are no towns or petrol stations along the Alpine Way and the last half of the road is unsealed. In winter this road is usually closed.

From the eastern part of Victoria (Gippsland area) you can take the Barry Way. From Buchan follow this narrow mountain road north for 178 km to Jindabyne then turn left and follow the Alpine Way for the last 36 km to Thredbo. This road is unsealed for much of its length and has very few petrol stations and stores along it as it passes through the rugged mountains surrounding the Snowy River.

Thredbo is well serviced by public transport with a regular daily bus, operated by Pioneer (☎ 13 2030 Australia-wide). Bookings are required in advance and the timetable varies from season to season.

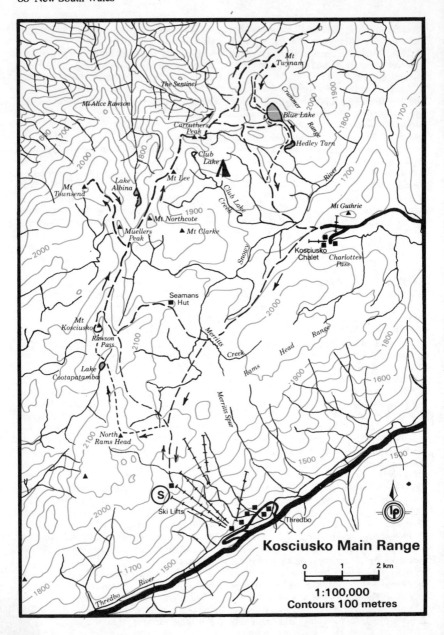

Mt Twynam

The Sentinel

Mt Alice Rawson

Crummer Range

Blue Lake

Carruthers Peak

Hedley Tarn

Club Lake

Mt Lee

River

Mt Townsend

Lake Albina

Club Lake Creek

Mt Guthrie

Mt Northcote

Mt Clarke

Kosciusko Chalet

Charlottes Pass

Snowy

Mueller's Peak

Seamans Hut

Mt Kosciusko

Rawson Pass

Merritts Creek

Rams Head Range

Lake Cootapatamba

Merritts Spur

North Rams Head

S

Ski Lifts

Thredbo

Kosciusko Main Range

0   1   2 km

1:100,000
Contours 100 metres

Thredbo River

Stage 1: Thredbo Village to Club Lake Creek

(17 km, 5-7 hours)

From the village a very steep 600-metre climb leads north-west to the crest of the Rams Head Range. The hillside has groomed slopes which are used for ski runs for the village during winter. A much easier alternative is to take the Crackenback Chairlift to the crest of the range for a moderate fee. This saves one to two hours of steep uphill walking and leaves you fresh to enjoy the rolling alpine meadows. The chairlift operates all year and if you keep your ticket a discount applies on the return journey.

From the top of the chairlift follow the main track north towards Mt Kosciusko. This descends gently before you cross a creek by a bridge. From there the walking track is an elevated steel walkway which protects the environment. At about 1½ km from the chairlift a rise is crossed and Mt Kosciusko can be seen ahead. From this point leave the track and walk west 300 metres across the open meadow to a band of rock. Climb this band using the grassy terraces and continue west for a ½ km past another rocky outcrop to the obvious rocky peak of North Rams Head.

This tower appears rather daunting, but is easily scrambled up without packs from most directions, the west side being easiest. From its summit most of the main range is visible and to the north is Mt Kosciusko, looking impressive from this viewpoint.

Collect the packs and turn north to follow the broad ridge which is covered with low grass and boulders. After 30 minutes, Lake Cootapatamba (or Lake May) can be seen in its glacially carved valley below Mt Kosciusko. Descend north-west directly toward the lake shore crossing extensive moraines in the valley. Walk around to its northern shore.

From the lake you can walk north up the valley to Rawson Pass and then west up the main track to the summit of Mt Kosciusko. Alternatively you can climb steeply north-west up onto the ridge for good views of the lake and then walk north up the grassy ridge to the summit.

The summit of Mt Kosciusko is the highest point of Australia and is a very popular day walk. There are usually other walkers there. From the top there are extensive views to the west.

From the summit, follow the old road down for one km. This road circles the mountain and, when it swings south, a foot track on the left leads to Mt Townsend and Lake Albina. This track is not always signposted. Follow this track north descending for two km to a saddle at the foot of Muellers Peak. At an obvious right-hand bend a very faint foot track heads north-west off the main track.

Leave the packs here and follow this faint track which crosses the rocky western slopes of Muellers Peak then climbs north into the saddle between Muellers Peak and Mt Townsend. The track becomes clearer to follow as it climbs north-west onto the plateau and then west to the summit of Mt Townsend (2210 metres). A short scramble leads to the top for a grandstand view of the area. From the summit the slopes fall steeply to the west and north and the view surpasses that from Mt Kosciusko.

If the weather is fine return to the packs via the summit of Muellers Peak; otherwise return by the same track. After you collect the packs, follow the main track north-east to Muellers Pass, some 500 metres away. Lake Albina appears in the valley to the north and can be visited as a sidetrip if time permits.

From the pass the track heads north-east for one km along the western slopes of Mt Northcote to Northcote Pass then more north-easterly to Mt Lee. Below, to the east, lies the Club Lake in a perfect bowl or cirque. Leave the ridge top track and descend steeply south-east to the flat valley floor below the lake. There are plenty of campsites near the streams above the creek junction.

Alternative Campsites
Lake Cootapatamba There are exposed campsites in the valley 300 metres below the lake. Camping beside the lake is not allowed for good environmental reasons.

Stage 2: Club Lake Creek to Thredbo
(21 km, 5-6 hours)
From the campsite walk north climbing steep open slopes up towards Carruthers Peak. Just before the top swing right onto the main ridge and follow the walking pads down east to meet an old road.

This road is followed north-east for 500 metres across a moor to a track junction. Follow the left track north-east which climbs gently for 2½ km to the plateau of Mt Twynham. The summit cairn is found on the rocks 200 metres right of the old road. The view of the Mt Jagungal area, to the north, is excellent.

From the summit, the easiest route to Blue Lake is to walk west for 300 metres then descend south-west into the valley, where you'll see the work that has been done to stop the extensive erosion. Descend steeply beside the creek to the marshy valley floor. Keep above the marsh and descend south-east on the rocks beside the creek to Blue Lake. The descent is quite steep in places so be careful to select a safe route. You reach Blue Lake at its western corner near the waterfall, an area which was once popular for camping. Unfortunately, the damage done by walkers here is evident and you will realise why camping beside this lake (and others) is now banned.

Follow the shore of the lake south-east to

Wombat

the outlet creek. Follow the west bank of Blue Lake Creek downstream for one km to Hedley Tarn, which is a series of shallow lakes. Leaving the tarns and the creek, walk south-west across a valley and up onto a large ridge to meet an old road that leads north-west to Carruthers Peak. Turn left (or south-east) on to this and follow it down to the Snowy River.

Cross Club Lake Creek first, then the Snowy River using the boulders and stepping stones. If the river is high it may be necessary to wade across. (In flood conditions it may be safer to follow the untracked Snowy River Bank upstream for four km to the bridge near Seamans Hut.) Continue to follow the old road east as it climbs steeply to the car park at Charlottes Pass. Turn right and pass through the locked gate onto the Mt Kosciusko road. This closed gravel road is now followed south-west for three km to the bridge crossing Merritts Creek (the second bridge 300 metres further on is over the Snowy River). At the first bridge an old snow pole line heads south-west.

Follow this pole line for one km to a wading crossing of the Snowy River. (If it is too deep don't cross but follow the bank upstream for one km and you will again meet the pole line as the river follows a large loop.) Continue to follow the pole line and it soon crosses the Snowy River again. The pole line then climbs uphill through a saddle and descends gently to meet the steel walkway of the Mt Kosciusko track.

Turn left and walk south one km to the Crackenback Chairlift at the start of the walk. Either walk steeply downhill to Thredbo or take the chairlift. If you present your original ticket the return fare is reduced.

Alternative Campsites
Snowy River You will find good flat campsites beside the Snowy River near the junction with Club Lake Creek. The shelter here from the prevailing weather is minimal.

Northern Territory

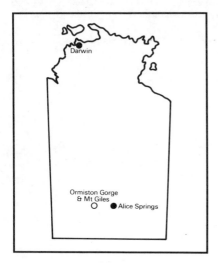

The Northern Territory, while part of the tropics, is the most barren and least populated area of Australia. The territory has a rich coastal band of vegetation along its northern boundary but further inland, in the central desert areas, the rainfall dramatically decreases. The interesting areas of the territory are well separated by extensive red plains.

Large sections of the territory are administered by the original residents, the Aborigines. This has a dramatic effect on bushwalking as, in many cases, you are not allowed to freely cross public land but must have the permission of the Aborigines. For many places it is almost impossible to obtain permission and, when it is given, their requirements must be followed.

In the southern part of the territory is the red centre with Alice Springs and Ayers Rock, also known by its Aboriginal name, Uluru. Most of the centre is a barren desert with low undulations of little interest for

bushwalkers. The exception is a string of ridges and mountains called the Macdonnell Ranges which have some interesting features to explore.

There are many spectacular and colourful gorges which are well worth visiting. Most gorges have permanent water, thus making bushwalking feasible. The largest gorge is at Ormiston and, combined with the nearby Mt Giles, constitutes an interesting and varied desert walk. There are many other walks that can be done in this range and the only limitation is the location of water. Currently, the Conservation Commission of the Northern Territory is constructing a 220-km extended trail along the Macdonnell Ranges. This will take several years to complete and, at present, only the first two sections near Alice Springs are finished.

Further north, the desert continues to the first permanently flowing river, the Katherine. This has carved a magnificent gorge which is protected by a national park. The best bushwalk in this park involves a walk to the top of the gorge then a return by following the river downstream. The upper section of the gorge has been closed to walkers, however, and you are now only allowed as far as Djuan Valley. This limits the walk. The other alternative is to follow the five-day trail to Edith Falls, but this is not a circuit and requires prearranged transport.

On the northern coastline, the Kakadu National Park has some interesting rugged areas for bushwalkers to explore. The south-eastern and eastern regions of the park include part of the Arnhem Land Plateau and is the best area to walk in. Access to the region is awkward, but if you are able to visit it do so, as the Aboriginal art is the best in Australia. All walking in Kakadu is subject to permits and restrictions and permission must be obtained in advance. Don't expect to be able to obtain permission on arrival.

Most walking in the dry season is confined to the gorges and streams where water and some shade can be found. The wet summer months are the best time to visit the plateau. Access can be very difficult, however, as helicopters have just recently been banned and the roads may all be flooded.

Other Suggested Bushwalks

Larapinta Trail This is the 220-km trail currently being built along the spine of the Macdonnell Ranges. Currently, the first 47 km from Alice Springs to Jay Creek have been completed and provide a three to four-day walk.

Redbank Gorge & Mt Sonder Explore the gorge the first day. Climb east onto Mt Sonder and descend eastwards to Ormiston Gorge. It is a two to three-day walk requiring a car shuffle in the Macdonnell Ranges, 100 km west of Alice Springs.

Tylers Pass to Glen Helen From Tylers Pass follow the Macdonnell Ranges east to Glen Helen. It is a three to five-day walk 120 km west of Alice Springs. It is also best done after recent rainfalls, and requires a long car shuffle.

N'Dhala Gorge From Ross River Homestead, walk south along the tracks to the gorge. Explore the gorge from a base camp and return north over the ridges to Ross River. This is a two to three-day walk, 60 km east of Alice Springs.

Katherine River From the camping ground, follow the track east for one day and turn left into Djuan Valley. Spend a day exploring the area before returning by either following the same track back, or by following the gorge downstream. This requires swimming or floating through the long pools. An easy to medium three to four-day circuit in the Katherine Gorge National Park, 350 km south-east of Darwin.

Edith Falls Wilderness From the Katherine Gorge camping ground follow the track north along the Crystal Brook Valley then west to the Edith River and the falls. This is a four to six-day walk in the Katherine Gorge National Park which requires a lengthy car shuffle or prearranged transport.

Jim Jim to Koolpin Creek From Jim Jim Falls, cross the plains south-west for six km then follow the gorges south for two days. Climb south-west onto the low watershed and head along this in a southerly direction for five km. Descend west to follow the obvious straight valley west for 15 km to Koolpin Creek. A further half day along the creek leads to the road. It's a four to six-day walk in the Kakadu National Park, 200 km east of Darwin, and it requires a long car shuffle using 4WD, or pre-arranged transport. Permission must be obtained in advance.

Western Falls Circuit From the end of Barramundie Ruins Rd, follow the valley south-west for six km to camp near the falls. Next day, visit the falls further west then follow the gorge south-east to camp on the plateau near another fall. Walk north-east across the plateau then descend a short gorge past many waterfalls to return back to the start. A medium three-day walk with reliable water, 30 km west of Jim Jim Falls in the Kakadu National Park.

ORMISTON GORGE & MT GILES

Much of the centre of Australia is barren, flat desert with only a few low hills. There are exceptions and, in the very centre, there are strings of ridges and mountains that are very rugged and beautiful.

The largest of these is the Macdonnell Ranges, conveniently situated near Alice Springs, the only major town in central Australia.

This range is composed of high ridges that run east to west and have been cut by streams to create impressive and beautiful gorges. The largest and most colourful of these is Ormiston Gorge with impressive scenery, permanent water and sweeping views from nearby Mt Giles. This walk, in the heart of Australia, is thoroughly recommended to all bushwalkers.

Features

The Macdonnell Ranges are composed mainly of quartzite rocks which originated as very ancient sandstones. These rocks have been subjected to great forces which have folded and uplifted them into high ridges. The rocks have been eroded, as is seen in the spectacular gorges for which this range is best known. Simpson's Gap, Standley Chasm, Trephina and Serpentine gorges are all popular. And, of course, there is Ormiston Gorge.

The climate of the range is arid, receiving rainfall at very irregular intervals. The plant and animal life is well-adapted to cope with the lack of water. The only vegetation on the hills and mountains are low shrubs and grasses, of which the spiny spinifex is the most common. In the gorges and along the watercourses are large river red gums and, close by them, grow white ghost gums (sometimes perched on the tops of cliffs and bluffs and other bizarre places).

In shady gullies there are ferns and palms, left over from an earlier period when the area received a much higher rainfall than it does today. The animal and birdlife is most active near the waterholes and is more varied and plentiful than you would expect in such a dry climate. After rainfall the area bursts into life as the vegetation takes advantage of the surplus water. A visit to any part of these colourful ranges is well worth the effort.

Standard

The suggested three-day walk has been given a medium standard. It is difficult to grade as the weather and water supplies have a great influence on the conditions. Day-time temperatures vary from 20°C to 40°C and there is little shade. Some of the walk is along well-marked tracks, part of it is over a flat spinifex covered plain, and the remainder is a rough rock scramble up Mt Giles. While most of the walk has no markers at all there are no navigational problems as all features can be easily seen through the sparse vegetation.

The new Larapinta Trail will eventually include much of this walk and will make navigation very easy. The current timetable for construction in this area is 1994 but that depends on funding, and may take longer.

Days Required

The itinerary is for three short days walking. This allows the group to rest during the heat of the day if necessary. In cool weather the walk can be completed in two days. Variations to the route depend greatly on the available water supplies.

Seasons

Winter is the best season for walking with mild to warm days and cool to cold nights. Sometimes the temperature falls below freezing at night and a suitable sleeping bag is essential. Spring and autumn are reasonable for walking while, in summer, the temperatures become very high and bushwalking is not recommended. Generally April to October are the best months for walking in the Macdonnell Ranges.

Equipment

Equipment needs for walking in this area are fairly simple. Sleeping bags should have long zippers for versatility and be suitable for heavy frosts. Footwear should be sturdy and light. Lightweight leather walking boots are the most suitable. Runners are not suitable as the sharp spinifex can puncture their soft uppers. Gaiters are advised for further protection against the spinifex.

Tents are unnecessary in this area as rainfall is very rare, but many people use ground sheets and sleep under the trees and bushes to keep the dew away. This option leaves you exposed to the insect life so a mosquito net might also be needed. If you are trying to save weight just take your tent inner, which will also protect you from the insects.

A foam mat is a good idea as the ground is usually very hard, You also need a wide brimmed hat, sunglasses and sunburn cream because of the harsh sun. For those with fair skin, long-sleeved shirts are recommended to prevent sunburn.

Some firewood can be found, but stoves are recommended as campfires have caused a number of bushfires in the ranges. Water bottles are essential and two litres per person should be plenty for use during the day. If the ranger advises that the Mt Giles spring is dry (a rare event) then sufficient water for the entire walk will need to be carried.

Maps

The only map available is the 1:250,000 *Hermannsburg*, published by NATMAP. This map is very simple and provides little detail. Fortunately, the navigation is easy and uncomplicated so the lack of good walking maps is unimportant.

The best information to the area is from the ranger who has his office in the Ormiston visitor centre (near the camping ground). He may also be able to tell you about the availability of water. A large colour photograph on the wall of the visitor centre shows the location of the route to Mt Giles. The display is also worth looking at as it illustrates many of the plants and animals that may be seen.

Permits

All walkers are required to obtain a free permit from the ranger before commencing an overnight walk. The ranger's office is at the display centre near the camping ground. If the ranger is not there he can sometimes be found at his residence 100 metres away to the south-east. For advance information it is best to contact the district office of the Conservation Commission of the Northern Territory (☎ (089) 51 8211), George Crescent, Alice Springs, 5750.

Access

Ormiston Gorge is 100 km due west of Alice Springs and has a sealed road to its entrance. From Alice Springs follow the Larapinta Drive west towards Hermannsburg. About 47 km from Alice Springs turn right onto the signposted Namatjira Drive and follow this beside the Macdonnell Ranges towards Glen Helen for 81 km. Turn right at the signposted road junction for the final eight km to the parking area and camping ground at the entrance to Ormiston Gorge.

There are no camping fees for staying overnight at the camping ground, which has toilets, showers and water. The closest store for food and petrol supplies is at Glen Helen, 12 km away by road. There is no public

transport to the park. Tour groups do visit this gorge occasionally and it might be possible to join a bus tour from Alice Springs. The return trip is not as easy to arrange, however, as the bus tours only visit the gorge as demand requires. The other possibility is to use a tour bus to Glen Helen and walk the last eight km from the road junction to the camping ground.

Stage 1: Ormiston Gorge to Giles Spring

(15 km, 4-6 hours)

From the display centre there are two tracks that can be taken into the gorge. The 'Ghost Gum Walk' starts 30 metres north-west of the display centre and climbs up and then along the western side of the gorge to descend to the stream bed in the centre of the gorge. The other track is simply signposted as 'Gorge Walking Track' and heads north from the display centre. This track follows the floor of the gorge upstream along the east bank. Depending on the height of the water it may be necessary to scramble up over some rock bands.

Both tracks join at a large permanent waterhole at the major bend where the gorge

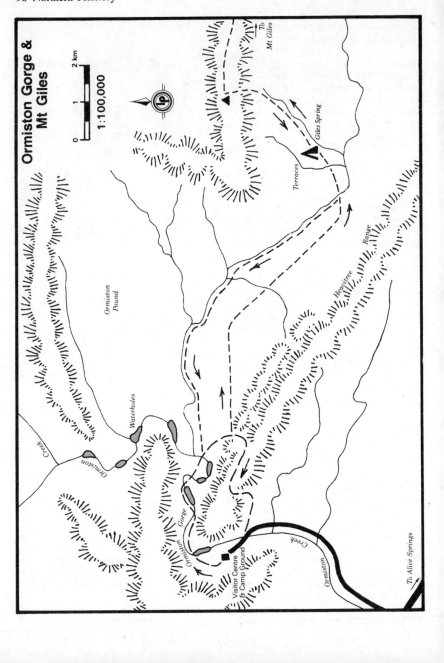

Ormiston Gorge & Mt Giles

1:100,000

0 1 2 km

To Mt Giles

Giles Spring

Terraces

Ormiston Pound

Waterholes

Ormiston Creek

Heavitree Range

Ormiston Gorge

Visitor Centre & Camp Ground

Ormiston Creek

To Alice Springs

Top: K Col, Mt Field National Park
Bottom: The huge granite bluffs of Frenchmans Cap

Top: Edeowie Gorge, Wilpena Pound
Left: St Mary Peak, Wilpena Pound
Right: Alligator Gorge, Mt Remarkable

Ormiston Gorge

swings east. Cliffs on both sides come down to the stream bed and you will need to swim across the creek to continue on. This is an easy pleasant swim through a deep pool.

Once past the bend the walking is easy along the south bank of the creek bed and some coloured markers show the track. The valley opens up and within one km you enter Ormiston Pound. This is a wide flat valley about 10 km across and the destination, Mt Giles is clearly seen due east.

Continue to follow the marked track which crosses the main creek three times. Beside the third crossing the track passes a waterhole then climbs away from the creek bed and heads in a south-easterly direction towards the hills of the Heavitree Range. About a 10-minute walk from the creek the foothills are approached and this is the best place to leave the track to walk towards Mt Giles.

From here cross the floor of Ormiston Pound – easy walking except for the sharp spinifex. Walk due east for four km across a succession of gullies and stony rises to a higher rise which provides views to the south-east. Walk south-east descending for one km to meet the south boundary fence of the park. Follow the fence due east to the main creek.

Cross the fence at the creek and walk eastwards climbing gently away from the creek up onto a broad terrace beneath the southern face of the Chewings Range. This terrace is dissected by some gullies running out of the range. Water is usually found in the second and third gullies and camp can be made near these streams.

Stage 2: Giles Spring to Mt Giles, return (8 km, 4-6 hours)

The ascent of Mt Giles from the campsite is a relatively straightforward scramble. From the campsite walk north-east to the foot of the range and climb up the spinifex-covered slopes towards a prominent bluff on the side of the range. Climb into the gully to the right of the bluff where there is shade and often water.

Climb up the gully and turn left into the first side gully. Ascend this gully and emerge on to the steep spur above the bluff. This spur is easily climbed onto the main ridge. Turn left and climb onto the summit marked by a trig point. This vantage point has excellent views of Ormiston Pound and the surrounding ranges.

This summit is not the Mt Giles that is marked on the map. The map refers to the flat-topped hill covered with trees three km to the east. The ridge can be followed east through three steep saddles to the tree-covered hill if desired. The trig point has better views and the return is by the same route back to the campsite.

Stage 3: Giles Spring to Ormiston Car Park

(14 km, 4-6 hours)

The return route to Ormiston Creek is via the same valley that was followed in. For variety follow the creek for the entire route. From the campsite follow the stream south to meet the main creek. Turn west then north-west following the southern bank of the main

creek into the pound. Several waterholes will be passed where the creek swings west again.

Continue to follow the creek west until it meets Ormiston Creek on the western side of the pound. Turn left and walk 500 metres south to meet the marked walking track just before a waterhole. Follow the walking track south-east away from the creek towards the hills. (This section was walked on the first day.)

Continue to follow the track as it climbs into a small valley in the southern wall of Wilpena Pound. The track then sidles west across another small valley then climbs onto the top of the ridge that forms the southern wall of Ormiston Pound. Follow the main track (there are several variations) west across the undulating terrain of the ridge.

Descend the south-west side of the ridge to cross Ormiston Creek and meet the main road 200 metres south-east of the display centre. Turn right and walk back to the camping area to complete the walk. Before leaving the park please inform the ranger on duty that you have returned.

Queensland

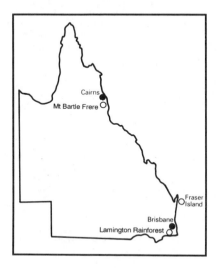

This hot north-eastern state is known as the Sunshine State. The humid coastal climate has encouraged a thick belt of tropical rainforest to grow along the eastern edge. Inland, dry plains and plateaus sweep westwards to the central deserts. The majority of these inland plains are large properties used mainly for grazing cattle.

Most of the bushwalking areas are in the forest covered mountains near the coast. With the high humidity, carrying a pack is often very hot work and bushwalks in the cooler southern half of the state are more popular. There are some excellent areas in the north of the state if the heat can be tolerated.

South of Brisbane, on the New South Wales border, is the most popular bushwalking area in the state. The McPherson Range (often called the Border Range) towers over the valleys providing some interesting bushwalking. Most of the range is covered with tall rainforests which often restrict

scenic views. Hidden in the forests, however, are beautiful high waterfalls and gorges. Some of the range is protected by national parks, of which the most famous park is Lamington.

In this area there is a well-developed and maintained track system which provides very easy walking to the major features in the northern half of the park. Walking along these rainforest tracks is very pleasant.

More rugged walking can be found in the southern half of the park which is a wilderness. The Lost World, Mt Widgee and the Stinson Stretcher Track to Point Lookout are popular with local walkers. The range continues further west and is known as the Scenic Rim. This connects to the spectacular complex of ridges and peaks called Mt Barney. In fine weather this steep peak is worth climbing.

North of Brisbane on the coast is the Cooloola National Park. This has a series of lakes and coastal forests with a newly constructed bushwalking trail crossing the park. It is interesting, but like many designed tracks it is a one-way route which requires a car shuffle as there is no public transport. A short way north of Cooloola is one of the most magnificent places in Australia, Fraser Island.

Fraser Island is the largest sand island in the world and is covered with tall rainforests, huge sand dunes and lakes. Most of this island was, until recently, managed by the Forestry Commission. During this time it was extensively logged for satinay. Now, with an impending declaration of World heritage status it looks as if it will be preserved.

The easiest and most enjoyable bushwalking is via the tracks in the centre of the island which enable visits to the many freshwater lakes. The route passes through many types of vegetation and is highly recommended. More adventurous bushwalkers can visit the northern third of the island. It is protected by a national park and is very scrubby, less frequented and difficult to access.

East of Fraser Island the Great Dividing Range swings inland for 500 km to the Carnarvon National Park. This inland park features the famous and spectacular Carnarvon Gorge, worth visiting if the roads are open. Other smaller parks east and north-east of Carnarvon can provide some interest for bushwalking.

The Great Dividing Range continues north following the coast. There are many small parks and areas that can be explored. The most significant park for bushwalkers in the north is the Bellenden Ker National Park, south of Cairns. This contains the state's highest mountain, Mt Bartle Frere, which provides a fine bushwalk if one follows rough tracks to its summit.

Further north there are some interesting areas but due to the heat, carrying a pack is not popular. Base camps are commonly used to explore areas in the far north. Around Cape York there is some excellent coastal walking but it is difficult to gain access and in some areas you will need permission from the local Aborigines.

Other Suggested Bushwalks

Hinchinbrook Island A medium four to five-day wilderness trail follows the east coast of this large island. Permits are needed and numbers are restricted. Fuel stoves must be carried as fires are totally banned.

Mt Barney From Cranes Creek walk north up onto the South-east Ridge and follow this to the East Peak of Mt Barney. Descend west to camp in the saddle. Climb the west peak then descend the South Ridge to the start of the walk. This is an easy two-day walk (with some scrambling) in the Mt Barney National Park, 100 km south-west of Brisbane.

The Lost World From Albert River climb north onto the Razorback, then follow this east to The Lost World. Cross the plateau and descend south-east to camp in the saddle. Explore Black Canyon as a sidetrip. Follow the Albert River back to the start. A medium to hard two to three-day walk in the Lamington National Park, 100 km south of Brisbane.

Binna Burra to O'Reillys From Binna Burra follow the Coomera Track, then the Border Track, to O'Reillys to camp. Follow the Blue Pool Track north to camp beside Canungra Creek. Follow the East Canungra Creek to Fountain Falls, climb north-east to Noowongbill Lookout and descend steeply north-east to the Coomera River. Follow the tracks back to Binna Burra. A three-day medium to hard circuit in the Lamington National Park.

Cooloola Wilderness Trail From Mullen car park follow the marked trail south-east across undulating country to Elanda Point on Lake Cootharaba. An easy two to three-day walk in the Cooloola National Park, 140 km north of Brisbane.

Isla Gorge From the car park, descend north into the gorge and up Kallaroo Creek to camp. Explore Observation Hill and Dyumbu Ridge as a sidetrip. Walk up Budyi Creek, south-east along the plateau and down Hewitts Creek to camp near Gamu waterhole. Follow the creeks and climb back to the car park. A medium three to four-day bushwalk in the Isla Gorge National Park, 400 km north-west of Brisbane.

Carnarvon Gorge Follow the gorge upstream to camp at Big Bend. Climb Battleship Spur, walk north-west to Mt Percy and descend Delay Ridge to Carnarvon Creek to camp. Follow the gorge back to the start. A medium three-day bushwalk in the Carnarvon National Park, 600 km north-west of Brisbane.

Sundown From Sundown Homestead, climb Mt Lofty then head west into the Severn River to Red Rock Creek, up the creek to the falls then down a creek to the start. This is a medium two-day bushwalk in Sundown National Park near the New South Wales border.

MT BARTLE FRERE

The Bellenden Ker National Park is an area of tropical rainforest and high peaks in far north Queensland. The park has a diverse

forest cover as it ranges from near sea level to 1600 metres in altitude. The area is undeveloped with only a few rough walking tracks for bushwalkers. The most popular bushwalk within the park is the long climb to the summit of Mt Bartle Frere, at 1622 metres, Queensland's highest peak.

Features

As with most natural areas close to the coast in north Queensland the park is covered in thick lush rainforest. This vegetation varies from the large leaved forest of the foothills to the dense, stunted growth crowning the ridges and high peaks. As a result of this luxurious growth, views of the surrounding countryside are very limited from within the forest. The only clear views on this walk are from a small patch of heathlands near the Upper Camp and from the massive boulder field just above.

Much of the forest was battered by a cyclone in early 1986 and this is evident. Regrowth initially consisted of a profusion of vines but the rainforest trees are now beginning to dominate and restrict the views lower down the mountain.

One tree that you should look out for and then avoid is the stinging gympie tree. This has large dark green leaves covered with fine needle-like barbs and it inflicts a painful, itching sting. Several saplings are growing near the walking track and care is needed to avoid these.

Life within the forests is rich. Huge colourful butterflies are common and the birdlife is both audible and easily seen. Most of the larger animals are only seen at night and include the common marsupials as well as rarer species such as the green possum and the tree kangaroo. Apart from the odd snakes there is little danger from the wildlife within this rainforest.

Standard

The route followed is along a well-marked but rough bushwalker's track. This track is not constructed but formed by the passage of many walkers. At times you have to climb steeply over exposed tree roots and large granite boulders. It is marked by coloured pieces of tape tied to trees and vines. The boulder field is marked by arrows painted on the rocks to show the easiest route. The walk is graded medium.

Days Required

Two days are needed to complete this walk. It can be varied by following a marked track from the summit leading west down to Lamins Hill, but this requires a lengthy car shuffle and is not suggested for a first visit. The walk follows the same track for the return as it is difficult to make a circuit of this bushwalk.

Seasons

The daily temperature in this area is fairly constant all year round varying between 25°C to 32°C. The humidity varies greatly and some seasons are more pleasant than others for walking.

Winter, the dry season, has the lowest humidity and is very suitable for walking, although the nights can be very cold, sometimes falling to freezing at the Upper Camp. The only detraction is that winter is the cane-burning season and the landscape is sometimes covered in a pall of smoke and haze.

Spring is the flower season and ideal for walking, while summer is very hot and humid being the wet season. To compensate, however, the waterfalls are at their best in summer and the whole rainforest is full of new growth. Autumn is also a good walking season with the creeks still flowing at high levels and the air is often clear, providing fine views.

Equipment

No special equipment is needed, but it is advisable to carry a waterproof jacket and a warm jumper as this mountain is often subjected to severe storms. At the Upper Camp, a stove is recommended as firewood is difficult to find.

Light boots are the best footwear – runners can be used but they lack traction on the exposed tree roots and sloping rock sections

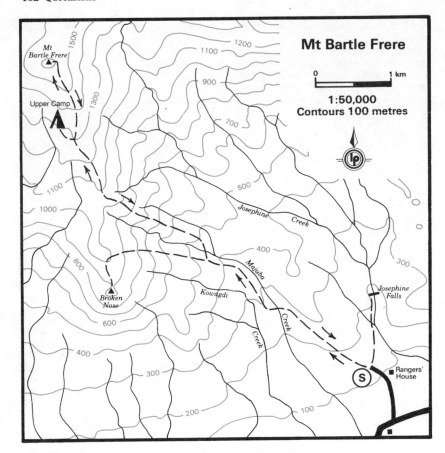

in wet weather. Take a good tent as the Upper Camp is exposed to strong winds.

Usually a water bottle is sufficient for carrying drinking water. On rare occasions the spring at the Upper Camp is dry (the park ranger will advise on this) and all water will then need to be carried from Majuba Creek.

Maps

The only map available is the 1:100,000 topographic map, *Bartle Frere*. This map does not show any of the walking tracks and has limited detail. It is produced by NATMAP Map Sales. Copies can also be purchased from any SUNMAP office in Queensland. The Cairns office is at 36 Shields St, just north of the mall.

A free leaflet, *Visitor Information to Bellenden Ker National Park*, is available from the ranger. This has some information on it and a useful sketch map showing the track location.

Permits

As with all Queensland parks, a free permit to camp in the forest must be obtained from the ranger. The rangers' office (☎ (070) 67 6304) is attached to the rangers' house beside

View of the coastal plain from Mt Bartle Frere

the road, 100 metres from the Josephine Falls car park. The rangers are helpful and will advise on the availability of water at the Upper Camp and of any changes in the track conditions.

Remember to inform the rangers of your return from the mountain. A permit can be obtained in advance by writing to The Ranger, Josephine Falls National Park, PO Box 93, Miriwinni, Qld, 4871.

Access

Mt Bartle Frere is close to the coast of north Queensland and 50 km due south of Cairns. The walk starts at the Josephine Falls car park, eight km west of the Bruce Highway.

From Cairns follow the Bruce Highway south for 57 km to Babinda and continue south along the highway a further nine km to the signposted side road to Josephine Falls. Turn right and follow the narrow sealed road for eight km to the Josephine Falls car park. There are no facilities at the car park and the closest shops are located at Babinda, 17 km away.

There is no public transport available to the start of the walk. Bus services run at very regular intervals along the Bruce Highway and, if they are used, it is necessary to walk the last eight km to the Josephine Falls car park. The road is interesting to walk along as it passes through cane fields but has little shade and can be very hot.

Several companies run buses along the highway from Cairns down to Townsville and on to Brisbane and bookings are essential. Traveland (☎ (070) 51 7433), 10A Shields St, Cairns, can reserve a bus seat.

Stage 1: Josephine Falls Car Park to Upper Camp

(7 km, 4½-6 hours)

At the Josephine Falls car park the walking track to Mt Bartle Frere is clearly signposted on the left. Follow this track which immediately enters the rainforest and continues over several low spurs and tiny creeks for 40 to 60 minutes to cross a major side creek. Cross this and almost immediately the track descends a little to cross the larger Majuba Creek. This flows through and past some very large granite boulders.

The track crosses the creek and climbs very steeply west past a small campsite to a ridge. The track now swings north-west and follows the rough, rocky top of a sharp ridge dividing two creek valleys. Follow this for 20 to 30 minutes to a good camping area and a signposted track junction. The left track leads to Broken Nose which is a rocky knoll on the southern ridge of Mt Bartle Frere.

At the junction turn right to the summit and descend to Majuba Creek and cross it. Collect drinking water as this is the last stream until the camp site is reached. Past the creek the track begins to climb steeply up a spur. Glimpses of the surrounding country can be seen through the trees. After one hour of climbing, the track winds past an enormous boulder that straddles the ridge. It is possible to scramble to the top of this for an excellent view of the valleys below. After another half an hour of climbing, the track swings north onto the main ridge of the mountain.

The track now climbs more gradually for a further 1½ to two hours to emerge from the forest onto a small heath-covered knoll with excellent views. There are several tracks and a signpost pointing west to water near the top of the knoll. Leave the main ridge and follow the water track west down to the obvious campsites on both sides of the spring. This is called the Upper Camp.

Water is available from the spring for 10 months of the year. This campsite is exposed and, in stormy weather, it is very windy and tents will need to be securely tied down. In fine weather the views of the sunrise and sunset are not to be missed.

Alternative Campsites
Big Rock This is a good camping area beside the 'Broken Nose' and 'Summit' track junction. It is about 1½ to two hours from the car park and there is permanent water here.

Stage 2: Upper Camp to the Summit, return
(1 km, 1½ to 2 hours)
If time permits the summit of Bartle Frere can be visited late in the afternoon of the first

day. The suggested itinerary is to visit it the morning of the second day and return to the car park by mid-afternoon.

From the Upper Camp climb east with packs for five minutes back to the main ridge and the water sign. Leave the packs here and turn left (north) and follow the track up the ridge to the extensive boulder field. The track climbs up and over the huge blocks and is clearly marked by painted arrows. There are excellent panoramic views from the boulders.

At the top of the rocks the track enters a short section of stunted forest then crosses open heaths to the final climb through forest to the summit of Mt Bartle Frere. There are no views from the top which is marked by a dead tree with name plates all over it. Return to the packs by the same track. Two other tracks join at the summit and walkers should make sure on the return journey that they are following the same track they climbed up.

Stage 3: Upper Camp to Josephine Falls Car Park
(7 km, 4-5 hours)
Collect the packs from the knoll near the Upper Camp, turn south and follow the track downhill into the forest. This is the same track as used on the ascent and it is followed for two to four hours back to the Broken Nose track junction near Majuba Creek. If the party has the time, Broken Nose requires an additional three to four hours return to visit as a sidetrip without packs.

From the track junction turn left (southeast) and follow the track past the campsites, back along the rocky ridge and down to cross Majuba Creek again. The last part of the track is easily followed back through the forest to the car park and the end of the walk.

If the weather is warm it is worth visiting Josephine Falls for a swim. The track to the falls is clearly marked and takes about 10 minutes to walk each way. The falls are a picturesque series of rocky pools and cascades surrounded by rainforest. Remember to let the rangers know you've returned before leaving the park.

FRASER ISLAND

This is the largest sand island in the world, covered in thick tall forests and lovely lakes. It is used extensively by commercial tour operators and receives relatively few visits from bushwalkers. The walking is excellent and a visit to this beautiful and unforgettable island is thoroughly recommended.

Features

Fraser Island is composed almost entirely of sand, resting on bedrock hundreds of metres below sea level. It is 120 km long and averages 14 km in width. A long wide beach sweeps the entire length of the east coast, while the west coast has short beaches and mangrove flats.

In the centre of the island the sand dunes rise to 240 metres and contain over 40 freshwater lakes. The high rainfall of 1500 millimetres has encouraged thick vegetation to grow and cover the dunes. This cover is varied, ranging from mangroves and scrubs to dense rainforest over 50 metres in height, all of which grow in pure sand.

Hidden amongst the dunes are a variety of perched lakes, which have formed above the water table in an impermeable pan basin, and other lakes which are 'windows' in the water table. Most lakes are tea coloured due to the organic matter in the waters.

In contrast to the diverse flora there is little wildlife. Dingos are the most numerous large animal and some are unafraid of man. There are also a few wild brumbies, usually seen on the eastern ocean beach. In the lakes, tortoises, fish and frogs are common. Birds are abundant with over 200 species having been recorded. Most of the island was managed by the Forestry Commission who until recently, selectively logged the forests and maintained the beauty spots. The area around Central Station (the forestry headquarters) is representative of most of the island.

Standard

For a reasonably flat island with ridges of only 240 metres above sea level, the walking is fairly tough because the island is all sand.

After a day's walking your legs will be tired. It is possible to take more than the three days suggested to make the walk easier. This would allow more time for swimming in the delightful lakes and exploring the lush rainforest.

The circuit is on walking tracks and sandy roads. Some care is needed with navigation as there are a few walkers' signposts missing. The suggested circuit is graded medium.

Days Required

The circuit requires three full walking days. It can be lengthened to four days with an overnight stop at Central Station. This would allow time to visit Pile Valley and to laze around and explore the lakes.

Seasons

This island can be walked at any time of the year. The climate is subtropical, being warm and pleasant most of the time. In the summer months of January and February, sudden and severe cyclones can occur. These tropical storms, with their gale force winds and heavy rain, will prevent walking until they pass. For the remainder of the year such storms are rare and the weather pattern of showers and rain is interspersed with spells of fine weather.

Equipment

No special hiking equipment is needed. Runners or sandshoes are the most suitable footwear (boots are too heavy in the sand). Although fires are allowed it is better to take a stove as wood is usually in short supply around the popular campsites. If using fires, care should be taken as the greatest threat to the island is from bushfires. Almost any tent or suspended sheet will suffice for overnight shelter. Fully enclosed tents will keep the insects away so, if you own one, take it.

Maps

The 1:50,000 forestry map, *Fraser Island south sheet*, is the best single map to use. It has no contour lines, but its detailed illustration of the maze of roads and tracks is reasonably accurate. It can be purchased from SUNMAP. They also publish a tourist map to Fraser Island and, while it is interesting to read, it has little practical use for bushwalkers.

The NATMAP 1:100,000 sheets are the only contour maps available. *Wide Bay* and *Happy Valley* are both needed to cover the walk. They can be purchased from both SUNMAP and NATMAP.

Information on the walking tracks of Fraser Island is available from the Department of Forestry (☎ (071) 23 7833), 123 Wharf St, Maryborough (postal address, PO Box 219, Maryborough, 4650), and also at Central Station (☎ (071) 27 9191) on Fraser Island.

Permits

Separate permits are required to visit the island and for camping overnight. The camping permit must be obtained in advance from the Forestry Office at Maryborough or Ungowa, or from the Hervey Bay City Council Office, (☎ (0710) 25 0222), 77 Tavistock St, Torquay, 4567. To obtain the permit by post write to The District Forester, (☎ (071) 23 7833), 123 Wharf St, Maryborough, 4650, Queensland. The permit tag must be tied onto the outside of your tent for inspection purposes.

The permit to visit the island is paid on the day of arrival and may be included with your transport cost or is available on all barges and tour boats.

Access

Fraser Island is 250 km north of Brisbane. From Brisbane follow the main highway north to Maryborough then turn right to Hervey Bay. Hervey Bay actually used to be three small towns Pialba, Scarness and Torquay. Older maps show these separately. The offices of all the boat and barge operators are here, as is the City Council office.

Regular bus services run from Brisbane to Townsville and Cairns with a scheduled stop at Pialba in Hervey Bay. Ansett Pioneer, Greyhound, McCaffertys, Deluxe Coachlines and VIP Express Coaches all operate several buses daily on this route. The

departure point is at the Pialba shopping centre. Bookings are best made with a tourist bureau or travel agent. The Hervey Bay Bus Service (☎ (071) 21 3719) operates several times daily from the corner of Tooley and Normanby Sts, Maryborough, and then on to Hervey Bay.

From Hervey Bay to the island, a variety of services operate and we suggest that you book your tickets at one of the travel agents in Hervey Bay. They know who is operating at the time and can do the ringing around for you. They can be found under 'Travel Agents' in the Yellow Pages of the local telephone book. For accommodation, Hervey Bay has nine caravan parks and many cheap motels and hotels.

Access to the island is by boat. Most services leave for the island between 8 and 9 am so an early start is advised, The cheapest form of transport is to board a barge at North Head, about 20 km south of Hervey Bay, as a passenger only. This requires private transport and you will be dumped on the island at Woongoolbuer Creek, about eight km from Central Station. If you can't get a lift with a private group you have a fairly uninteresting walk.

The other alternative is to join a tour group to the island. In most places it is unusual for bushwalkers to do this, but for Fraser Island it is a very practical solution to the access problems. We found the tour operators to be very friendly and quite co-operative in allowing us to break our visit the first day and rejoin another group at the same place, or by arrangement elsewhere, several days later.

There is no extra charge for this and in fact they seem keen to help anyone who wants to have a good look at their island. They collect and return you to where you are staying in Hervey Bay by bus, provide transport to the island by ferry or barge, provide transport on the island and one lunch for a reasonable fee.

Most tours run through Central Station to Eurong, a holiday resort on the east coast. As tours continually change their itineraries and dates of operation, select a group that can leave you, and later collect you, at Eurong.

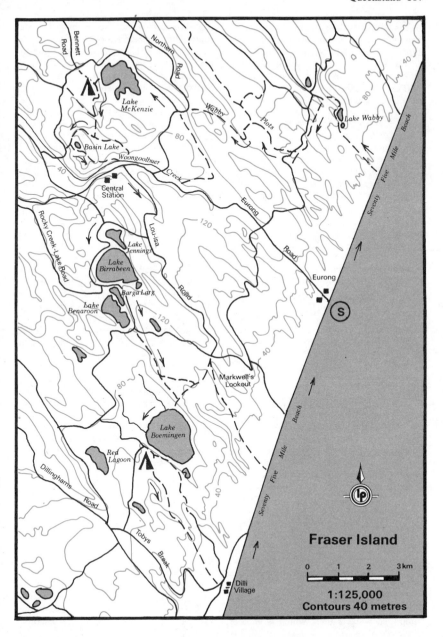

Fraser Island

0   1   2   3 km

1:125,000
Contours 40 metres

This is where the travel agents will help as they know the current schedules. If a stop at Eurong is unavailable then arrange for Central Station to be your walking start and end. The circuit passes through both Central Station and Eurong. Tour groups and barges leave on most days throughout the year.

Stage 1: Eurong to Lake McKenzie
(19 km, 5-7 hours)

From Eurong walk north along the wide sandy beach for 3½ km to a signpost pointing out the track to Lake Wabby. With some tours the driver may be willing to drop you there, saving the walk along the beach.

Leave the beach and follow the well-defined walking track in a north-west direction for three km to Lake Wabby. The track passes through light ti-tree forests. When you reach the lake the track becomes less defined and you can walk along either shore. The left side (west) passes through the forest while the right side (east) climbs onto the steep sand dune for good views of the lake. The right side of the lake is the more scenic route.

The sand dune is actually a large sand blow that is advancing and slowly engulfing the lake at the rate of four metres a year. Camping is not allowed anywhere near this lake.

At the northern end of the lake an unmarked foot track heads north then swings westward and climbs a ridge to a car park. Turn right onto the road and follow it for 30 metres to a signposted walking track on the left. Follow this track, which is an old disused road, south-west for 2½ km to a walkers' signpost in the centre of the track.

The signpost is not clearly marked and it is essential to turn right (west) here and follow a poor footpad through the scrub for 60 metres to meet a vehicle track and walkers track junction. If you miss the signpost and meet a vehicle track, turn sharp right and walk back north along the road for one km to the track junction.

The signposts at this junction are more obvious. Cross the road and walk west on the signposted walkers track which is another

closed road. This track passes through some lovely rainforest and after five km you reach a track junction. There is a walkers' signpost in the scrub on the left. Follow the left track and another 10 minutes of walking brings you to a major sandy road. Continue straight ahead on the road and turn right after five minutes as indicated by the walkers signpost.

This road is followed north-west for two km to Lake McKenzie. At a sharp right bend you'll see the lake through the trees. Leave the road here and push 10 metres through the light scrub onto the sandy lake shore. Follow the shore west for one km to a sandspit point. Cross the point and the marsh behind to the beach and walk south for 300 metres along the sand to the walking track markers near the edge of the scrub. Turn right to leave the lake and follow the track west 200 metres through light forest crossing a road to the signposted 'Walkers Campsite'.

The toilet and shower block is 50 metres away to the north-west and there is a tap for water on the edge of the general car camping area, past the toilet block. The marked walking trail follows the road all the way to the camping area, but it is far more pleasant to follow the lake shore as described.

The walkers' campsite is well sheltered with many flat sites and is close to the amenities. It is set apart from the car camping area and makes a pleasant overnight stop.

Alternative Campsites
Ocean Beach Windy sites are found all along the edge of the beach. Water is obtained from soaks in the sand.

Lake Wabby Camping is totally banned near this lake. If the party is at Lake Wabby late in the day, collect water from the lake and camp on the walking track past the Lake Wabby car park.

Stage 2: Lake McKenzie to Lake Boemingen
(22 km, 5-7 hours)

From the walkers campsite return to the shore of Lake McKenzie and follow the sandy beach 500 metres south to a walkers' signpost. Leave the lake and follow the walking track through light forest for about 10 minutes to a vehicle track. Turn left onto this and walk south for approximately 20 minutes past a small marshy lake to a signpost indicating a small walking track on the right.

Follow this walking track uphill a few minutes to another old vehicle track and continue straight ahead down this road for five minutes to a T-junction. Turn right and follow this road (at first west then south) for 15 minutes to the signposted walking track to Basin Lake. Turn left and descend to the lake shore.

Turn right and walk 500 metres around the sandy shore to the signposted track near the south-eastern corner. This is a good swimming spot. Leave the lake and follow the walking track south-east for 30 minutes through light forest to Woongoolbuer Creek. Cross the creek on a log bridge and follow the track on the right uphill to Central Station and the main road. This is seven km (a two to 2½-hour walk) from Lake McKenzie and has a camping area if needed.

Central Station has an interesting display in the forestry information centre and camping permits can be obtained here. It is better, however, to get your permit before arrival as the rangers are not always on duty. If available, collect a brochure, *Lake Boemingen Trail*, for use later in the walk. It is not necessary to have this brochure, but it helps to explain the different forest types and other interesting features along the way.

From the Central Station information centre, follow the main road east for five minutes to the Lake Birrabeen turnoff. Turn right and follow the main road south-east towards Lake Birrabeen through tall forest. Despite the occasional passing vehicle it is a lovely walk.

After three km follow the main road to the right at an unmarked road junction. After 4½ km from Central Station depart the main road and follow the signposted walking trail on the left, along an old closed road around the side of Lake Jennings. This lake has only a short sandy beach and is less attractive than

Australian Pelican

others. The old track joins another main road which follows the southern shore of Lake Jennings then turns south towards Lake Birrabeen. The lake is soon in view. Leave the sandy road at the second closed side track and follow the sandy lake shore of Lake Birrabeen for 1½ km. This lake is very large and beautiful.

Leave Lake Birrabeen at its southern end at the first old road (not signposted) and walk uphill to join a major vehicle track. Turn left onto this road and follow it eastwards for two km, at first east then south-east along the shores of Barga Larg (a marshy depression) then Lake Benaroon to a multiple track junction. From here a walking track leads directly to Lake Boemingen, but it is poorly marked and you may have difficulty following it. The easier route is to follow the main road to the right for seven km to the campsite on the south-western shore of the lake.

If using the walking track start at the signpost at the multiple track junction. The faint track heads south initially then turns south-east for 1½ km to cross a forestry road. The continuation from here can be very difficult to find and if it is lost then the forestry road can be used. The walking track continues for 1½ km and ends at another forestry road. Turn right (south-west) onto this to reach the northern shore of Lake Boemingen.

If using the forestry track from where the walking track crossed it, turn left onto the vehicle track and walk east for 10 minutes. Ignore the minor dead end road on the right. After another 1½ km the forestry road meets another old road. Turn right and within 15 minutes it passes the other end of the walking track and continues on to Lake Boemingen.

This lake, covering 200 hectares, is the largest perched lake in the world. Follow the wide sandy western shore of the lake and walk up to the road at the end of the beach. The campsite is a short distance to the left along the road.

The campsite is a large open area with views of the lake. Toilets are 100 metres south-west between the two roads. The area is shared with vehicle campers.

Alternative Campsite
Central Station There is a camping area with tap water, showers and toilets on the south side of the clearing.

Stage 3: Lake Boemingen to Eurong
(17 km, 4 to 5 hours)
The track from the lake to Dilli Village has nature trail markers along it. A free brochure, available from Central Station, describes the variety of vegetation seen. From the camping area above the south-western edge of Lake Boemingen, walk 30 metres east to find the signpost and walking track entry point. This track immediately climbs away from the lake and heads south-east. It is well defined and easy to follow.

After two km, a high point is reached from where glimpses of Lake Boemingen, the large nearby sand dune and the approaching ocean can be seen. The track then descends gradually through varied flora for a further three km to meet a major sandy vehicle track. The old walking track continues straight ahead, but is hopelessly overgrown. Turn left onto the vehicle track and a 100-metre walk

will bring you into Dilli Village. This is a private camp and has no public facilities.

From the camp it is possible to follow the vehicle track north for two km to the ocean beach. The more interesting route, however, is to walk east across the lawns of the village and follow the signposted track to the ocean beach. This track crosses a creek on a log bridge then wanders out to the wide ocean beach. This part of the beach was sand mined for minerals at one stage and as a result the sand dunes are unnaturally flat.

Turn left and walk north for 10 km along the sand to Eurong. Two major creeks are passed and these are easily waded across. This beach is used extensively by vehicles and a lift to Eurong is an alternative if you find the beach tiring.

Eurong is clearly seen and has a well-stocked kiosk for the public. Buses leave from here to the barge landing at Woongoolbuer Creek in the early afternoon of most days. The return bus and boat trip should have already been organised before the walk began.

LAMINGTON RAINFOREST CIRCUIT
The Lamington National Park is an extensive area of rainforest on the New South Wales and Queensland border, with the best network of graded walking tracks in Australia. Walking and camping in the subtropical rainforest of the park is easy and pleasant. Two highly commercial resorts cater for most visitors, but the park is large enough for everyone to enjoy.

Features
The Lamington National Park is an area of mountain ridges and peaks, high cliffs, deep gorges and many waterfalls. A high rainfall has encouraged the thick forest to cover virtually all of the ridges and valleys.

The rocks in the area are volcanic and originate from a huge shield volcano centred on Mt Warning. The rock is exposed along the New South Wales and Queensland border as an extensive cliff wall. There are magnificent views from lookouts along this escarpment and also from the lookouts along the eastern edge of the park.

The thick forests are a haven for many of the smaller native animals. Snakes, goannas, lizards and crayfish are frequently seen while walking along the tracks, and birdlife is abundant throughout the park. In the spring, the diversity of the wildflowers is an added attraction.

Standard

This national park has an excellent network of well-maintained and well-signposted graded walking tracks. These visit most of the major features, and walking along these trails is easy with gentle climbs and descents.

For a first bushwalking visit there is plenty to see by using the well-established track system. For repeated visits, walking off the trails is allowed and encouraged for bushwalkers, although it can be quite difficult pushing through the rainforest. The suggested walk uses the good track system and is graded easy.

Days Required

The walk takes three days and visits all the major features of the eastern side of the park. You can extend the trip using the trails, continuing along the Border Track from Mt Merino, then via Toolona Gorge to O'Reillys to camp. Return via the Border Track and the Coomera River (not to be missed!) to Binna Burra. This adds two more days to make a five-day circuit.

Seasons

This walking area is suitable for all seasons. The winter months are probably the most ideal with many dry sunny days, cool nights and clear views from the lookouts. The absence of ticks and snakes also makes trips at this time of the year more enjoyable. The spring months are the best time to see the wildflowers.

Late spring and early summer is hot and dry with high temperatures and frequent severe storms and is the least pleasant time to go walking. Late summer is the hot, wet season with many storms and showers. It is

a pleasant time, however, to walk in the park as the waterfalls and creeks flow well and the rainforest is at its best. Unfortunately, at this time leeches and ticks are common.

Equipment

Lamington is in the sub-tropical zone and is usually warm during the day and cool at night. Most walkers wear shorts and open shirts or T-shirts. A wool jumper or shirt is useful for cool nights. Many walkers wear sandshoes or runners on the trails, but boots are better if you have them, as the tracks in the rainforest are usually very muddy and slippery.

Almost any tent or arrangement that keeps you dry will suffice for an overnight shelter. Most locals simply use two nylon sheets; one for the ground and the other tied to the bushes and trees as a simple shelter.

It is a good idea to carry water for drinking as creeks are not at regular intervals. Also, carry stoves as fires are not encouraged and any dead wood is usually saturated.

Maps

This park is well mapped. If you are staying on the graded tracks then the 1:25,000 Forestry Commission map, *Lamington*, is ideal and the only map required. It shows all the tracks and features accurately. It has form lines (rough contours) and depicts vegetation types. You can buy it from SUNMAP.

If detailed contour lines are required then the 1:25,000 topographic maps, *Beechmont* and *Tyalgum* cover the walk. These are also from SUNMAP.

Another map available at Binna Burra (the start of the walk) is the *Binna Burra Track Map*. This map shows all the graded tracks in the eastern part of the park and is sufficient on its own for a walk using the tracks. It is available at varying prices and is cheapest at the display centre of the Lamington Natural History Association, near the Binna Burra Lodge.

Permits

A free permit is required for camping overnight within the park. This can be obtained from the Binna Burra rangers' station

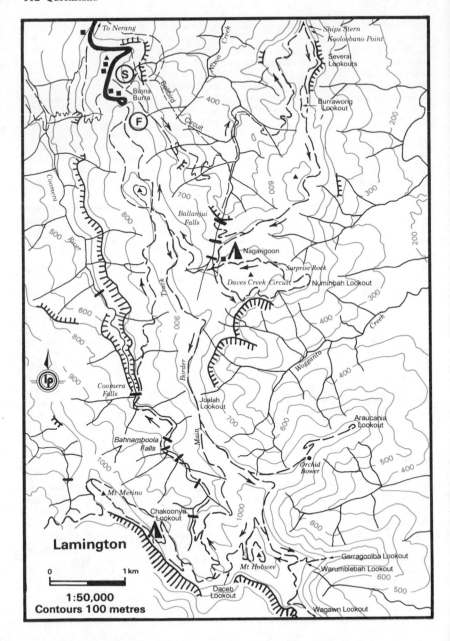

To Nerang

Mixort Creek

Ships Stern
Kooloobano Point

Several
Lookouts

(S)

Binna
Burra

Belbird

Circuit

400

Burrawong
Lookout

200

(F)

Coomera

700

600

300

200

River

500

800

Ballanjui
Falls

Nagarigoon

Surprise Rock

Numinbah Lookout

Daves Creek Circuit

Creek

300

(lp)

600

800

Track

Border

006

900

Woggonna

400

400

600

Joalah
Lookout

700

Araucania
Lookout

Coomera
Falls

500

Bahnamboola
Falls

Main

Orchid
Bower

400

1000

▲ Mt Merino

Chakoonya
Lookout

1000

600

Lamington

0   1 km

1:50,000
Contours 100 metres

Mt Hobwee

Daceb
Lookout

Garragoolba Lookout

Warumblebah Lookout

600

Wagawn Lookout

500

Top: The Acropolis from the Labyrinth, Pine Valley
Left: Cradle Mountain, Overland Track
Right: Mt Hyperion, from Pelion Gap, Overland Track

Top: Lake Hanson, near Cradle Mountain, Overland Track
Left: Autumn colours, Waterfall Valley, Overland Track
Right: Lake Will and Barn Bluff, Overland Track (TW)

(☎ (075) 33 3584), one km back down the road from the Binna Burra Lodge. Bush camping is not allowed within two km of Binna Burra or O'Reillys, within 30 metres of a watercourse, or on the major graded walking tracks.

Access

The Lamington National Park is 90 km south of Brisbane, and in the mountains behind Surfers Paradise. Binna Burra is the start of this walk and the name of a commercial lodge at the end of the access road.

From Brisbane follow the highway south for 64 km to Nerang then turn west and follow the Nerang Valley road for eight km to a road junction. Turn right at this junction and follow the narrow sealed road which climbs steeply for 19 km to Beechmont. Turn south onto the road to Binna Burra and follow it for 11 km to the parking area near the kiosk at the end of the road.

Public transport to Binna Burra is available several times a week from Brisbane via Nerang and returns the same day. It leaves from the Queensland Travel Centre (☎ (07) 221 6111), 196 Adelaide St, Brisbane.

All buses can be met at 61 Price St, Nerang, one hour after the Brisbane departure time. The lodge at Binna Burra also runs a private bus to Coolangatta Airport on Sunday and inquiries regarding this are best made with the lodge.

Binna Burra Mountain Resort is an expensive mountain hotel that employs professional guides. It also manages the camping ground and kiosk. If you are arriving late in the afternoon it is a good idea to book a campsite in advance by phoning the Binna Burra Lodge (☎ (008) 074260). Near the lodge there is a display centre run by the Lamington Natural History Association which has a good range of pamphlets (for a small donation). The closest food and petrol is available from Nerang, 38 km away.

Stage 1: Binna Burra to Nagarigoon Hut

(17 km, 4-5½ hours)

From the car park near the camping area walk back down the sealed road for 300 metres to where the road joins the side road to the lodge. At this junction, on the east side, is the start of the walking track to Bellbird Lookout and the Ships Stern. Follow this well-graded walking track south-east for one hour (ignore the side track to Bellbird Lookout) to a major track junction. Turn right for the Ships Stern (left is the Bellbird Circuit) and within 10 minutes another junction (to Lower Ballanjui Falls) is reached.

Leave your pack here and follow the right track upstream along the creek (for 10 minutes) to the foot of the Ballanjui Falls (a very high set of falls that tumble over the cliffs above).

Collect the packs and follow the left track for the Ships Stern. This follows Nixon Creek downstream for 15 minutes. Before leaving the creek, collect water for the afternoon. The track then climbs gradually for one hour up onto the northern end of the Ships Stern range, to a track junction. A five minute sidetrip on the left track brings you to Kooloobano Point for excellent views of the Nerang Valley.

Return to the track junction and follow the other track south along the eastern edge of the Ship Stern Range where there are several lookouts with excellent views to the east. You will reach a track junction 20 minutes from Kooloobano Point. Either track can be followed south, but the right-hand track provides a better view to the west from Burrawong Lookout.

Just past the lookout the two tracks join again and the trail zig-zags sharply down to a saddle where a signposted side trail leads east downhill for 600 metres to the Macrozamia Grove. This is nothing special as there are many of these plants in the rainforest elsewhere in the park.

The main track continues south-west for two km through a section of rainforest to the track junction leading to the Upper Ballanjui Falls. Leave your packs here and follow the switchback track down to the top of the same falls that were visited earlier. On the way down there are several other falls worth exploring. They are all signposted and close to the track.

The main falls are very high and dangerous if wet. If you look carefully at the high amphitheatre of cliffs you will see why the track does not descend to the foot of the falls. The return sidetrip should take 45 to 60 minutes.

Collect the packs and walk south-west along the main trail for 20 minutes to Nagarigoon Falls. The track zigzags up on the left to the top of the falls and Nagarigoon Camp is the large clearing to the east of the track. An old hut, which is locked, sits in the centre of the clearing and is for use by national park staff only. There is a permanent toilet on the northern edge of the clearing. The clearing is ideal for camping, and water is available from the creek 100 metres to the west.

Stage 2: Nagarigoon Camp to Merino Lookout

(22 km, 5-6½ hours)

Leave the packs at the camp as the first two hours' walking are on the Daves Creek circuit. This is well worth walking as the vegetation is very different to that found elsewhere in the park.

From the camp, follow the track south past the top of Nagarigoon Falls to a track junction. Turn right at this junction back towards Binna Burra and after 100 metres turn left at the next junction onto the Daves Creek Circuit. The track initially climbs south-east then descends out of the rainforest into open heathlands. The track surface becomes very slippery so be careful while it follows the edge of the scarp east past several lookouts to the end of the ridge.

The Numinbah Lookout is at the east end of the ridge and provides excellent views. From here the track returns west by following the ridge crest through light eucalypt forest to Surprise Rock; a trachyte dyke. There are two tracks around its base and the right-hand track along the northern side is better. You can easily scramble up the dyke at the eastern end where the track first meets it.

Continue west along the base of the rock to meet the other track and walk for a further 20 minutes west along the main track to a track junction. This is the same junction as met two hours previously and the camp and packs are 200 metres to the right.

After collecting the packs return to the track junction, turn right and 100 metres further on turn right again towards Binna Burra. The track now crosses the creek and drinking water should be collected as you cannot rely on finding water for the next two hours.

The main trail is now followed towards Binna Burra for another 20 minutes, then a sharp left turn is made onto the Main Border Track. This follows the crest of a broad ridge in thick rainforest. After 30 minutes you reach Joalah Lookout which is worth a stop. Lunch can be eaten here if the leeches are not too aggressive!

After another 15 minutes turn left for Wagawn. A further 15-minute walk in the rainforest leads to the Araucaria Junction. Araucaria Lookout can be visited as a sidetrip, but it is a five km return walk; otherwise miss this lookout and visit the Wagawn Lookout which has different views. Turn right at the Araucaria Junction and after 15 minutes through rainforest the Mt Hobwee Circuit junction is reached.

An excellent sidetrip leaves from this junction and will take 1½ hours return if all the lookouts are visited. Leave the packs at the junction and carry water containers for filling for the night's camp on this sidetrip. Walk south towards Wagawn and 300 metres down the track cross a small creek. Fill the water containers here from this semi-permanent creek and leave them for collection on the return.

Ten minutes from the packs, a track on the left leads to several lookouts worth visiting, taking about 30 minutes return. The first, Warumblebah Lookout, and the third Garragoolba Lookout, have fine views. The track continuation from the first lookout is not obvious and is 20 metres back from the lookout. Return to the Wagawn Track.

Continue south towards Wagawn. The track zigzags down to the crest of the ridge and the rocks known as Wagawn Lookout.

In clear weather there is a spectacular view to the south over the valleys of NSW and of Mt Warning. Return along the same track (collecting the water containers) to the packs at the Mt Hobwee Circuit junction.

Turn left towards Mt Hobwee and in 15 minutes you will reach the sidetrack leading to the summit. If you have time (the campsite is 50 minutes away) follow the well graded track left to the summit of Mt Hobwee. Two lookouts are passed on the ascent and the track does a complete spiral around the hill. Views from the top are only fair because of the vegetation. Return to the packs at the main track. Turn south-west and the track gradually descends, passing Dacelo Lookout to meet the Main Border Track after 20 minutes. If time is short, camp can be made in the forest 100 metres down the track towards Binna Burra.

Turn left (west) onto the Main Border track and follow this track for 20 minutes to the Merino Lookout junction. Turn left and climb towards Merino Lookout passing several lookouts on the way.   •

The Merino Lookout is found 250 metres to the left on a signposted side track and has fine views over New South Wales. There is room for five tents at the lookout and all water has to be carried from the creek on the Wagawn Track.

Alternative Campsites
Mt Hobwee Very rough camping near the summit. The views are fair and water has to be carried from the Wagawn Track.

Border Track, Hobwee Circuit Junction Reasonable tent sites are available in the thick forest north of the junction. Water is taken from the Wagawn Track. Use this only in emergencies as it is beside the Main Border Track where camping is not normally permitted.

Stage 3: Merino Lookout to Binna Burra
(14 km, 4-5 hours)
From the lookout return to the Main Border Track. A short sidetrip left (for five minutes) to the Chakoonya Lookout is worthwhile. From here you can see the tall towers of Surfers Paradise in the distance.

Return to the track junction and continue east along the Main Border Track towards Binna Burra to the Hobwee Circuit Junction (retracing yesterday's steps). Turn left towards Binna Burra following the Main Border Track and after 15 minutes turn left onto the Coomera Circuit.

This track descends to the valley floor and then follows the Coomera River downstream past many waterfalls. Some of these are best viewed from the short signposted side tracks. There are many suitable places for lunch beside the stream.

The track crosses the river several times. About 500 metres past Bahnamboola Falls the river is crossed for the last time and the track then climbs gently. Below, the river enters a narrow canyon known as the Coomera Crevice and disappears from sight. The valley then opens up into a large amphitheatre. From the Coomera Lookout the 64-metre-high Coomera Falls can be seen tumbling into the 160-metre deep valley. This view is not to be missed.

From the lookout the track climbs gradually for 3½ km to meet the Main Border Track. Turn left and follow the Main Border Track north for two km through lush rainforest to the end of the walk at the car park above the camping ground near Binna Burra.

South Australia

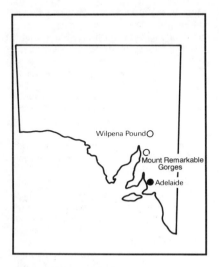

Wilpena Pound ○

○ Mount Remarkable
Gorges

● Adelaide

This state has a low population density as much of its area is arid farmland and desert. There are no high mountain ranges or thick forests but there is a series of interesting desert ranges with many small gorges and rock faces. The resulting colourful landscapes are worth visiting. The best known ranges are the Flinders Ranges which run from Adelaide north for 800 km. The Flinders Ranges have low mountains and ridges which have been deeply dissected by streams, creating the many gorges for which it is famous.

Small parts of these ranges are preserved in a few national parks. Mt Remarkable National Park contains a couple of narrow, colourful gorges and usually has water for most of the year. This small park is very popular with bushwalkers from Adelaide and, in two days, it is possible to visit most features in the park.

Further north, the Flinders Ranges become higher and more impressive. The range widens into several broad ridges which enclose the famous 'pounds' for which the area is known. These were formed by the uplifting and sinking of the land leaving broad basin shaped valleys. The best known and largest of these, Wilpena Pound, is protected within the Flinders Ranges National Park. This area is so popular with bushwalkers, that camping within Wilpena Pound is restricted to one area only. The most popular walk climbs St Mary Peak and visits Edeowie Gorge.

In the northern Flinders Ranges there is another park which protects more gorges and peaks. This is the Gammon Ranges National Park. This provides some excellent longer bushwalks for experienced walkers. It is an ideal area to explore from a base camp. In other areas of this state there are some isolated parks of interest to bushwalkers such as Flinders Chase National Park on Kangaroo Island and Deep Creek Conservation Park Park (both south of Adelaide).

There are several easy two-day bushwalks in these parks. On the western side of Spencer Gulf is the Lincoln National Park. This provides some good coastal walking along old tracks and roads, but it is 700 km by road from Adelaide.

There is some pleasant bushwalking in South Australia. Its ranges are not high but they are colourful and provide ideal walking in the winter months when the wetter eastern states are less appealing.

Other Suggested Bushwalks

Telowie Gorge From the ranger station walk south then west along the Barbecue Track into the forest park to camp. Follow the watercourse of Telowie Creek through the gorge and back to the start. This is an easy two-day bushwalk, 20 km south of Mt Remarkable National Park.

Edeowie Gorge & Black Gap From Wilpena Pound follow the track past Cooinda Camp into Edeowie Gorge. Walk down the gorge climbing past all the waterfalls to camp. Walk south along the foot of the range to camp beside the creek at Black Gap. The walk heads east through Bridle Gap back to Wilpena Pound. A medium three-day circuit walk around Wilpena Pound.

Gammon Ranges From Weetootla Well follow Balcanoona Creek north-west to Bunyip Chasm. Then follow the ridges to Mt John Roberts and cross the valleys to Cleft Peak and Rover Rockhole. Follow Italowie Creek and then head over Red Hill back to the start. A four to five-day walk in the northern Flinders Ranges, 500 km north of Adelaide.

The Heysen Trail This is a 800-km walking and bridle trail that starts from Cape Jervis, south of Adelaide and follows the Flinders Ranges north to Mt Hopeless in the desert. A lot of the trail passes through farmlands and has minimal track markers. There are other more interesting long-distance walking trails in Australia.

WILPENA POUND

Wilpena Pound is an outstanding natural basin in the Flinders Ranges National Park. This park of 780 sq km is a mosaic of steep sawtooth ridges, rocky gorges and broad undulating plains in the dry ranges of South Australia. The park lies on the southern edge of the large arid deserts that cover most of Central Australia.

The park has a semi-arid climate. Major attractions for bushwalkers are the peaceful tree-lined gorges, extensive views from craggy peaks, and abundant wildlife.

In early 1988, Wilpena Pound was extensively burnt by a naturally occurring bushfire. Although 70% of Wilpena Pound was burnt, the positive outcomes that result from bushfire will ensure that it remains a beautiful area to visit. The bush will regenerate quickly, wildflowers in the area will be better than before and nomadic species of native birds will be attracted to the pound because of the new growth.

Features

Wilpena Pound is an enormous natural amphitheatre in the central Flinders Ranges. It is oval in shape; 16 km long and six km wide. The interior of the pound is a long undulating plain covered with grasses and thin forests of native pine. The watercourses, which are usually dry, are lined with large river red gums.

From the outside, the pound has a rugged appearance, with a continuous line of jagged ridges and peaks encircling it. These high cliffs are composed of red quartzite.

The Aboriginal name, 'Wilpena', means the place of bent fingers and indeed the pound does resemble a cupped hand.

Geologically the area is very interesting, with Pre-Cambrian quartzite rocks which have been extensively folded and tilted. The rock strata stands out clearly as the hills have only a thin vegetation cover. There are several basins of which Wilpena Pound is the largest. A unique feature is the superabundance of Pre-Cambrian fossils embedded in the quartzite rocks.

Early this century Wilpena Pound was used for grazing, then growing wheat; it is now preserved within the Flinders Ranges National Park. Wildlife in the area is usually abundant. Kangaroos and emus graze on the grasses and lizards and birds are seen during the day. The smaller animals are usually seen around sunset and early in the evening.

Standard

The two-day walk is of a medium standard. It follows well-defined and marked tracks, except in Edeowie Gorge where the creek bed is followed. This involves easy walking over small boulders and stones, and beneath trees.

Days Required

This walk generally takes two days. Fast walkers can complete it in 1½ days by visiting Edeowie Gorge on the first day.

Seasons

From May to October the mild temperatures are suitable for walking. From November to

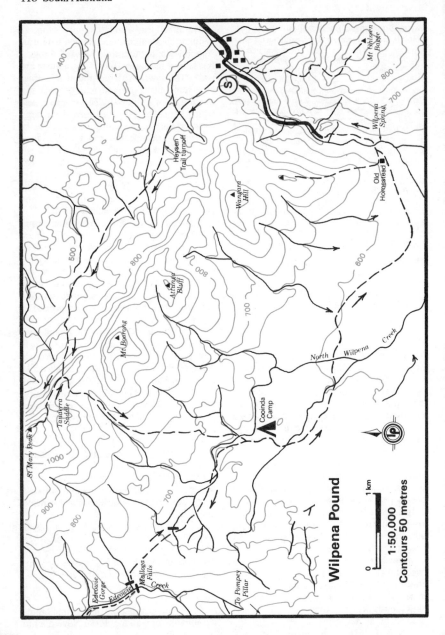

Wilpena Pound

1:50,000
Contours 50 metres

0 ——— 1 km

April the weather is too hot and dry to be pleasant for walking. Also, water holes and springs are more likely to have water in the cooler months.

Equipment

No special equipment is needed for walking in Wilpena Pound. Runners or light boots are ideal footwear. A shady hat and sunscreen should be carried as it can be very hot even during the winter.

All water required during the day will have to be carried, so check the availability of water near Cooinda Camp with the ranger before leaving. If the rockhole is dry then all water for the entire two days will need to be carried.

Campfires are allowed at established fireplaces, but the rangers request that a stove be carried and used if the party has one.

Maps

The 1:50,000 topographic map, *Wilpena*, covers the entire route. This is available from the South Australian Department of Lands (☎ (08) 226 3905), 12 Pirie St, Adelaide, 5000.

The National Parks Service also produces a small leaflet, *Bushwalking in the Flinders Ranges*, which offers some advice on equipment needed. This leaflet can be obtained at the rangers' office at Wilpena Pound (☎ (086) 48 0048) or by contacting the National Parks & Wildlife Service (☎ (08) 216 7777), 55 Grenfell St, Adelaide (postal address: GPO Box 667, Adelaide, 5001).

Permits

You need to get a permit from the ranger at Wilpena Pound and, if following the main tracks, the system is simple. At the rangers' office at the entrance to the Wilpena Pound Camping Area fill in your 'Bushwalking Itinerary', a short and simple form that requires the leader's name, contact person and your intended itinerary. This is left at the office and upon your return to the office you should find your form, write on it that you have returned and leave it in the designated box.

Within Wilpena Pound the only camping area that bushwalkers are allowed to use is Cooinda Camp. Outside Wilpena Pound, dispersed camping is generally allowed. If you intend to explore further than the main tracks it is important to discuss your route with the rangers (☎ (086) 48 0048) as water can be difficult to find and they may be able to give advice. Permission is readily given provided that there is water available and there is no fire danger.

Access

Wilpena Pound is 350 km north of Adelaide in South Australia. From Adelaide follow either of the two main highways north towards Port Augusta. Eight km south of Port Augusta, turn right to Quorn, then Hawker, and on towards Wilpena Pound. The road is sealed all the way to the park entrance and camping ground.

If you arrive late at night, campsites are available for $5 at the Wilpena Pound Camping Area. This is a large commercial camping area at the end of the road with toilets, showers and a kiosk (open during day-light hours only).

The park has public transport access by bus twice weekly from Adelaide. This service is run by Stateliner (☎ (08) 212 1505 for reservations). The bus leaves Adelaide from the bus terminal at 111 Frankland St. The bus departs Wilpena Pound at the motel south of the kiosk.

Stage 1: Wilpena Campground to Cooinda Camp via St Mary Peak

(11 km, 3-4½ hours)

From the shop near the camping ground follow the road south-west for 100 metres to a car park. Turn right onto the walking track which is marked as the 'Direct Track to St Mary Peak'. This track has markers which are blue triangles on a white background.

Follow this walking track north-west and ignore the Heysen Trail turnoff to the right. The track follows a fence line for four km (one hour) climbing over some small ridges with views of St Mary Peak ahead. About one hour from the start the track leaves the

The track to St Mary Peak

fence and climbs steadily for 40 minutes to Tanderra Saddle. The last section of the track involves some simple scrambling up short cliff lines.

From the saddle, St Mary Peak can be climbed as a sidetrip taking 40 to 60 minutes return. Leave the packs at the saddle (there is a sheltered flat area 20 metres north of the track junction) and follow the well-marked and used track north to St Mary Peak. This involves some rock scrambling which should not be attempted in wet weather. The track needs to be carefully followed climbing the steep ridge then bypassing a cliff near the top by descending west along a narrow ledge.

The peak is the highest point of the Flinders Ranges and has extensive views to the north and east. Below to the west the red cliffs of Edeowie Gorge can be seen and to the south the flat centre of Wilpena Pound is

visible. Follow the same track back to Tanderra Saddle to retrieve the packs.

From the saddle follow the marked track south-west then south for three km (one to 1½ hours) to the usually dry North Wilpena Creek. Cross the creek and continue south-west 100 metres to the Edeowie Gorge track junction.

Cooinda Camp is the large flat area 50 metres east of this track junction. This is the only camping area allowed within Wilpena Pound. Usually the creek is not flowing and water can be found at a large semi-permanent waterhole a fair distance from the camp.

To find the waterhole walk 700 metres north from the track junction along the Edeowie Gorge track to a pine track marker post. Leave the main track and descend 20 metres to the right to the large rock hole. This is marked on the *Wilpena* map. In dry weather this hole is sometimes empty; seek the advice of the rangers on water availability before starting the walk.

Sidetrip: Cooinda Camp to Edeowie Gorge, return

(6-11 km, 2-6 hours)
The sidetrip to Edeowie Gorge is worth walking. Fast parties can visit it on the first afternoon, but most groups will walk it in the morning before leaving for the return to Wilpena. If two nights are spent at Cooinda Camp then the gorge and Pompey Pillar can both be visited in the one day.

Leave the packs at the campsite and follow the Edeowie Gorge track north-west for two km to a large rock cairn at a broad saddle. This track is not as clearly defined as the St Mary Peak track and some care is needed to follow it. The track now descends gradually north-west for ½ km into a creek. Turn left and follow the creek bed downstream climbing around a small waterfall to meet Edeowie Creek. Immediately upstream is the deep fissured slot of Malloga Falls. The creek is usually dry, making for easy walking. This is about one hour from Cooinda Camp.

If you have enough time, follow the rocky creek bed downstream a further 2½ km to

Glenora Falls. This takes a further 1½ to two hours each way and gives an excellent view of the gorge. Climbing down these falls can be dangerous and is not recommended. Return to Cooinda Camp by the same route.

Sidetrip: Cooinda Camp to Pompey Pillar, return

(9 km, 3-5 hours return)
If another night is to be spent at Cooinda Camp it is worthwhile climbing Pompey Pillar, the second highest peak in Wilpena Pound. This peak has no tracks to it so you have to push through the scrub to climb it. From the camp, walk north-west along the Edeowie Gorge track for 20 to 30 minutes. Leave the track and climb west through the scrub for 2½ km following a broad trackless ridge to the summit. Care will be needed to avoid the thickest patches of scrub. The climb will take approximately three to five hours return from the camp.

Stage 2: Cooinda Camp to Wilpena via the Pound

(9 km, 2-3 hours)
This is an easy half-day walk, even after a morning visit to Edeowie Gorge.

From the track junction near the campsite walk south along the walking track. This very soon becomes an old vehicle track which you follow for 5½ km (about 1½ hours) to the old homestead ruins near the Wilpena Spring. The homestead was built in 1911 as part of a wheat farm which harvested some good crops; it was later abandoned after a flood destroyed the access road. The large clearings in Wilpena Pound are also left from this farming venture.

From the old homestead the return track of 2½ km to the Wilpena camping ground is clearly signposted. Following the track, cross the creek and climb up to a closed road and walk north to a car park. A further 15 minutes along the gravel road leads northeast to the camping ground and the shop at the start of the walk.

MT REMARKABLE GORGES

The Mt Remarkable National Park is a small area of natural bushlands in the southern Flinders Ranges. It is one of the few remaining wilderness areas near Adelaide and is highly regarded by local walkers. Despite its small size there is some excellent walking.

Features

This park is in the boundary zone between the arid north and the wetter southern regions of South Australia and many types of flora grow here. The park encompasses dry woodlands of mallee and eucalypts and cool gorges filled with native pines and river red gums. Some of the park is reclaimed farmland and is regenerating with native scrub and forests.

Wildlife is varied and prolific with kangaroos, wallabies and possums as well as snakes, lizards and goannas. You're quite likely to encounter the inquisitive emu (particularly near the car parks), so keep an eye on your lunch as they'll eat anything. There are also plenty of smaller birds.

The exposed cliffs in the gorges and valleys of the park are formed of folded red quartzite rock. There are no high peaks to climb but the ridges provide fine views of Spencer Gulf and the surrounding areas.

Standard

The tracks are all well defined in this park and navigation is easy. The standard depends on how far you wish to walk each day – the two-day walk is of medium standard. It can be lengthened to an easy three-day walk.

Days Required

The two-day walk includes Alligator Gorge on the first day and Hidden Gorge on the second. If three days are planned, then Alligator Gorge can be visited as a day trip from Teal Dam for the second day of walking.

Seasons

In summer, overnight camping is not permitted in the park because of the risk of bushfires. In other seasons bushwalking and bushcamping are permitted. Autumn has warm, mild weather, but there is a shortage of water and it is usually necessary to carry all water that is required.

In winter the creeks have some water in the pools and occasionally are flowing. The days are cooler, often cloudy and very pleasant for walking. In spring the creeks usually still have some water in the pools and the wildflowers are abundant.

Equipment

No special equipment is needed for bushwalking. Runners or light boots are ideal footwear. Water must be carried during the day and in dry seasons water for the entire trip will need to be carried. Sufficient water containers should be taken and the ranger can advise where water may be found. Campfires are allowed at established fire-places.

Maps

The 1:50,000 topographic maps, *Melrose* and *Wilmington*, cover the entire park. The Melrose map is very accurate, but the Wilmington map is missing the track on The Battery. You can buy both from the Department of Lands (☎ (08) 226 3905), 12 Pirie St, Adelaide, 5000.

The national park leaflet, *Walking Trails in Mt Remarkable National Park*, is also very useful, showing all the trails on a sketch map. This can be obtained from the rangers at Mambray Creek (☎ (086) 34 7068) or by contacting the National Parks Service (☎ (08) 216 7777), 55 Grenfell St, Adelaide (postal address: GPO Box 667, Adelaide, 5001).

Permits

Permits for overnight bushwalking are available from the rangers at Mambray Creek (☎ (086) 34 7068), RMB 7, Port Germein, 5495. The fee is $1 per tent per night. Overnight camping is only allowed at five areas within the park. This, however, gives plenty of scope to vary the walk.

When obtaining the permit the rangers can advise the walking party of the current water situation.

Access

Mt Remarkable National Park is 250 km north of Adelaide and 50 km south-east of Port Augusta. Mambray Creek, the southern access point into the park, lies five km east of the Adelaide to Port Augusta highway. Daily interstate bus services use this highway and can deposit you at the turn-off. This is not a scheduled stop and the pickup at the completion of the walk must be arranged in advance.

Pioneer and Greyhound Australia (☎ 13 1238), 111 Franklin St, Adelaide, both run services that pass the Mambray Creek turn-off.

You can also catch a train to the tiny town of Mambray Creek. You need to let the railways know in advance, however, because the town is not a scheduled stop. From the turn-off it is a dusty five-km walk along a gravel road to the start of the walk.

Stage 1: Mambray Creek to Teal Dam (13 km, 3-4½ hours)

From the car park follow the fire trail (closed to vehicles) up the valley of Mambray Creek towards Alligator Gorge. The valley has many large red gums and is a pleasant walk. There are two 'walkers only' track deviations on the right worth walking along, and which soon rejoin the fire trail. After a 45-minute walk there is a track and creek junction.

Turn left on the Alligator Creek track and cross two creek beds, which are usually dry. About 10 minutes from the junction the fire trail ends and a walking trail is followed upstream for another one hour to the Hidden Gorge Track junction. This section is a very pleasant walk with the track crossing the stream numerous times and with many red cliffs and bluffs above.

From the junction continue straight ahead towards Kingfisher Flat and Alligator Gorge. After five minutes, you will pass Hidden Camp and another fire trail begins. This fire trail follows the valley for about 15 minutes. It then climbs sharply onto a spur and continues along the valley well above the river for a further 30 minutes to the fire trail junction at Kingfisher Flat.

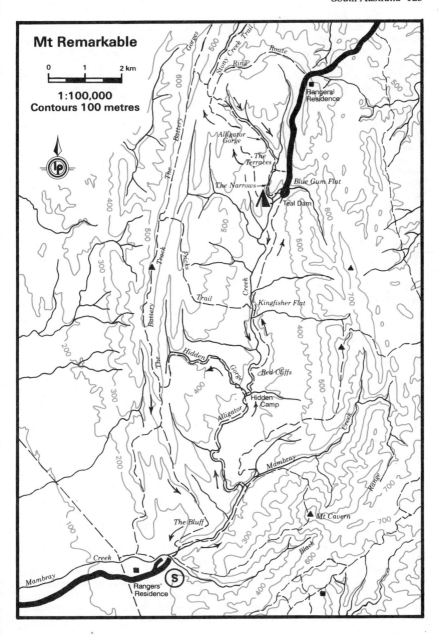

Mt Remarkable

0   1   2 km

**1:100,000
Contours 100 metres**

Gorges

Stony Creek Trail

Route

Rangers'
Residence

Alligator
Gorge

The Terraces

The Narrows

Blue Gum Flat

Teal Dam

The Battery

Pichis

Trail

The Battery Track

Creek

Kingfisher Flat

Hidden

Gorge

Red Cliffs

Hidden
Camp

Alligator

Mambray

Range

The Bluff

Mt Cavern

Black

Creek

Creek

Mambray

Rangers'
Residence

S

Continue straight ahead and follow the fire trail north for three km to the car park and picnic ground at Blue Gum Flat. Turn left at the first fire track and walk down to Alligator Creek below Teal Dam. Campsites near the creek are good with water from pools in the creek. In dry seasons water may need to be carried to this camp area.

If you arrived at the campsite early then Alligator Gorge can be visited in the afternoon.

Alternative Campsites
Hidden Camp This is a good camping area with water available from pools in the creek. These may be empty during a dry spell. This is one to 1½ hours before Teal Dam.

Kingfisher Flat There is good camping near the creek, about 30 to 40 minutes before Teal Dam.

Sidetrip: Alligator Gorge Return Walk
(8 km, 2-3 hours)
Leave the packs at the camp site, then walk west following the fire trail. This track climbs a ridge to the north-west for 3½ km to the junction with the Stony Creek and Ring Route tracks.

At this junction there is a signposted walking track on the right to Alligator Gorge. Follow this track (which is poorly marked) downhill into the top of the gorge. If the track is lost, head straight downhill to the creek and then down the creek to rejoin the track. You now simply follow the bed of the creek downstream. There is no track as such, but is mostly very easy walking with the occasional pile of loose stones to descend and cross.

As you walk further downstream the gorge becomes more impressive. After about one hour The Terraces are reached. These are a series of sloping flat rocks in the creek. Shortly after these, the gorge joins with a major creek. A well-formed and signposted track is now followed downstream to a track junction. The left track leads uphill to a car park. Follow the right hand track along the floor of the gorge towards The Narrows.

The most spectacular part of the gorge is now entered and the rock walls close in to a chasm about two metres wide. Often a pool of water blocks the gorge here. Splash on through the pool and continue down the creek bed to where the valley widens out again.

A marked walking track begins here and leads up to the picnic area at Blue Gum Flat. Ignore the track and continue downstream in light forest for 150 metres to the camping area below Teal Dam.

Stage 2: Teal Dam to Mambray Creek
(16 km, 4 to 5 hours)
From the Teal Dam camping area follow the fire trail east up to Blue Gum Flat. Turn right and follow the fire trail south to Kingfisher Flat, then further south to Hidden Camp. Five minutes' walk past the camp you will meet the track junction to Hidden Gorge (1½ hours from Teal Dam and the same track as previously walked).

Turn right at the track junction and follow the well-formed walking track north-west towards Hidden Gorge. The track generally follows the usually dry creek bed. Gradually the cliffs become higher as the track penetrates deeper into the gorge. The red walls of the gorge tower above small forests of native pines. At one point the walls rise sheer on both sides with a narrow gap between them.

Beyond this the gorge becomes wider and a further 15 minutes' walk upstream, a large rockfall blocks the valley. This is bypassed by climbing up on the left side. Continue up the valley being careful not to head up a minor side creek on the left. A walkers' track sign indicates the correct way. Eventually the valley opens out and then divides. The marked walking track turns south and climbs steeply up a spur, sidles into a saddle and then makes a short final ascent west to meet The Battery Track. This is about 1½ to two hours from Hidden Camp.

Opposite the junction with The Battery Track is a signposted lookout, worth visiting (without the packs) for a clear view of Spencer Gulf and the three cities known as the Iron Triangle.

Return to the junction, collect the packs and walk south for one km along The Battery Track past the fire lookout tower to a sharp right bend where a marked walking track leaves the fire trail. Turn left and follow this foot track south down a long ridge. This ridge has several good views of Spencer Gulf and the park.

About 2½ km from the fire trail, there is a short climb onto The Bluff, a small hill overlooking Mambray Creek. From the top of The Bluff the track swings south-west and descends for one km to an open grassy area near a vehicle track. Follow the walking track which turns south and descends to the fire trail along Mambray Creek. Turn right and a five-minute walk brings you to the car park from where the walk began.

Tasmania

The tiny island state, Tasmania, has the most challenging and interesting bushwalking country in Australia. Every summer bushwalkers converge here to experience the difficulties and rewards of walking in Tasmania. Tasmania has large tracts of natural bushlands, in fact about a half of the state remains relatively undisturbed. These large wilderness areas are located close to the cities (everything in Tasmania is close!) and have reasonable access. The wilderness is so famous that the south-western section has been declared a World Heritage area.

Bushwalkers on their first visit to Tasmania are often surprised by the complexity and steepness of the terrain in the mountain ranges. The highest peak is only 1700 metres in elevation yet large cliffs of 300 to 500 metres are common and smaller cliffs border almost every ridge. Surrounding these rugged ranges are thick forests, tenacious scrub bands and broad open buttongrass plains. Recent ice ages have sculpted the higher regions creating the maze of lakes, ridges, cirques and sharp peaks that Tasmania is renowned for.

The weather is variable with both heat waves and blizzards occurring each summer. All bushwalkers must be well-equipped and well prepared to cope with all extremes. For the hardy walker, however, the rewards are great, as the scenery and wilderness are incomparable.

The South West National Park occupies the entire south-western corner of the state and is the largest wilderness area in Tasmania. It provides some of the most exciting and challenging bushwalking that can be found. It is a large park and most trips into it require at least one or two weeks. The variety in this park is one of its most outstanding features.

The southern coastline is a series of sandy bays flanked by abrupt high headlands. Inland from the beaches are wet, buttongrass plains. Further north there is the vast natural harbour of Port Davey, formed when the rising waters of the last ice age drowned a river valley. From the harbour the jagged outline of some of the major mountains and ranges in the park can be seen.

The Western and Eastern Arthurs, the Southern Ranges, the Frankland Range and the Mt Anne Range all provide excellent walking. Traditionally, the walking routes through the mountains follow the crest of the ranges and are very exposed to the unpredictable weather. A visit to the higher areas is for the experienced bushwalker only.

Through all this wilderness there is only one marked track which has several names. The track follows the southern coastline, then follows the plains north, then swings east following the base of the Western Arthurs and along the Huon River valley to the roads. There are also a few well used, easily followed but very rough routes, which pass through rugged country. Climbing cliffs and descending steep dangerous gullies is normal walking in these ranges.

The most spectacular walk in this park and in fact all of Australia is undoubtedly the Western Arthur Traverse. This rugged, exposed walk has become very popular. All bushwalkers who intend to visit this range should get the *South West Tasmania* guide book by John Chapman. Due to its popularity, walkers have caused significant erosion in this range and at present a strict permit system is being considered. Anyone intending to visit this or any of the the other high ranges would be well advised to contact the Tasmanian Department of Parks, Wildlife & Heritage for the current situation. This walk has not been described in this guide as walkers are being encouraged to visit other spectacular places which have better tracks to them.

The other popular extended bushwalk in the South West National Park is the combination of the South Coast and the Port Davey tracks. This excellent route visits many of the beautiful bays along the southern coastline and then follows the river valleys inland. As it has only two short high-level sections it is less exposed to extreme weather conditions. For the first extended walk in this park, this route is recommended and described here.

In the northern part of the South West National Park there is a small range with a circuit walk visiting Mt Anne, the highest peak in the area. It is a good walk for parties who either do not have the time or experience for the longer traverses. The circuit is, at times, as exciting and dangerous as any of the other high level routes in the south-west.

Not all walkers who come to Tasmania are prepared for the extreme weather and there is some pleasant easy alpine walking to be done on the track system in the Mt Field National Park. This is situated beside the main access road to the south-west and provides views into that area. A series of huts provide basic shelter and many of the tracks follow the valleys providing shelter and a gentle introduction to Tasmania.

North of the South West National Park is the Wild Rivers National Park which protects the Franklin and Jane rivers as they flow through spectacular gorges. This park was created after a long and bitter conservation battle over the proposal to dam all the rivers for hydro-electric power generation. The conservationists eventually won and the proposal was abandoned. The classic trip through this park is to raft down the Franklin River. The Franklin River trip is not described in this guide as it not a bushwalk – information on this two to three-week adventure is readily available.

In the centre of the Wild Rivers National Park is Frenchmans Cap. This rocky crag towers above the region and the southern side has been carved away by glaciers forming Australia's tallest cliff face. Good views of this cliff and the surrounding ice carved landscape are obtained from the walking track to the peak. This walk has been included here as its one of the best shorter walks to be done.

Further north is the famous Cradle Mountain-Lake St Clair National Park. This contains Australia's best known walking track, The Overland Track, which starts in the north and follows an interesting route south through a varied wilderness area. Craggy peaks, alpine moors, dark forests, spectacular waterfalls and numerous lakes are some of the features of this walk. The track itself is well-marked and easily followed.

A system of open huts operates in the park although they cannot be relied upon as they are usually full in the warmer months. There are many other good bushwalks to be done in and around this park and to the east is the Walls of Jerusalem National Park. There are several routes between the two parks. The *Cradle Mountain – Lake St Clair National Park* guidebook has a few suggestions for experienced bushwalkers.

Most of the eastern side of the state is less spectacular and of less interest to bushwalkers. The exception to this is a peninsula of red granite protected by the Freycinet National Park. This park provides easy walking along a well-defined track system. As this region receives a much lower rainfall than the western half of the state it is popular with bushwalkers who have been washed out of the more rugged areas.

There are many other extended bushwalks that can be done in Tasmania by experienced walkers who are looking for further challenges.

Other Suggested Bushwalks
South West
Federation Peak From Scotts Peak follow the tracks to Cracroft Crossing then south along rough routes to Federation Peak. Return by the same route. A difficult eight to 12-day walk. Permits are expected to be imposed on this walk.

Western Arthur Traverse From Scotts Peak walk south to the range and follow the eroded track east along the crest of the range. Overuse by bushwalkers has led to a need for permits and it is expected that these will be difficult to obtain as numbers have to reduced dramatically. A hard nine to 12-day walk in the South West National Park.

South West Cape Circuit From Melaleuca walk south to New Harbour then west to South West Cape. Then head north along the coast to Noyhener Beach. Walk east across the plains and ridges to Melaleuca. A medium six to 10-day circuit in the South West National Park. Access is by light airplane or by the tracks that pass Melaleuca.

Southern Ranges Traverse From Lune River, follow the range west to Precipitous Bluff then down to the coast and back east along the South Coast Track to Cockle Creek. A hard eight to 11-day walk near the southern coastline.

Frankland Range Traverse From Strathgordon follow the crest of the Wilmot and Frankland ranges south to Scotts Peak Dam. A hard eight to 12-day walk along the western side of the Lake Pedder Dam. Not a circuit and requires transport to Strathgordon to be arranged.

Central Western Area
Denisons, Spires & King William Ranges
From the Strathgordon Road follow a track north to the Denisons. Climb onto the range and continue west to the Spires. Follow the river valley north-east, follow an old mining exploration road north then follow the crest of the King William Range north to descend to the Lyell Highway. A medium to hard eight to 12-day bushwalk in the centre of the state. It is not a circuit and buses regularly pass both ends of the route.

Cradle Mountain & Central Plateau
Falls of Jerusalem to Cynthia Bay From Lake McKenzie cross the exposed Central Plateau south-west to the Walls of Jerusalem National Park. Continue south-west past several lakes and down to meet The Overland Track. Follow the tracks south to Cynthia Bay. There are a variety of routes that can be followed and all of them are good. A medium nine to 14-day bushwalk. It is not a circuit and transport must be arranged for the northern end.

Pine Valley & The Labyrinth Use the boat across Lake St Clair to Narcissus Hut. Follow the tracks north to Pine Valley and climb The Acropolis. Climb up into The Labyrinth to camp. Follow the range south over Mt Gould, descend to the valley and follow the tracks via Lake Petrarch back to Cynthia Bay. A medium four to seven-day bushwalk in the southern half of the Cradle Mountain-Lake St Clair National Park.

Penguin to Cradle Mountain A solid six-day walk from the coast through the Leven Canyon and over Black Bluff Range. It provides an interesting alternative approach to The Overland Track.

East Coast
Douglas-Apsley Traverse A new national park near Bicheno provides a classic three-day walk in dry forests. It is very different to the rest of Tasmania and suitable for all seasons.

THE OVERLAND TRACK
The Overland Track is Australia's most famous walking track. It traverses the Cradle Mountain–Lake St Clair National Park which is a rugged wilderness area replete with spectacular scenery. It is one of the most interesting and enjoyable walks in Tasmania and is also a mecca for foreign bushwalkers.

Features
The Cradle Mountain-Lake St Clair National Park is known locally as 'The Reserve'. The

Top: K Col, Mt Field National Park
Bottom: The huge granite bluffs of Frencmans Cap

Top: Wineglass Bay, Freycinet Peninsula
Bottom: Mt Anne and Mt Lot, South West National Park, Tasmania

park's 1260 sq km include a mixture of rugged peaks, forested valleys and alpine moorlands. Most of Tasmania's highest peaks are within its boundaries including Mt Ossa, the state's highest. Scattered across the park are numerous waterfalls, tarns and lakes. Most of the landscape results from the last ice age when an ice cap covered most of the reserve.

The park has high rainfall and wild weather. Water is abundant and the vegetation is well adapted to the tough conditions. Pandanni, native pines, scoparia and fagus (the only deciduous native) are familiar to bushwalkers who visit the park.

Wildlife in the reserve is abundant and easily seen. Around the huts wallabies, possums, native cats, tiger cats and the occasional Tasmanian Devil are seen at night.

Along the track are obvious signs of wombats, although they are less frequently seen. Birds that are often seen include currawongs, eagles and parrots. There are three species of snakes and all are poisonous and should be left alone. Lizards, frogs and leeches are common.

Standard

The Overland Track is signposted and easy to follow. The well-trampled track is in fairly good condition considering how much rainfall the region receives. An extensive rebuilding programme in recent years has repaired and improved much of it so that parts of the track are easy walking along elevated boardwalks and bridges. Other sections are badly eroded with deep mud and slippery exposed roots.

Most parties carrying packs average about three km per hour along the track. The northern half of the park is exposed to the extreme weather that can occur and can be dangerous in severe storms. For this reason the recommended walk is from north to south so that the exposed areas are crossed in the first few days. If a day or two of the itinerary is lost early in the trip the schedule can be easily altered. The recommended walk is for seven to 10 days and has been graded easy to medium.

Days Required

The Overland Track can be completed in five days and many parties do just that and race through the park. The park, however, has many interesting features to be explored and more time is needed to appreciate them. The described walk visits a number of the easily accessible major features and requires eight days to complete.

Some leeway is required for poor weather and you should carry an extra two days' food. If the weather remains fine the extra food will allow more time to explore Pine Valley. The walking times and distances shown for each day include the recommended sidetrips. If you have time, additional sidetrips and the time they take are noted as extras.

Seasons

Summer is the most popular season to walk The Overland Track as the weather is fairly stable and generally mild. During these months the sun shines frequently, but wild storms, persistent rain and snowfalls do

Bennett's Wallaby track pattern

occur and all parties must be prepared for cold wet conditions.

In autumn the temperature gradually drops and the days are often cloudy. Heavy mists, fogs and frosts are common. For most of winter the higher areas are snow covered and cold winds bring heavy rain and snowstorms. Many of the streams flood and can be difficult to cross. Winter is for very experienced walkers.

With spring the weather gradually improves. Strong cold winds are still common and the streams remain at high levels, but the sun shines more frequently. In late spring the flowering season begins and continues for most of the summer.

Equipment

All parties venturing into this park must be well-equipped and fully self sufficient. The Overland Track has numerous huts along it and these are free for all walkers to use. Unfortunately, a party cannot rely upon using the huts each night as they are often overcrowded during popular periods and in wet weather. All groups should carry good tents that are able to withstand heavy rains. Most campsites are well sheltered.

A groundsheet is a useful extra for keeping clothing and sleeping equipment clean in huts and also as a second layer on the tent floor to keep water out. Sleeping bags should be suitable for temperatures below freezing and most walkers choose superdown.

Warm clothing of wool or high quality synthetics is needed. A balaclava, or a wool hat and scarf are essential and warm gloves should be carried as well. Full wet-weather

clothing of waterproof pants and jacket are also necessary.

For footwear, good solid leather boots perform best in the wet muddy conditions. Some walkers use runners, but have many problems; they also become potentially dangerous when snowfalls occur. Most walkers carry a pair of runners for use around camp.

There is plenty of water available along the track so a small ½-litre waterbottle is adequate.

Stoves must be carried as most huts are equipped with pot belly stoves which are unsuitable for cooking. Campfires are totally banned as the park has been declared a fuel stove only area. Enough fuel should be carried for the entire trip.

Maps

The 1:100,000 special topographic map, *Cradle Mountain-Lake St Clair National Park*, is the map to have. It is produced specially for bushwalkers and shows all tracks, huts and interesting features of the park. On the back of this map are some notes on the park and The Overland Track and some general advice for walkers. This map is published by TASMAP. It can be purchased in most bushwalking shops in the eastern states of Australia.

An alternative set of 1:100,000 topographic maps are produced by TASMAP. They have little use for Overland Track walkers. Three maps, *Sophia, Mersey* and *Nive*, are required to cover the track.

A new set of topographic maps at 1:25,000 scale are being produced. These maps cover the entire track and while they are excellent they are not needed by The Overland Track walker. *Cradle, Will, Achilles, Cathedral, Du Cane, Olympus* and *Rufus* cover the track. They are also available from TASMAP.

For more detail of sidetrips from The Overland Track and other walks that may be done in the area, the guidebook *Cradle Mountain-Lake St Clair National Park* by John Siseman & John Chapman is recommended. This can be bought in most Australian bushwalking shops.

Tasmanian Devil track pattern

Permits

Permits are required to walk The Overland Track. The fees charged are $20 per adult and $10 per child. For a family the maximum fee is $50. The fee is reasonable considering the amount of track work and is paid at the ranger station near the start of the walk. For shorter walks a fee of $4 per night per adult applies. For information about the track contact the Cynthia Bay rangers (☎ (002) 89 1115 or 89 1138) or the Waldheim rangers (☎ (003) 63 5187).

During popular periods a ranger is stationed in the park and may ask to see permits. The rangers strongly request all walkers to carry tents and all parties must carry stoves. Do not rely upon the huts as they may be full. The track is open all year for bushwalkers.

Access

The Cradle Mountain-Lake St Clair National Park in the centre of the highlands of Tasmania is 160 km north-west of Hobart and 70 km south-west of Devonport. The Overland Track is not a circuit and requires the use of public transport or a very long car shuffle. During the summer period special bus services operate to both ends of the walk. In other seasons a regular service passes near both ends of the park and requires a short walk to the start.

The northern access point is Cradle Valley (marked as Waldheim on some maps). This is 85 km from Devonport by road. The most direct route from Devonport is to follow the highway west for 13 km to Forth, then turn south to Lower Wilmot, Wilmot and on to Cradle Valley. The last 30 km is unsealed.

The rangers' office is near the visitor information centre just inside the northern border of the park. If you arrive late in the day you can camp at the Cradle Mountain Campground which is located beside the main road two km north of the park border. Camping fees are moderately expensive ($12 for a two-person tent site) but the facilities are excellent and unusual in the effort that has been put to make the camp blend into the surrounding forest. Bunkhouses are also available for $18 per night if you don't wish

to camp. Basic food like milk, bread, some groceries and dairy products can be purchased at the campground. Takeaway meals are available from Charlies Place which is located beside the airstrip 500 metres south of the camp entrance.

If you are after a more classy form of accommodation then consider either the Lemonthyme or the Cradle Mountain lodges. Prices range from a reasonable $60 per night. Currently the Cradle Mountain area is being redesigned and this may result in changes.

The southern access point is Cynthia Bay, six km north of the Lyell Highway, the main road from Hobart to Queenstown. From Hobart follow the Lyell Highway towards Queenstown for 167 km to Derwent Bridge. Turn north and follow the road for six km to Cynthia Bay.

The rangers' office is next to the main car parking area. In the same building there is a kiosk which sells takeaway meals, souvenirs and basic food supplies. Currently a new car park and buildings are being constructed 100 metres to the south. For late arrivals, Cynthia Bay has a large camp ground and cabins with toilets, showers and a laundry. Fees for use of the camp ground are paid to the rangers. Overland Track walkers are allowed to camp without any extra fees at Fergy's Paddock (beside The Overland Track), a five-minute walk west of the rangers' office. This has toilets only.

During the summer months, access by public transport is available to both ends of The Overland Track. The northern access point of Cradle Valley has daily bus services from the start of December to the end of February. These are operated by Mountain Stage Line, Maxwells Coaches and Tasmanian Wilderness Transport from both Launceston and Devonport. As well Redline Coaches now use the new link road to the west coast for their regular Devonport to Queenstown bus route and they call at Cradle Mountain Lodge on this run. As timetables vary from season to season the simplest method for booking a bus is to contact The Backpackers Barn at Edward St, Devonport

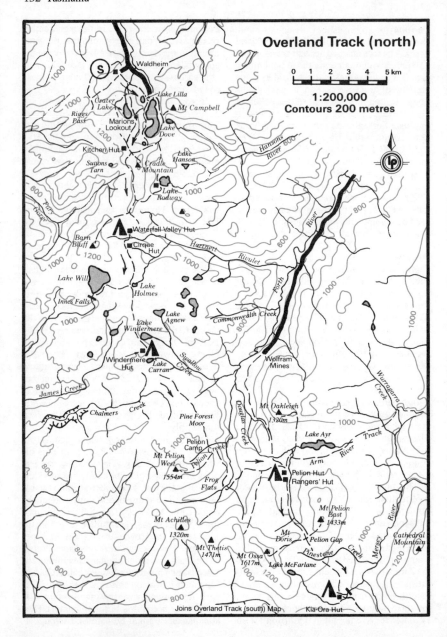

Overland Track (north)

0 1 2 3 4 5 km

1:200,000
Contours 200 metres

Waldheim

Lake Lilla

Crater Lake

Mt Campbell

Riggs Pass

Marions Lookout

Lake Dove

Hansons River

Kitchen Hut

Lake Hanson

Suttons Tarn

Cradle Mountain

Lake Rodway

Waterfall Valley Hut

Barn Bluff

Cirque Hut

Hartnett Rivulet

Forth River

Lake Will

Lake Holmes

Innes Falls

Lake Agnew

Lake Windermere

Commonwealth Creek

Windermere Hut

Lake Curran

Swallow Creek

Wolfram Mines

Wurragarra Creek

James Creek

Chalmers Creek

Pine Forest Moor

Douglas Creek

Mt Oakleigh 1320m

Lake Ayr

River Arm Track

Pelion Camp

Pelion Creek

Mt Pelion West 1554m

Frog Flats

Pelion Hut
Rangers' Hut

Mt Achilles 1320m

Mt Pelion East 1433m

Mt Doris

Pelion Gap

Cathedral Mountain

Mt Thetis 1471m

Mt Ossa 1617m

Pinestone

Mersey River

Lake McFarlane

Kia-Ora Hut

Joins Overland Track (south) Map

(☎ (004) 24 3628), as they are agents for all the buses. They also sell liquid fuel and have storage facilities if needed.

The southern access point of Cynthia Bay has two main services. They are Mountain Stage Line (☎ (003) 34 0442), PO Box 433, Launceston, and Cradle Mountain Coaches (☎ (004) 24 3628). Both operate a regular service from October to March from Cynthia Bay directly to Launceston and Devonport. Liquid fuels and storage facilities for luggage are also available and in other seasons the bus can be chartered by personal arrangement.

The other service operates all year as it is the main bus service from Hobart to Launceston. This is operated by Redline Coaches (☎ (002) 34 4577) from Tuesday to Saturday all year round. This service passes through Derwent Bridge six km south of Cynthia Bay. The bus leaves Hobart from the Transit Centre at 199 Collins St at 8.30 to arrive at Derwent Bridge about midday. The bus from Queenstown leaves the depot at Orr St at 9 am and leaves Derwent Bridge for Hobart at 10.15 am. The Saturday bus leaves Queenstown at 1 pm and leaves Derwent Bridge at 2.30 pm for Hobart. The current fare from Hobart to Derwent Bridge is $20 per person.

Stage 1: Cradle Valley to Waterfall Valley Hut

(13 km, 5-6½ hours)
The start of The Overland Track is near the old Waldheim lodge, originally built by Gustav Weindorfer (the park's founder) as a guesthouse. Waldheim Lodge is located on the signposted side road in the park. Currently management are considering a traffic plan for the park and it is to be expected that the start will be accessed by a shuttle bus. Private vehicles are likely to be banned from parking near the lodge. Before starting walkers should realise that they are not allowed to camp before reaching Waterfall Valley. Once past there, dispersed camping is allowed through the park.

To the left of Waldheim is a sign which simply states 'Start of Walking Tracks'.

Follow this track south-east through a small patch of forest then across an open buttongrass valley on a raised boardwalk. Ronny Creek is crossed on a good bridge and then the track divides. The signposted Overland Track turns right, but ignore this and turn left for Lake Lilla and Lake Dove. This is an interesting track with more views and will rejoin The Overland Track near Marions Lookout.

Follow the track south-east for 1½ km (ignore both turns to Wombat Tarn) to Lake Lilla. Cross the outlet creek and follow the track above the eastern shore of Lake Lilla and over a low saddle down to Lake Dove. Turn right at the track junction near the lake and walk south for 200 metres to the sandy beach and old boatshed site. In calm weather the views and reflections of Cradle Mountain are excellent from this lake.

Continue to follow the track south from the boatshed for another 400 metres to a track junction. Turn right and a steep climb south-west leads up onto Marions Lookout. Just before the lookout you will meet the track from Crater Lake. Continue south over the rocky bluff of Marions Lookout and follow the track south-west for one km to a track junction. Turn left and walk 200 metres to Kitchen Hut about two to 2½ hours from the start. This hut is very small and is for emergency shelter only. In poor weather it is a popular lunch site.

The packs can be left here for the sidetrip to the summit of Cradle Mountain (1½ to two hours return). From Kitchen Hut follow The Overland Track south-east for 100 metres and turn left onto the signposted track to Hansons Peak. The track to Cradle Mountain is almost immediately on the right (the signpost is usually missing). Turn right and follow this track uphill to the scree slopes. From here the track is marked with red painted arrows and traverses the boulder fields southwards to the summit tower where there is a bronze plaque which names the surrounding peaks.

Return to Kitchen Hut by the same track. If the peak is covered in cloud an alternative sidetrip is to follow the cairned track south-west from the hut down through a small valley to Suttons Tarn. This takes about one hour return from Kitchen Hut.

Collect the packs at Kitchen Hut then walk south-east 100 metres to the track junction and turn right along The Overland Track. Follow the track south for 2½ km along the western slopes of Cradle Mountain before making a short climb onto Cradle Cirque and the track junction to Lake Rodway. Turn right and follow The Overland Track south-west along the open and exposed ridge called Cradle Cirque. After 800 metres the track junction to Barn Bluff is met.

If you have enough time the ascent of Barn Bluff is worthwhile, adding two to three hours extra to the day's walk. The sidetrack to Barn Bluff follows the open ridge south-west for 1½ km then climbs south up the dolerite scree slopes to the summit. Return by the same route to the track junction.

From the Barn Bluff track junction turn left and follow The Overland Track south-east for one km along Cradle Cirque to a fine view of Waterfall Valley. The track then descends steeply south-west for ½ km down muddy eroded tracks to the open plain of Waterfall Valley. Turn right and follow the signposted side track to Waterfall Valley Hut. This small hut has bunks for eight people and an open fireplace. Excellent tent sites are 50 metres upstream of the hut in the forest and there is a permanent toilet 10 metres uphill from the hut. The water supply beside the hut door is often polluted and so it is best to collect water at the top of the camping area 50 metres upstream.

Alternative Campsites

Kitchen Hut Walkers are not allowed to camp in this tiny refuge and should only stay here in emergencies.

Cirque Hut This is a 15-minute walk south of Waterfall Valley Hut beside The Overland Track. It is a modern hut which will sleep about 30 people; it also has two pot belly stoves for heating and there's a toilet east of the hut. Unfortunately, the ground around

this hut is very boggy and camping here is not recommended.

Stage 2: Waterfall Valley Hut to Windermere Hut

(13 km, 5-6 hours)

From Waterfall Valley Hut walk 400 metres east back to The Overland Track. Turn right and follow this south for five minutes to the second creek crossing. Drop the packs here for a short sidetrip to a lovely waterfall. Follow the north bank of the creek down steeply for 100 metres then scramble down on the right to the base of the waterfall. This is one of the most beautiful falls in this area. There are many more falls in this valley which you can explore. Return to collect the packs.

Cross the creek and continue south for 10 minutes along The Overland Track to the boggy plain near Cirque Hut. The hut is 150 metres east of the track. From here The Overland Track rises gently over an open exposed moor for two km to Lake Holmes. Just west of the lake is a track junction to Lake Will and Innes Falls. The sidetrip is worthwhile and will take two to 2½ hours return.

Drop the packs and follow the track west past several small tarns to meet Lake Will at a small beach. Turn south-west and follow the lake shore to the outlet creek. Innes Falls are 200 metres downstream from the lake. Return by the same track.

Collect the packs, then continue to follow The Overland Track south for 1½ km over a high exposed ridge. This ridge provides extensive views in fine weather. From the ridge crest the track descends quickly then continues south for two km to the western shore of Lake Windermere. Follow the shore south and leave the lake at its south-west corner near some campsites.

Walk south-east across buttongrass slopes for 10 minutes to Windermere Hut. This modern hut will sleep about 40 people and has one pot belly stove for heating. The toilet is south-east of the hut. There are campsites near the hut and beside the lake shore.

Alternative Campsites There are several places which could be used on the moors. All these are exposed to the wind and are, therefore, best avoided in poor weather.

Stage 3: Windermere Hut to Pelion Hut
(14 km, 4½-6 hours)

From the hut follow The Overland Track south-east through light forest. It soon swings south and descends to cross the outlet creek of Lake Curran one km from the hut. The track then climbs gently for three km at first south then south-east, to the exposed Pine Forest Moor. You'll meet a track junction just before a forest. The signposted sidetrack to the left is to the Forth River Lookout. This takes only five minutes for a reasonable view.

Back at the track junction follow The Overland Track south-east into the forest. The original track can still be seen on the right where it follows the western edge of the forest. This has very deep mud and should not be used.

Follow the marked track south through the forest for one km to open moors. The track crosses these moors south for one km then gently descends through light forest for 500 metres to cross Pelion Creek. A short climb leads to a track junction; the sidetrack on the right leads to Pelion Campsite.

Continue on The Overland Track for five minutes to another track junction. The right-hand track leads uphill to Mt Pelion West. This sidetrip will add an extra four to five hours to the day's walk and should only be attempted by experienced scramblers as the summit plateau is a maze of large dolerite boulders.

Continue to follow The Overland Track south through thick forest as it descends gradually for 2½ km to Frog Flats. Walk east across the river flats and cross the Forth River on a bridge. At 720 metres above sea level this is the lowest point on The Overland Track. The track continues east crossing the remainder of Frog Flats then swings north-east and climbs for two km through forest to a track junction on the scrubby Pelion Plains. The sidetrack to the right leads to Mt Thetis and is a full return day trip.

Continue east on The Overland Track for

a further 15 minutes to Pelion Hut. This hut is a tin shed that sleeps 16 people and has one pot-belly stove for heating. There are also good campsites near the hut and at Douglas Creek, 100 metres east. A permanent toilet is west of the hut. If the party is extending the length of the walk then this is an ideal place to spend two or even three nights. Other walks in the area include a four to five-hour return trip to Mt Oakleigh, two hours return to Lake Ayr and a nine to 10-hour return trip to Mt Thetis and Achilles.

Alternative Campsites

Pelion Creek This is about two to three hours south of Windermere Hut on a signposted side track. It has good shelter for three tents.

Frog Flats An extensive region of grass flats which make excellent tent sites, but beware as the area is prone to flooding.

Stage 4: Pelion Hut to Kia-Ora Hut
(13 km, 5-6 hours)

From Pelion Hut walk south past the Rangers' Hut (locked and not for use by walkers) to join The Overland Track. Follow the track south through forest for 2½ km to cross a large creek on a good bridge. The track then climbs steeply for 1½ km through forest patches to Pelion Gap.

From the gap the views are spectacular: ahead is Cathedral Mountain; behind are the pinnacled cliffs of Mt Oakleigh with Barn Bluff and Cradle Mountain in the distance; to the east is Mt Pelion East and west behind Mt Doris, is Mt Ossa, at 1617 metres, the highest peak in Tasmania. This is one of the best views from The Overland Track itself. Even better views are obtained by a short climb south-east onto the slopes of Mt Pelion East.

If the weather is good the packs can be left at the gap for a 2½ to three-hour return sidetrip to Mt Ossa. From the signposted junction in the gap follow the track to the west. This climbs steadily around the southern slopes of Mt Doris to a saddle. From the saddle the track climbs steeply up a scree-

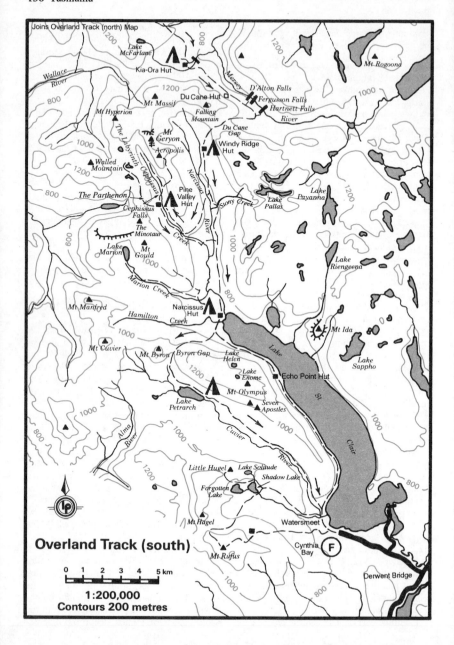

Joins Overland Track (north) Map

Lake McFarlane
Kia-Ora Hut
Mt Rogoona
Mersey
D'Alton Falls
Mt Massif
Du Cane Hut
Fergusson Falls
Mt Hyperion
Falling Mountain
Hartnett Falls
River
The Labyrinth
Mt Geryon
Du Cane Gap
Windy Ridge Hut
Acropolis
Walled Mountain
Cephissus
Narcissus
Lake Payanna
The Parthenon
Pine Valley Hut
Stony Creek
Lake Pallas
Cephissus Falls
The Minotaur
Creek
River
Lake Riengeena
Lake Marion
Mt Gould
Marion Creek
Mt Manfred
Narcissus Hut
Lake Sappho
Mt Ida
Hamilton Creek
Mt Cuvier
Mt Byron
Byron Gap
Lake Helen
Lake Enome
Echo Point Hut
Lake Petrarch
Mt Olympus
Seven Apostles
Lake St Clair
Alma River
Cuvier River
Little Hugel
Lake Solitude
Shadow Lake
Forgotten Lake
Watersmeet
Mt Hagel
Cynthia Bay
F
Mt Rufus
Derwent Bridge

Overland Track (south)

0 1 2 3 4 5 km

1:200,000
Contours 200 metres

filled gully towards the summit. The top of the gully appears to be impassable, but the route is well cairned and some mild scrambling leads to a small plateau with a tarn.

The summit cairn of Mt Ossa is 100 metres north of the tarn. Return to Pelion Gap by the same route. If Mt Ossa is covered in cloud then Mt Pelion East may be worth climbing instead. This takes 1½ hours return to the gap and is an easy climb to the east with a final short rock scramble to the summit.

At Pelion Gap collect the packs and follow The Overland Track south-east, descending for 1½ km into Pinestone Valley. This part of the track is eroded and usually muddy. Wade across Pinestone Creek and the track continues south-east for 2½ km through mixed forest and moors to Kia-Ora Hut. There are a couple of creek crossings 50 metres before the hut (normally crossed by low wooden bridges). If heavy rains have fallen the bridges may be submerged and in this case the creeks can be crossed with difficulty 20 metres upstream in the forest.

Kia-Ora Hut is a new hut which can sleep 24 people. Reasonable tent sites exist in the light forest near the hut. The toilet is on the buttongrass plain west of the hut. Water is available from Kia-Ora Creek, some 50 metres south of the hut.

Alternative Campsites

There are many campsites on this section of the track. Suitable sites are found near Douglas Creek, near Pelion Gap (fine weather only) and in Pinestone Valley.

Stage 5: Kia-Ora Hut to Windy Ridge
(11 km, 5-7 hours)

From Kia-Ora Hut follow The Overland Track south-east for 50 metres to the bridge across Kia-Ora Creek. After crossing the bridge follow The Overland Track south-east for two km (about 45 minutes) through mixed forest to Du Cane Hut. This is an old hut, set in a large clearing, built of timber shingles and registered by the National Trust. The hut has many holes in the roof and walls and is not really suitable for staying in, even

in emergencies (the stars can be seen through the roof).

From the hut door The Overland Track descends east to the edge of the clearing then swings south-east into a dark myrtle forest. About 1½ km from the hut is the track junction to D'Alton and Fergusson Falls. These falls are well worth visiting as a side-trip, taking about 1½ hours return to visit all the falls.

All walkers need to be careful as the narrow side tracks are poised on steep slippery slopes. Leave the packs at the junction and descend steeply north-east down a rough track. After 150 metres there is a poorly marked track junction (often the signpost is missing). Turn right and follow the unmarked track upstream for five minutes to a large boulder wedged high above the Mersey River in a narrow gorge. The boulder forms a natural bridge and, taking care, use it to cross to the north-east bank of the river. Walk 50 metres upstream for a good view of Fergusson Falls.

Return to the poorly marked track junction and follow the other track downstream. This immediately crosses a small creek and 50 metres further there are good views of the D'Alton Falls on the right. A rough track continues downstream for a further 400 metres to a ridge where the 40-metre-high Cathedral Falls can be seen. The track descends down a gully to the river where the less spectacular Boulder Falls can be seen. Return to the packs by the same tracks.

Collect the packs and follow The Overland Track south for one km (25 to 30 minutes) to another signposted track junction. This track leads to Hartnett Falls which should not be missed. The return sidetrip will take about one hour. Leave the packs at the junction and follow the track north-east for 800 metres to the top of the falls. For the best views walk downstream following the track near the cliff edge. This descends to the river and a short walk upstream leads into the spectacular gorge at the base of the falls. Return by the same track to The Overland Track.

Pick up the packs and continue following

Black Currawong

The Overland Track west, climbing gently for two km to Du Cane Gap. Views from this gap are restricted due to dense vegetation. From the gap the track descends steeply through forest for two km to Windy Ridge Hut. This hut is a modern timber construction and will sleep 24 persons comfortably. It has a pot-belly stove for heating. The toilet is just north of the hut.

Water for the hut is available from a plastic pipe or from the small spring 200 metres south along the main track. Campsites around the hut are poor; good campsites are 300 metres north along the main track around the ruins of a previous hut.

Alternative Campsites
Hartnett Falls This is a 20-minute walk from the main track with good tentsites near the top of the falls.

Campfire Creek Good campsites are scattered near this creek, close to The Overland Track, about 10 minutes east of Du Cane Gap.

Stage 6: Windy Ridge Hut to Pine Valley Hut
(8 km, 2½-3½ hours)
From Windy Ridge Hut continue south along The Overland Track for two km to a track junction signposted 'Pine Valley'.

If going direct to Narcissus Hut: If you don't have the time to head to Pine Valley and have to continue to Lake St Clair then follow the track south. Stony Creek is crossed before another track, about two km further on leads off to the right to Pine Valley. Continue via wet plains which are often crossed by raised boardwalks to the swing bridge across Narcissus River. It is one km from here to Narcissus Hut.

If going to Pine Valley: Leave The Overland Track and turn right onto the track to Pine Valley. Follow this track south-west for three km through mixed forest to another junction on the east side of Cephissus Creek. Turn sharp right and follow the signposted track north-west, for two km to an area of open forest beside Cephissus Creek. Cross the creek and walk 50 metres west to Pine Valley Hut.

This is a new hut that sleeps 24 people. You can collect water from the tank at the hut. There are plenty of excellent campsites in the forest beside Cephissus Creek, 50 metres west of the hut.

The walk from Windy Ridge to Pine Valley Hut is a pleasant half day's walk so you have time to climb The Acropolis in the afternoon if the weather is good.

Alternative Campsites There are several dry areas of forest along the track where you can make camp if necessary.

Sidetrip: The Acropolis
(6½ km, 3½-5 hours)
If the peaks are clear leave the packs at the campsite and follow the signposted track north from Pine Valley Hut. After 250 metres you pass the small, but attractive Cephissus Falls. About 800 metres past the falls the track crosses the creek to a signposted track junction. The left track is to the Geryon Campsite which is used mainly by rock

climbers. Follow the right-hand track north-east for one km climbing gently, then steeply up onto the top of the flat ridge south of The Acropolis. From here, there is a good view of both the area and the rocky mass of The Acropolis.

The track turns north and follows the flat, open ridge for one km to the foot of the bluffs. From here the track is marked with cairns as it traverses the scree slopes on the eastern side of the cliffs. The track winds north under the cliffs for 400 metres then a steep scramble leads to the summit plateau. Some walkers will need help to ascend the short cliffs on the final climb.

The summit cairn is 100 metres north of the ascent route. The view from the top is excellent with cliffs, tarns and peaks in all directions. Return to Pine Valley Hut by the same route.

Sidetrip: The Labyrinth
(7 km, 3-5 hours)
If the weather is OK a visit to The Labyrinth is a good walk for the morning before leaving for Narcissus Hut in the afternoon. The Labyrinth is a plateau covered with many small lakes and tarns and has fine views of the surrounding peaks and cliffs.

Leave the packs at the campsite, then walk north from the hut for 30 metres along the Acropolis Track to a signposted track junction. Turn west (left) and follow The Labyrinth track into the forest. It soon begins to climb steeply into the saddle south of The Parthenon. The track turns north and traverses the western slopes of The Parthenon, then descends to the south-eastern end of Lake Ophion in The Labyrinth.

If you have the time it is worth walking one more km to Lake Elysia. Follow the northern shore of Lake Ophion and a cairned track leads north-west to the western shore of Lake Elysia. The views and reflections here on a calm day are magnificent. Return to Pine Valley by the same track.

If the party has spare days then more time can be spent on The Labyrinth climbing all the major peaks and exploring the lake system. *Cradle Mountain-Lake St Clair*

National Park, by John Siseman & John Chapman gives detailed notes.

Stage 7: Pine Valley Hut to Narcissus Hut
(9 km, 2½-4 hours)
From Pine Valley Hut follow the main track back through the forest and down the valley. This is the same track that was used on the way in. Turn right at the track junction after two km to cross Cephissus Creek. The track continues south-east for a further 1½ km through scrubby forest to again cross the creek. The next km leads through some small plains providing views of the surrounding mountains and this lead to the suspension bridge across the Narcissus River.

The track soon joins with The Overland Track; turn right and follow the main highway south for a further four km to Narcissus Hut. This is a corrugated iron hut which can sleep 24 people. The toilet is 50 metres north of the hut. There are plenty of campsites on the flat plain around the hut.

Stage 8: Narcissus Hut to Cynthia Bay
(19 km, 7-9 hours)
The recommended walk is via the Cuvier Valley and, while it is longer than the alternatives, it is far more scenic. The first alternative is to take a boat ride down Lake St Clair. This operates during the summer months on most days. The operator usually leaves a notice in the hut announcing when the next service is due. A radio installed in the hut can also be used to notify the operator that the boat is needed. The fee for the journey to Cynthia Bay is $20 per person, if there's a full boat. In other seasons the boat will operate by prior arrangement or by radio call.

If walking, leave Narcissus Hut and follow The Overland Track south-west for 300 metres to a track junction. Turn left and continue to follow The Overland Track south-west, crossing Hamilton Creek on a long raised bridge. One km from the creek crossing there is a track junction in the forest. The left hand track is the main Overland Track and follows the shore of Lake St Clair south for 14 km to Watersmeet. This track has very few views and, if followed, it takes about five to six hours to walk from Narcissus Hut to Cynthia Bay.

The recommended route turns right at this junction and climbs west through the forest for two km to Byron Gap. From this gap a final view is seen of the Du Cane Range to the north. Frenchmans Cap to the south is also visible. Descend south from the gap for two km to the buttongrass plains at the northern end of Lake Petrarch. The track skirts the northern shore of the lake through forest to the short beach on the south-eastern shore. From the lake the track follows the open Cuvier Valley south-east for nine km to enter the forest and meet The Overland Track (which sidled the shore of Lake St Clair from Narcissus Hut).

Follow The Overland Track south for 400 metres and cross the Cuvier River by a large bridge at Watersmeet. The Overland Track now becomes a vehicle track which you follow south-east for one km (ignoring the sidetracks) to Cynthia Bay. At the end of the walk remember to sign out in the log book near the rangers' office.

Campsites and hut accommodation are available at Cynthia Bay upon application with the ranger. Overland Track walkers can camp at Fergy's Paddock for free – this is five minutes' walk west from the rangers' office. Toilets are the only facilities.

Alternative Campsites
Lake Petrarch Good campsites are found at the southern end of the lake.

Echo Point If following the lake track there is a small hut and plenty of campsites two to three hours from Narcissus Hut.

FRENCHMANS CAP
This dominating peak towers above the Franklin River area in western Tasmania and is extremely popular with bushwalkers. It is composed of white quartzite rock which shines in the sun giving the impression it is permanently snow covered. Walkers approach the mountain along a well-used

track and there are two huts en route. The views around the peak and from the top are exceptional and well worth the walk.

Features
Glaciers have carved out the white quartzite rock leaving behind Tasmania's highest cliff on the east face of the peak. The surrounding ridges bear obvious glacial scars with tarns, cirque cliffs and erratics abounding. Erosion is still active and visible on the slopes around Barron Pass. The approach track passes through many different vegetation zones and is quite interesting.

Standard
The track into the peak is easy to follow and walk except when under snow. It is slowly being repaired to prevent further erosion and most of the work has been done in the higher alpine area of the park. In the valleys the track is often very muddy and walkers are requested to walk through the mud rather than try to find a route around. It is intended to repair the entire track although this will take several years.

There are two huts on the track but all walkers should take a tent as they are often full during the summer. The walk is subject to Tasmania's fickle weather and walkers should expect everything from rain and cold to heatwaves.

Days Required
The suggested minimum is three days, returning along the same track. There are several possible variations but these are only suitable for bushwalkers experienced in off-track walking. As the peak is often covered by swirling cloud it is suggested to allow four to five days, thereby improving your chances of obtaining clear views.

Seasons
Frenchmans Cap can be visited in all seasons as the track has a flying fox and a bridge over the two larger streams. This provides access all year except in extremely high flood levels. Like all places there are periods when your chances of fine weather are more likely

View from Frenchmans Cap

and these are usually the best time to visit. Late summer provides the best chance of fine stable weather and is understandably the most popular. In winter the peak is usually covered by snow and a visit then is only recommended for those with snow experience. Autumn and spring are reasonable although the chances of good views are reduced.

Equipment

Good clothing is essential for walking to this peak as the track is very exposed from Barron Pass onwards. Outer garments should be both windproof and waterproof and both pants and jacket are recommended. If tents are taken past Lake Vera they must be of high quality and able to withstand strong winds, hail and snowfalls. A groundsheet, in addition to the tent floor, is very useful for keeping dry. Sleeping bags should be suitable for temperatures below freezing (superdown is preferred by most).

Warm clothing of wool or high quality synthetics is needed and a balaclava and gloves are essential. Some people walk in runners, but have many problems in cold wet weather and do lose them in deep boggy holes. Good solid boots are the only suitable footwear for all the conditions that are encountered.

Stoves and enough fuel for the whole trip must be carried as the track has been declared a 'fuel stove only' area. Fires are not permitted for any purpose.

Maps

The 1:50,000 *Frenchmans Cap* map produced by TASMAP is all that's needed as it covers the entire walk and includes useful notes on its reverse side specifically for bushwalkers. This is available from map and bushwalking shops in south-eastern Australia. The TASMAP 1:100,000 *Franklin* is also suitable as it shows the tracks although it contains less detail. More walks around the area are detailed in *South West Tasmania*, by John Chapman. This can be bought in most bushwalking shops in Australia.

Permits

No permits are currently required for bushwalking to Frenchmans Cap. This policy is currently under review and it may become necessary to control numbers by issuing permits. Before planning to walk here it is advisable to contact the Department of Parks, Wildlife & Heritage (☎ (002) 30 2620), GPO Box 44A, Hobart, 7001, to determine the current situation.

Access

Frenchmans Cap is located 30 km south-east of Queenstown in western Tasmania. The closest road is the Lyell Highway which links Queenstown to Hobart. A regular bus service along this highway provides all-year access.

From Hobart follow the Lyell Highway toward Queenstown for 173 km to Derwent Bridge then a further 30 km to the signposted start of the track. A car park is located a short distance west along the highway. From Queenstown follow the Lyell Highway east for 44 km to cross the Collingwood River. Continue east for nine km to the signposted start of the track as above.

Redline Coaches run a daily service along the highway from Tuesday to Saturday (no buses run on Sunday and Monday) and this service continues through Queenstown to Strahan. From Hobart the bus leaves from 199 Collins St (☎ (002) 31 3233) at 8.30 am and passes the track at about 1 pm on the way to Queenstown. On Saturday the bus stops less frequently and passes the track at about noon. From Queenstown on Tuesday to Friday the bus leaves from Orr St at 8.30 am to pass the track at about 10 am on the way to Hobart. The Saturday service leaves Queenstown at 2.30 pm to pass the track at about 3.15 pm. The fare from Hobart to the track is currently $25.

Stage 1: Lyell Highway to Lake Vera
(9 km, 4½-6 hours)
Walk south-west along the track and descend gently to the banks of the Franklin River. Wade across the river or use the flying fox to cross to the southern side. The well-defined

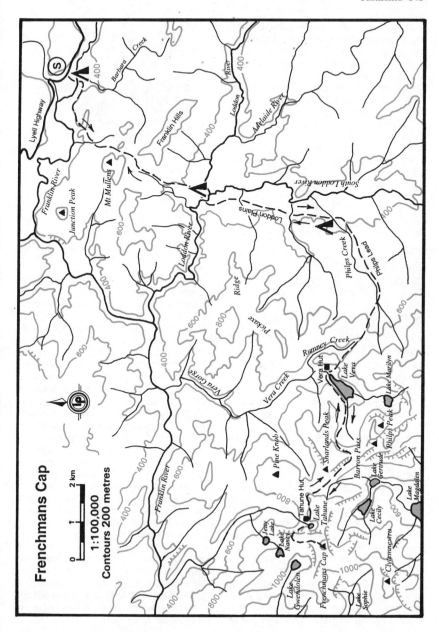

Frenchmans Cap

1:100,000
Contours 200 metres

0   1   2 km

track crosses a plain then climbs steadily for one hour to a saddle south of Mt Mullens. In fine weather this provides the first views of Frenchmans Cap and the spectacular crags around the mountain. The track continues south-west descending to the forested banks of the Loddon River. An excellent campsite exists here if needed.

Cross the Loddon River using the suspension bridge and the track swings south crossing the often muddy Loddon Plains for four km to Philps Creek. Past the creek the track turns south-west and follows the narrow buttongrass valley of Philps Lead for two km before entering the forest. A short climb over a low saddle leads to the buttongrass of Rumney Creek then a short descent north-west in forest will take you to the Lake Vera Hut.

This is a modern hut that can accommodate 16 people. The solar powered toilet is interesting and hopefully will solve one of Tasmania's bushwalking problems. Campsites near the hut are limited but there are several good sites 200 metres away on the north side of the creek.

Alternative Campsites
Loddon River Sheltered sites are found near the bridge on the northern bank.

Philps Creek Reasonable sites can be found near the creek on the Loddon Plains.

Stage 2: Lake Vera Hut to Frenchmans Cap, return
(20 km, 7-9 hours return)
The track to Frenchmans Cap climbs up through the rugged Barron Pass and most walkers find this a difficult section to carry packs along. While there is a small hut at Lake Tahune most walkers reduce the difficulties by leaving their packs behind and visiting Frenchmans Cap as a full-day trip.

From the hut use the bridge to cross Vera Creek then head westwards along the northern shore of Lake Vera. This section is slow as the track sidles a steep hillside and undulates markedly as it passes obstacles. This leads to a small wet flat at the western end of

Common Brushtail Possum track pattern

the lake. The track then enters the rainforest beside the creek. Some ladders aid on the hardest sections as the track climbs steeply into Barron Pass. A large landslide is crossed near the top illustrating that natural erosion is still active.

The views from the pass are wonderful as lakes and the surrounding spires provide a setting for the impressive view of the huge cliffs on Frenchmans Cap.

From the pass the track descends west a short way before traversing the steep slopes below Sharlands Peak. After one rough km this leads to the open ridge on the north-west side of Sharlands. This is easily descended to Artichoke Valley which is actually a swampy terrace.

At the northern end of this feature the track ascends a gully then traverses rough slopes west towards Lake Tahune. Steps aid in the difficult descent through the cliffs to the hut near the outlet creek. Twelve people can cram inside this small hut. Campsites are available 50 metres to the west near the lake. The adjacent toilet is a solar-powered model which was transported here by helicopter.

Cross the outlet creek and climb west up the scree slopes to the saddle known as the North Col. Turn south following the track to the cliffs. A chimney is ascended before you follow a series of open ledges to the final slopes which lead to the summit cairn. In fine weather the view is extensive as half of Tasmania can be seen. Return to Lake Vera by following the same track.

Top: Prion Beach, South Coast Track
Bottom: Coal Bluff, South Coast Track

Top: Walkers on Mt Feathertop
Bottom: Winter snow on Mt Feathertop (JW)

Stage 3: Lake Vera to Lyell Highway

(9 km, 4-5½ hours)

Follow the same track back down Philps Lead and across the Loddon Plains, climb past Mt Mullens and back to the Franklin River near the highway. If catching a morning bus, reasonable camping is available near the river crossing. From there it is only a 10-minute walk to the highway.

MT FIELD NATIONAL PARK

Created in 1916 this, one of Tasmania's oldest parks, has been progressively enlarged since. It has had a chequered history as, in 1949, a swap was made where a block of the tallest trees were logged in exchange for another block of mixed forest. Despite this there is some very pleasant easy walking offering excellent views for bushwalkers. A well-developed track system exists to most of the higher features and while each place can be visited on one-day walks, it is well worthwhile linking them together for some easy overnight walking.

Features

The core of this park is an elevated plateau which was extensively glaciated in geologically recent times forming many of the features. Lakes, tarns, boulder fields, cirques and cliffs are all remnants of the weathering action of ice and are readily seen. The plateau is a mixture of alpine moors and heathlands. On the lower slopes grow the swamp gums (known elsewhere in Australia as mountain ash) which are the worlds tallest hardwood trees, reaching heights above 100 metres. Some important features are located near the entrance as, in addition to the well-known Russell Falls, the park includes the two deepest caves in Australia at depths of over 300 metres.

Standard

Well-marked walking tracks are easily followed. The suggested walk is graded easy to medium as it does pass through an alpine region which is subject to Tasmania's fickle weather.

Days Required

It takes two full days to walk the tracks as described. If a late start is made from Lake Dobson then it may be better to change it into three easy days.

Seasons

Late summer is the best period to visit any of Tasmania's alpine regions and this applies also to this park. Other seasons are suitable as the tracks are clearly marked so walking is reasonable from late spring through summer to late autumn. In winter, the higher region of the park is usually covered by snow and is unsuitable for bushwalking.

Equipment

Good clothing is essential for walking in the higher parts of the park. Outer garments should be both windproof and waterproof and both pants and jacket are recommended. Tents must be of high quality and able to withstand strong winds, hail and snowfalls. Sleeping bags should be suitable for temperatures below freezing.

Warm clothing of wool or high quality synthetics is needed and a balaclava and gloves are essential. Some people walk in runners, but have many problems in cold wet weather and do lose them in deep boggy holes. Leather boots are the only suitable footwear for all conditions that may be encountered. Stoves and sufficient fuel must be carried as the track has been recommended as a 'fuel stove only' area.

Maps

The 1:50,000 *Mt Field National Park* map produced by TASMAP is the best one to take. It clearly shows all the tracks and on the reverse side includes useful information for bushwalkers. It is available from most map and bushwalking shops in south-eastern Australia. If it is out of print, the 1:100,000 *Tyenna* is a reasonable substitute as it shows most tracks. This is also produced by TASMAP.

Permits

No permits are required for bushwalking in

this park but all walkers are requested to register their details with the duty rangers at National Park before setting out.

Access

Mt Field National Park is located 75 km west of Hobart and lies between the Maydena-Strathgordon Road and the Lyell Highway. Access to the park is from the Maydena Road through the tiny settlement of National Park. From Hobart follow the Lyell Highway north-west for 37 km to New Norfolk. When the highway turns right to cross the bridge over the Derwent River leave it to continue straight ahead towards Maydena. Continue west for 40 km to National Park, turn right and, in one km, enter the camping ground near the park headquarters.

Access by public transport is good in summer with one company operating a bushwalkers' bus service through National Park and onto Scotts Peak Dam in the south-west. This runs on Saturday, Sunday, Tuesday and Thursday, leaving 60 Collins St, Hobart at 9.30 am and passing National Park at about 10.40 am. The return service (on the same days) leaves National Park at 2 pm for Hobart. Fares are currently $25 per person each way. In other seasons buses can be chartered from Invicta (☎ (008) 03 0505), 60 Collins St, Hobart, 7000.

The camping ground is part of the National Park and costs $6 to put up a two person tent. Bookings should be made in advance for the Christmas and Easter holiday periods with the Ranger-in-Charge, (☎ (002) 88 1149) Mt Field, PO Box 41, Westerway, 7140. Full camping facilities are provided. A kiosk provides basic stores and takeaway meals. More substantial meals are available at the restaurant beside the trout farm, just outside the park entrance.

The walk described begins at Lake Dobson which is located 14 km from the camping ground at the park entrance. This is accessed by the gravel road that climbs up onto the plateau and is followed to the car park at Lake Dobson. Most walkers who come by bus will stay overnight at the camping ground and may be able to arrange a lift with another camper. Otherwise it is a dusty plod up the road to the top.

Stage 1: Lake Dobson to Twilight Tarn
(15 km, 6-7 hours)

If staying at the camping ground it is worthwhile walking the short circuit to Russell and Lady Barron Falls. This gives excellent views of some 90-metre-tall trees giving a different perspective of the park's features.

The actual walk starts from Lake Dobson, 14 km from the campground. Begin by walking west from the public shelter on the Pandanni Grove Nature Trail. Ignore both turns on the left to the Wellington Ski Club then turn left onto Urquhart Track to begin climbing away from the lake. This rises to meet the closed road that accesses the ski lodges above. Follow this road uphill to the second sharp bend and continue straight ahead towards Mawson Ski Club. Pass this lodge and several others to the end of the road and the start of the walking tracks.

Seal Lookout is soon passed providing excellent views of the lake in the deep glacial carved valley below. Continue on to the track junction to the Tarn Shelf on the Mawson Plateau. Turn left to follow the track that climbs onto the Rodway Range. A very rocky track leads north-west over Mt Rodway then descends west into K Col. At the junction keep left to walk to the Peterson Memorial Hut. This tiny A-frame hut is for emergency use only.

From here, if the weather is fine, there is an excellent sidetrip to the summit of Mt Field West which takes three to four hours' return. Leave the packs at the hut or hide them in the nearby rocks. Then follow the marked track west past Clemes Tarn. Continue north-west past Naturalist Peak to a plateau covered with tiny tarns. Past these the track scrambles west to the rocky tower of Mt Field West. The view is extensive and looks into the World Heritage area. Unfortunately, it is marred by the extensive logging seen below in the Florentine Valley. Return to K Col to collect the packs.

Return east back towards the Rodway Range to the first track junction and turn left

Mt Field
National Park

1:75,000
Contours 100 metres

Lake Newdegate, Mt Field National Park

towards Newdegate Pass. This track heads north and gently ascends into the pass. A short scramble to the left leads to The Watcher which provides grandstand views of the Lawrence Rivulet valley below. Follow the track east through the pass where extensive use of boards protect the fragile landscape. A gradual descent follows and some boulder fields are crossed to the outlet of Lake Newdegate. The Lake Newdegate Hut located to the left, is suitable for an overnight stop although there is presently no toilet.

To continue, turn left at the track junction and and follow the track past Twisted Tarn and on through light forest to Twilight Tarn, 50 minutes from Lake Newdegate. The hut is located on the other side of the tarn and was originally built in the 1930s as a ski lodge. It has three major rooms and provides a reasonable overnight stop. Campsites near the hut are also available.

Alternative Campsites
Newdegate Hut A rough hut near the lake; currently it has no toilet.

Stage 2: Twilight Tarn to Dobson Road
(14 km, 5-7 hours)
From Twilight Tarn follow the marked track eastwards and descend for 30 minutes to cross the plain near Lake Webster. The track enters the forest and divides. Follow the left track which leads to a bridge crossing a creek. A steady climb then passes through ti-tree then eucalypt forest to Kangaroo Moor. The track at first follows the right-hand edge of the open plain then crosses over, on cording, to the northern side. Near Lake Fenton it enters open forest and sidles well above the lake to the dam wall at the eastern end. The wall was built in 1939 to supply water for the town of National Park.

Turn left at the track junction near the dam wall and head north-east towards Mt Field East. At the first track junction it is worthwhile leaving packs behind and following the right-hand track uphill for 25 minutes to Seagers Lookout. This provides good views of Lake Fenton. Return along the same tracks to the junction to collect the packs.

Turn north and follow the track towards Mt Field East. This is poorly marked and care is needed to follow it as it climbs across some boulder fields then descends gently to Windy Moor. Easy walking leads to the track junction below Mt Field East. Scramble north up scree slopes for 300 metres to the summit. In fine weather the major mountains of the south-west are easily identified. Return to the track junction south-east of Mt Field East.

The track swings south-east across the moor then descends steeply down through boulders in the forest and passes Lake Raynor on an unmarked side track. This leads to the hut at Lake Nicholls. This hut is in good condition. Continue to follow the track south as it passes through more forest past the side track to Beatties Tarn and out onto the Lake Dobson Road. From here it is 8½ km down the unsealed road to the camping ground near the park entrance.

MT ANNE CIRCUIT

Mt Anne is the highest peak in the South West National Park; its sharp profile and huge cliffs dominate the area. Mt Anne is part of a small range of peaks capped with red dolerite, in stark contrast to the surrounding white quartzite ranges.

The circuit walk of this small range, while short in length, is at times as exciting as any other trip in the south-west. In fine weather the scenery and views are superb.

Features

This small range has a series of open plateaus connected by razorback ridges. Along the edge of the plateaus and ridges, columnar cliffs of red dolerite fall steeply into the surrounding valleys. The plateaus are covered with low, stunted shrubs and random piles of dolerite scree. In the valleys the vegetation varies with the soil type. On the dolerite slopes thick forests stand while only rough grasses and shrubs grow on the quartzite ridges.

Most of the landforms are products of relatively recent glaciation. The glaciers and ice-carved valleys from the range leaving spectacular cliffs and creating the three-km-long Lake Judd. Several small lakes and

tarns are also glacial remnants. As is normal for this area of Tasmania, wildlife is rare and most walkers only see birds and lizards.

Standard

Between Condominium Creek and Mt Anne there is a good track. Beyond Mt Anne the circuit becomes rough and is not a track, but a rough well-worn route created by the passage of many bushwalkers. Steep boulder hopping is required to negotiate Mt Lot and some parties will need to use a rope to lift and lower packs. The route is not hard to follow, with cairns and muddy trails showing the way.

The circuit is exposed to extreme weather conditions which can occur at any time of the year, so all parties should be able to cope with being very wet and cold. Navigation can be difficult in poor weather. The walk is graded medium. Walkers with less experience are advised to only attempt to follow the track as far as Mt Anne and return along the same route. This is still an enjoyable walk.

Days Required

The recommended time for the circuit is three to four days. This allows a little time to explore the area and for delays caused in the event of poor weather. The circuit, however, can be walked in two days using private transport or hired cars. If using Bushwalkers Transport (the bus company) then allow three or four days for the walk and for time to make connections with the minibus.

Seasons

Tasmanian walkers visit Mt Anne all year round because it is close to the road and there is a small hut on Mt Eliza. For fine weather, however, the best time to go is in late summer. December and January are also suitable although the weather is less stable.

Throughout summer (at irregular intervals), the range is buffeted by severe storms that bring rain, hail and snowfalls. These can be so severe that parties cannot continue and even the best equipment can be destroyed by the winds. All walkers must be well equipped for this circuit.

In the other seasons fine weather is rare. The plateaus are often covered in thick cloud and severe storms occur frequently. In winter the plateaus are usually covered with snow. A visit to the range in autumn, winter or spring is interesting but recommended for experienced walkers only.

Equipment

Good equipment is essential for walking this circuit. Tents must be of good quality and able to withstand strong winds and snowfalls. A groundsheet placed on top of the tent floor will make the tent more waterproof. Sleeping bags should be suitable for temperatures as low as freezing point and warm clothing and full wet-weather jackets and pants are essential. Solid boots are also recommended.

Fuel stoves are essential for all parties as the range has been declared a 'fuel stove only' area. It is also advisable to carry a 20-metre rope to use as a safety line on the final climb to Mt Anne and for packhauling near Mt Lot.

Maps

The 1:25,000 *Anne* and *Scotts* maps produced by TASMAP are highly recommended as they clearly mark the walking tracks and routes. The older 1:100,000 topographic maps, *Old River* and *Wedge*, also cover the circuit but do not show all the features of the area. The maps are all published by TASMAP. You can buy them in most bushwalking shops in the eastern states of Australia. More detail of this walk and other walks in the area are described in *South West Tasmania* by John Chapman.

Permits

No permits are required for walking in this range at present but this situation may change as management plans are presently being formulated. All walkers intending to walk this range should check the current situation with the Department of Parks, Wildlife & Heritage, 134 Macquarie St, Hobart (☎ (002) 30 6285).

Access

Mt Anne is 75 km west of Hobart in the South West National Park. Access is via the Strathgordon Road. From Hobart the roads are followed through New Norfolk to Maydena then to Frodshams Pass, 121 km from Hobart. Turn left onto the gravel Scotts Peak Road and follow this south for 20 km to Condominium Creek. There is a large car park on the south side of the creek.

If you are arriving in the evening there is a good camping area beside Condominium Creek, 30 metres east of the car parking area, and there's a toilet beside the main track. The walk finishes at Red Tape Creek, on the Scotts Peak Road, nine km south of Condominium Creek. A car parking area is 100 metres north of the creek, and campsites are not very good in the area.

The closest petrol and food supplies are at Maydena, 51 km away. If the party is using private transport a short car shuffle to leave a vehicle at Red Tape Creek, is a good idea.

From early December to early March access is easy using the regular mini-bus service which operates on Tuesday, Thursday, Saturday and Sunday. The service is run by Invicta (☎ (008) 03 0505) and leaves at 9.30 am from the office at 60 Collins St, Hobart. The arrival time at Condominium Creek is about noon and departure time for Hobart is about 12.40 pm on the days mentioned above. The bus can pick up walkers at Red Tape Creek which is the end of this walk at about 12.35 pm.

There is a fee of $35 per person each way. At other times of the year the mini-bus can be booked by special arrangement with Invicta. Unfortunately, they don't sell liquid fuel or supply a secure place for luggage. Fuel can be purchased in the bushwalking shops in Hobart which are now open seven days a week during summer.

Stage 1: Condominium Creek to High Camp Hut

(3 km, 1½-2½ hours)
From the car park, follow the board covered track east across the buttongrass plain. The track then climbs east up an open ridge for

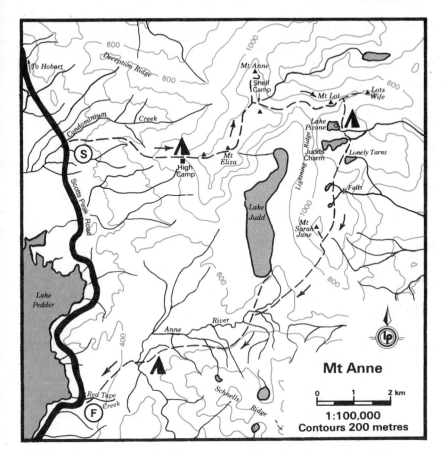

1½ km where it descends briefly to a saddle. A short climb south-east leads onto a large ridge which you follow for one km to the treeline. This marks the boundary between the dolerite and quartzite rock bands.

The small High Camp Hut (map ref 510429) is in the trees on a signposted side track 30 metres south of the main track and a scenic toilet is 10 metres south-west of the hut. Exposed campsites are in small alcoves near the hut, and water is obtained from the tank at the hut.

The walk from the road to High Camp Hut is very short, but it is the usual first camp if using the minibus. The next campsite is about two hours walk further and has only fair shelter. In poor weather it is advisable to stop at High Camp.

Stage 2: High Camp Hut to Lake Picone
(9 km, 6-9 hours)

From the hut follow the track east climbing steeply in light forest then rocks to the summit cairn of Mt Eliza (about ½ to one hour). From the summit follow the cairned track north-east, then north, across the open plateau. The plateau has many tiny tarns and the views from the eastern edge looking down into Lake Judd are worth deviating to see.

Continue to follow the cairns across an extensive boulder field on the west side of the north peak on the plateau (map ref 532441). At the end of the boulder field climb onto the top of the ridge crest (map ref 528444). This takes about 1½ to two hours walking from the hut.

The packs can be left here for the sidetrip to the summit of Mt Anne which will take one to two hours return. From the packs follow the cairned route north along the ridge top and into the saddle underneath the summit tower. The cairned track swings east and climbs the scree-covered slopes to the foot of a short gully on the south-east corner of the peak. The route now becomes steep and exposed and you should use a safety line if the peak is wet or has snow on it.

Following the cairns, climb up the short steep gully then traverse to the left along a series of ledges. The route climbs directly up for three metres then traverses back to the right, across the sloping terraces above the gully to the exposed ridge. Carefully sidle right over large sloping boulders to a short ramp. Climb the ramp and at the top of it ascend directly to the summit. A log book is kept in the summit cairn.

Return via the same route to collect the packs. From the ridge crest descend east five metres then sidle south-east descending along the base of the cliffs for about 15 minutes. The cairned route then leads to the slabs and tarns of Shelf Camp. Tents are best placed on the slabs to reduce impact on the environment.

From Shelf Camp the route traverses the rough slopes east to the jagged ridge crest that leads towards Mt Lot. It is easiest if the set of terraces which descends gently are followed thus avoiding the huge boulders which crown the ridge. Sidle the steep northern faces of a large knoll on the ridge to a saddle. Walk east over a another knoll to an awkward descent. Sidle the rest of the ridge on the north side until a fine view of Lots Wife is obtained.

Ahead lies The Notch (map ref 542444).

Do not try to sidle into it but rather climb up above and descend the ridge into this narrow saddle. There are several cairned tracks in this area.

The remainder of the ridge leading to Mt Lot is the hardest, most dangerous part of the circuit and some parties may need to use a rope for lifting people and packs. From the slot there are two routes. The most awkward is to climb directly east for five metres to the ridge above. The other route is to descend the gully on the south side for about 60 metres until an exit to the left (east) is possible to the scrubby slopes. Climb directly up to the ridge crest to join the direct route out of the slot.

The ridge is now followed east. The route weaves between huge blocks along the ridge. It is very exposed and most parties need to haul packs in several places. Eventually the summit of Mt Lot is gained. This peak has fine views of the surrounding area. From the Shelf Camp to the summit of Mt Lot will take two to three hours to walk.

Below, to the south-east is Lake Picone and there are two routes that descend to it. If the party is short of time, descend south down Lightning Ridge to a small knoll, then descend south-east to the open ridge between Lake Picone and Judds Charm. Follow the ridge east to find campsites near the outlet creeks of both lakes. This will take one to 1½ hours from the summit of Mt Lot.

The other route is slower but allows the party to climb Lot's Wife as a sidetrip. From the summit of Mt Lot descend the eastern ridge to the first saddle. Pass the rocky tower ahead by descending on the south side of the ridge then traverse the slopes under the cliffs of the knoll to regain the ridge crest. Descend easily east to the main saddle between Mt Lot and Lot's Wife.

If climbing Lot's Wife, leave the packs here and follow the obvious ridge east and climb the rocky tower using the second gully on the north side. The return sidetrip will add 1½ to two hours extra to the day's walk. After collecting the packs descend south through light forest to clear buttongrass leads. Follow the grassy leads south to the outlet of Lake Picone (about two to 2½ hours from the summit of Mt Lot). Lake Picone has reasonable tent sites near the outlet creek and fair shelter.

Alternative Campsites

Shelf Camp This has rough exposed tent sites and is not recommended in poor weather. It is two to 2½ hours' walk from High Camp.

Judds Charm This is the next lake south of Lake Picone and has a few reasonable tent sites. It is a 15-minute walk further on from Lake Picone.

Stage 3: Lake Picone to Anne River Crossing

(11 km, 4½-6 hours)
From the outlet creek of Lake Picone climb south to the ridge. Follow the crest of this ridge south-east to cross the outlet creek of Judds Charm. Climb west up the open ridge overlooking Judds Charm to the open plateau. Walk south for two km over this undulating plateau passing two small lakes to the south-east side of Mt Sarah Jane. Leave the packs and scramble easily to the summit of Mt Sarah Jane. This will take 40 to 60 minutes return.

Collect the packs then walk south-west to the edge of the plateau. Follow the plateau edge south-east for 500 metres to where the cairned track descends south-west. Descend following the rough track to the open buttongrass plains near the Anne River.

The track follows the river bank south-west to meet a major track. This is the Lake Judd Track. Turn left onto the Lake Judd Track and follow it south-west over the buttongrass plains then west through light forest to the cable crossing over the Anne River (map ref 498377). Good sheltered campsites are on the east bank of the river.

If you plan to use the minibus you should camp here. If you have enough time an easy sidetrip to Schnells Ridge is worthwhile. Climb the open slopes east of the campsite to the top of the ridge. In fine weather the views are excellent. This will take two to three hours return.

If you are using private transport then an extra 30 to 40 minutes walk leads to the road at Red Tape Creek.

Stage 4: Anne River Crossing to Red Tape Creek

(2 km, 30-40 minutes)
Cross the river by wading or using the cables. Follow the track west into a low saddle where it swings south-west and gradually descends to the end of the walk at Red Tape Creek. This is nine km south of the start of the walk at Condominium Creek. The minibus passes here at about 12.35 pm on its way back to Hobart.

SOUTH-WEST BEACHES & PLAINS

This excellent long walk traverses the magnificent south coast and river plains of the South West National Park in Tasmania. The track is easy to follow and crosses varied country, ranging from sandy ocean beaches and open buttongrass plains to high rugged ridges and rainforests.

The route described is the combination of the South Coast and Port Davey tracks. These two tracks form a very popular walk in the South West National Park and this walk is easier and less demanding than other long bushwalks in this area. The walk passes through one of the most magnificent wilderness areas in Australia and is recommended to all bushwalkers.

Features

The southern coast of Tasmania is a series of sandy beaches and sheltered bays tucked between high rugged headlands. To the east these headlands are composed of fluted red dolerite rock which is exposed as impressive vertical cliffs on South Cape and South East Cape. Further west the rock changes to white quartzite which is also exposed in impressive cliffs on the Ironbound Range.

The headlands jut out into the Southern Ocean and have to be climbed over as they are impassable at sea level. These headlands have formed because the sea has risen since the last ice age, drowning the coastal plains. The bays of Cox Bight and Surprise Bay are excellent examples of drowned plains. All along the coast a thick band of dense coastal scrub lines the beaches. Behind this scrub band are patches of open buttongrass plains and thick rainforests. From the high ridges there are good views of the inland ranges.

The Port Davey Track crosses the narrow opening of the large drowned river plain called Bathurst Harbour then continues north along river valleys. These valleys are usually wide open buttongrass plains with thickets of scrub and forest along the watercourses. The track passes through the natural break between the White Monolith and Western Arthur Ranges to the flat inland plains. From the track there are good views of the rugged white quartzite ranges which dominate the inland area.

Most of the creeks and rivers crossed have tannic-stained waters caused by the acidic grasses and plants that grow in the area. This water looks strange but is fine for drinking. There is some native wildlife around the coast and on the inland plains although, as the larger animals are nocturnal they are rarely seen.

Seabirds are common along the coastline, and some parrots and other ground birds live on the plains. Many other birds live in the scrub and forests and are occasionally seen by the casual observer.

Orange-bellied Parrot

winds are commonly encountered on this crossing.

The remainder of the walk has no problems caused by the weather, apart from floods. The streams and rivers do rise quickly after heavy rain, but they also fall rapidly so wait for the level to drop if a stream is flooded.

There are two very deep crossings at Bathurst Narrows and New River Lagoon. These are easily made by rowboat unless there is a strong tide. Most of these problems only occur occasionally during the summer and most parties will encounter few difficulties.

Days Required

The detailed 12 to 14-day itinerary uses the Invicta Transport minibus service as it is not a circuit walk. The two tracks can be walked in nine days by fit parties, but this does not allow time to wait out poor weather conditions and flooded rivers.

A food supply can be sent in advance by light aeroplane to Melaleuca or Cox Bight and many parties take advantage of this and plan a leisurely walk of 15 to 18 days. There are many sidetrips to walk and interesting features to explore and any extra days allowed for are easily filled if the weather permits.

Seasons

As with all bushwalks in the South West National Park, summer is the best season for this walk. The weather is often fine along the

Standard

This walk is graded medium if you follow the suggested itinerary. As there are many alternative campsites the standard can be varied to suit the party. The tracks are easily followed as they are well trodden and have occasional markers to show the route. Since the declaration of the World Heritage Area funds have been used for a lot of track maintenance work and this has improved conditions for walkers. Most of the very deep mud has been either covered with boardwalks or the track has been re-routed to a new alignment. There is a high-level crossing of the Ironbound Range and sleet and strong coast and occasionally warm enough for swimming in the cold ocean waters. Also, many of the storms pass over to batter the high ranges while down on the beaches it is overcast but still pleasant. The high-level crossing of the Ironbound Range receives the full brunt of the fickle weather and sometimes it is necessary to wait a day or two for better conditions before attempting the crossing.

In other seasons it is still possible to walk this track without the need for special equipment. Stream levels, however, often remain very high and any party attempting an autumn, winter or spring visit should be composed of very experienced bushwalkers capable of crossing flooded streams. The weather is often very wet and stormy and private transport arrangements to both ends of the walk will need to be made. During the summer the minibus operates to both ends of the track on a regular basis.

Equipment

As with any bushwalk of several weeks duration, all equipment must be good quality and in good order. After a week of walking it is the wrong time to discover that the tent leaks badly and your equipment is unsuitable. Tents must be of good quality, able to stand up to strong winds and, most importantly, keep out heavy rain. A groundsheet placed inside on top of the tent floor will make the floor more waterproof (all tent floors are easily damaged and can leak).

Sleeping bags should be adequate for temperatures just above freezing. Warm clothing and full wet-weather clothing (jacket and overpants) is essential. Leather boots are recommended but lightweight models will suffice. Some walkers wear runners, only to lose them in knee deep mud where they are almost impossible to find. While there is now less mud than there once was it will be many years before its all removed. A warm hat or balaclava and gloves are recommended. Water is readily available at all major campsites but a small water bottle may be carried for drinking water during the day.

Stoves are highly recommended as fire-wood is becoming more difficult to find and the Department of Park of Parks, Wildlife & Heritage is considering a total fire ban. The Ironbound Range has been declared a 'fuel stove only' area and no fires are allowed there for any use. An experienced walking party may wish to carry some light rope to assist in crossing flooded streams. Most groups are encouraged not to carry a rope but wait for water levels to drop as this is the easier, safer and lighter alternative.

Maps

The 1:100,000 topographic maps, *Old River*, *South East Cape* and *South West Cape*, cover this walk in good detail. The track is shown in its correct location on these maps except for the area near Junction Creek.

A newer topographic 1:100,000 map, *South Cape*, replaces the two Cape maps by printing both areas on a single sheet of paper. This map, however, does not show vegetation detail but shows the Land Tenure details (which authority is in charge of the land) instead. Most walkers prefer the vegetation information but it is a question of expense and personal preference.

All the recommended maps are published by TASMAP. They can be purchased at most bushwalking shops in south-eastern Australia.

More walks in the south-west are detailed in the guide book *South West Tasmania*, by John Chapman. This is available at most bushwalking shops in Australia.

Permits

No permits are currently required for walking in the South West National Park. Management is currently looking at levels of use and bushwalkers can expect permits and fees to be introduced. For the current situation contact the Department of Parks, Wildlife & Heritage, 134 Macquarie St, Hobart (☎ (002) 30 6285), GPO Box 44A, Hobart.

Access

This bushwalk follows the southern coast then the inland plains of the South West

National Park in Tasmania. It is not a circuit walk and requires the use of the bushwalkers bus service or private transport to complete. During the summer the bus operates on a regular timetable. In other seasons the bus can be booked by private arrangement.

The eastern access point is Cockle Creek, 126 km south of Hobart by road. From Hobart follow the Huon Highway south through Huonville then Geeveston to Dover and follow the signposted roads towards Hastings Caves. Drive through the tiny town of Hastings, and 1½ km past the town, turn left and follow the gravel roads south for 23 km through Lune River and Catamaran to the end of the road at Cockle Creek.

There are no facilities of any sort at Cockle Creek. If arriving late at night tents can be pitched in the sand dunes north of the bridge. From early December to mid-February there is a regular bushwalkers' bus service to Cockle Creek. This is operated by Invicta (☎ (008) 03 0505), 60 Collins St, Hobart.

The service currently operates on Monday, Wednesday and Friday leaving the bus depot at 60 Collins Street at 9.30 am. The arrival and departure time at Cockle Creek is 12.30 pm on the days mentioned above. The fare is $35. In other seasons the bus can be booked by private arrangement with Invicta.

The northern access point is Scotts Peak Dam on the southern edge of the Lake Pedder Dam. From Hobart follow the highway north-west to New Norfolk then follow the Strathgordon Road west through Maydena to Frodshams Pass, 121 km from Hobart. Turn left onto the gravel surfaced Scotts Peak Road and follow this for 35 km to the end of the road, two km past the Scotts Peak Dam wall. There are no facilities at the car park. If arriving late at night then the Huon River Camp (on a side road just west of the dam wall) has shelter, toilets and water. Management has proposed moving the track so that it starts from the Huon River Camp. Follow any signs they may erect.

From late November to early March, Invicta run a regular bus service four days a week to Scotts Peak Dam. This is the same service used for access to Mt Anne. It leaves 60 Collins St, Hobart at 9.30 am on Saturday, Sunday, Tuesday and Thursday and arrives and leaves Scotts Peak Dam at about 12.30 pm. The fare is $35.

Other access points in the heart of the south-west are the beach at Cox Bight or the airstrip at Melaleuca (separated by a couple of hours walk). Both are reached by light aeroplane and are half way along the suggested walk. Tiny commercial airplanes land here irregularly throughout the summer period. It is necessary to book for all flights and prices vary considerably depending on the numbers in the party and the availability of aircraft.

Two companies provide this service. Par-Avion (☎ (002) 48 5390), PO Box 334, Rosny Park, 7018 and TASAIR (☎ (002) 48 5088), GPO Box 451E, Hobart, 7001. Both of these companies can also fly supplies of food into Melaleuca or Cox Bight and will quote a price per kg. All parcels must be securely packed (both for transporting and to keep out animals) and need to be delivered to the airline several weeks before the expected collection date. All parcels should be clearly labelled with the leader's name and expected date of collection.

Stage 1: Cockle Creek to South Cape Rivulet

(12 km, 3-4½ hours)

The walk starts at the bridge over Cockle Creek. Cross the bridge and follow the vehicle track on the southern bank upstream for 100 metres to a closed gate. Pass through the gate into a clearing and follow the foot track to the information shelter. After filling out the log book follow the track south-west over a low rise through light forest for 1½ km to where the trees abruptly end. Here the track swings left and follows the southern edge of Blowhole valley for five km to Jeephead Camp.

Continue to follow the track south-west for one km to South Cape Bay, turn right (west) and follow the cliff tops, then descend to the sand. Follow the sandy beach west for one km to Lion Rock and just past this is a rocky wall forming an obstacle. If the tide is

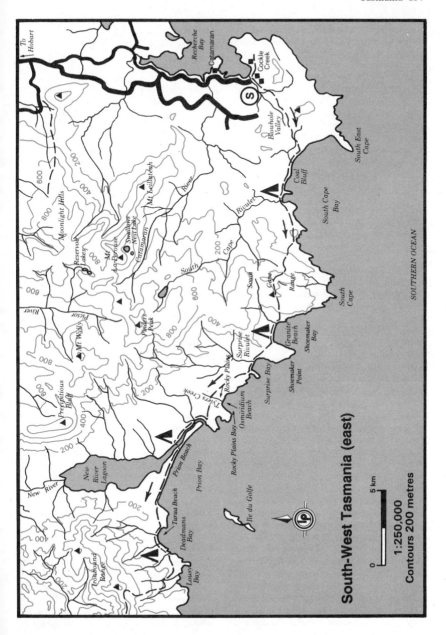

South-West Tasmania (east)

1:250,000
Contours 200 metres

0 ━━━━ 5 km

To Hobart

Recherche Bay
Catamaran
Cockle Creek
(S)
Blowhole Valley
South East Cape
SOUTHERN OCEAN
Coal Bluff
South Cape Bay
Moonlight Hills
Mt Bell
Mt Leillateah
River
Rivulet
Reservoir Lakes
Swallows Nest Lake
Catamaran
Mt La Perouse
South Cape
South Cape Range
South Cape
Pindars Peak
River
Pictor
Mt Wedd
Granite Beach
Shoemaker Beach
Shoemaker Point
Shoemaker Bay
Surprise Rivulet
Precipitous Bluff
Rocky Plains
Surprise Bay
Tylers Creek
Osmiridium Beach
Rocky Plains Bay
New River
New River Lagoon
Prion Beach
Prion Bay
Ile du Golfe
Turua Beach
Deadmans Bay
Ironbound Range
Louisa Bay

low climb over a low rocky saddle and scramble along the rocks under the wall to the next beach. If the tide is high use the signposted cut track which climbs inland high above the rocky wall over the top of Coal Bluff (where there are good views).

Past the rocky wall a rough track follows the rocky shore under Coal Bluff for one km to a sandy beach to meet the diversion route. Walk west along the sand, climb over the small headland and along the next beach to the large stream called South Cape Rivulet. There are good campsites on the east bank of the lagoon.

Alternative Campsites
Jeephead Camp Good shelter and water are found at the end of the old vehicle track, one km north of South Cape Bay.

South Cape Headland Good shelter is available on the headland one km east of South Cape Rivulet. Water is taken from the Rivulet, a 10-minute walk to the west.

Stage 2: South Cape Rivulet to Granite Beach
(10 km, 5-7 hours)
Cross South Cape Rivulet to the west bank. This crossing can be difficult at high tide or at flood levels. A signpost indicates the start of the track which heads west into the rainforest. About half an hour from the rivulet there is a good view of the coast from three metres above the track. Continue on through the forest for another 40 to 50 minutes over some hills. The track then descends to cross the open buttongrass plain of Blackhole Creek. It then climbs for 1½ km in forest to a dry ridge which has a reasonable campsite. Past the ridge descend for 15 minutes to a small creek where water is usually found.

The track now swings north and climbs onto the forested top of the South Cape Range. This part of the track is usually very muddy and it is a relief when the track swings west to the open Flat Rock Plain. This has tremendous views of the coast to the west. Cross the plain and descend steeply west

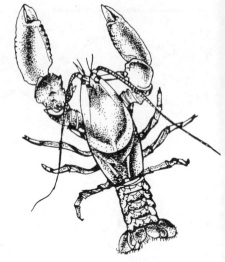

Yabby

following the muddy track through the forest to enter Granite Beach at its east end beside the waterfall. There are good camping areas beside the track, 200 metres east of the waterfall.

Alternative Campsites
Blackhole Plain Several sites are available with good shelter on both sides of the plain, but there's no reliable water supply here.

Trackcutters Camp This camp is on the dry ridge, 3½ hours from the rivulet. The water source is a 15-minute walk west along the track.

Stage 3: Granite Beach to Prion Boat Crossing
(12 km, 4-6 hours)
From the waterfall at the east end of Granite Beach traverse the rounded stones, then the sand of the beach, to its west end. This will take 30 to 45 minutes. The track leaves the beach and climbs north-west over the ridge of Shoemaker Point. As it descends on the west side there is a good view of Surprise

Bay and the coast. Continue to descend, passing some campsites to enter Surprise Bay at the east end of the beach. This is about one to 1½ hours from the campsite at Granite Beach.

Cross Surprise Rivulet which can be difficult at high tides or if the stream is in flood. Walk along the sand to the west end of the beach. The track leaves the coast here and passes through light forest for two km to the open Rocky Plains. The track, marked by stakes, crosses these plains north-west with good views of the coast and Precipitous Bluff.

Osmiridium Beach is off the track and worthwhile visiting. Just before Tylers Creek leave the South Coast Track and walk south for 15 minutes along the east bank of the stream to the campsite in the forest. This is an excellent site for lunch. The beach and bay are interesting and worth exploring. Return to the main track by the same route.

The South Coast Track continues west into light forest to the top of the dunes overlooking Prion Beach. Follow the crest of the dunes north-west then descend to the sand at Milford Creek. Crossing this creek may involve some deep wading depending on tide and flood levels.

On the west bank the track starts again and climbs steeply onto the top of the lightly timbered sand dunes. The track follows the crest west through ti-tree for one km then descends to the sandy lagoon shore. This is followed north-west for 10 minutes to the row boats. There is a good camping area in the scrub behind the boats. Water from the lagoon is usually brackish and fresh water can be collected from a creek 10 minutes' walk north of the camping area.

Alternative Campsites
Osmiridium Beach You can camp beside Tylers Creek in the sand dunes behind the beach. Water is taken from Tylers Creek.

Eastern Prion Good campsites are found on top of the ridge where the track enters the east end of the lagoon. Water is obtainable from unreliable soaks on the lagoon shore.

Stage 4: Prion Boat Crossing to Deadmans Bay
(9 km, 2½-3½ hours)
Cross New River Lagoon using the rowboats. Please ensure that at least one good boat is left upside down on each shore, tied up close to the scrub where it is well out of the reach of tides and floods. Most parties will take about one hour to complete the crossing as it is necessary to cross three times. As this day's walk is short, some time may be spent exploring the sand bar or rowing around the lagoon before leaving for Deadmans Bay.

Walk south across the sand to the ocean beach. Turn right and walk west for five km along Prion Beach to its west end. This takes 45 to 60 minutes and has good views of the surrounding mountains and ridges. The marked track begins at the rocky creek gully at the end of the sand. Follow the track west through forest for two km to Turua Beach.

Walk west along the sand around the small rocky headland to the second sandy beach. The track heads inland just before the rocks at the western end of the beach. Follow the forest then buttongrass to the small rocky cove known as Little Deadmans Bay. A poor three-sided shelter hut is located beside the track east of the bay. It is anticipated that this hut will be eventually removed. Follow the track down to the stony shore and scramble along this for 100 metres to the large creek and good campsite.

Alternative Campsites
Western Prion Camp on the grassy flats at the western end of the sand. It is exposed to the southerly storms. Fetch water from the gully where the track leaves the beach.

Turua Beach A good camping area is located in the scrub belt on the east side of Deadmans Creek in the western part of the bay.

Stage 5: Deadmans Bay to Louisa River
(12 km, 6-9 hours)
From the campsite beside the large creek in Little Deadmans Bay the track heads inland.

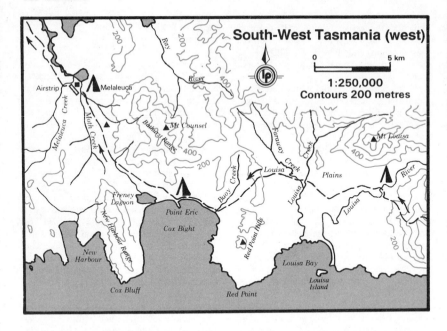

South-West Tasmania (west)

0   5 km

1:250,000
Contours 200 metres

Airstrip
Melaleuca
Melaleuca Creek
Moth Creek
Bathurst Range
Mt Counsel
Ray
River
400
200
Faraway Creek
Louisa Creek
Louisa Creek
Plains
Mt Louisa
400
River
Freney Lagoon
New Harbour Range
Point Eric
Cox Bight
Buoy Creek
Red Point Hills
Louisa
200
New Harbour
Louisa Bay
Louisa Island
Cox Bluff
Red Point

It crosses a small plain and climbs west on to a large spur where there is a view of Lousy Bay. The track continues climbing in very wet and muddy rainforest for four km to the High Campsite on top of the range. Past the camping area the track leaves the trees and becomes very exposed as it follows the crest of the Ironbound Range west for three km. The track has been extensively repaired in recent years and large sections of boardwalks make for easy walking.

In fine weather, the views are excellent but often wind-driven rain, sleet and sometimes snow make the crossing miserable. The descent is down a steep stony spur for three km to the Louisa River. The original track continued straight across the river and the river crossing was sometimes very dangerous. The present track turns right and follows the river north 400 metres to a safer crossing in the forest.

There are campsites on both sides of this crossing but it is best to cross before camping if possible. This river is very prone to flash floods and the crossing is dangerous at high-water levels. At high flood levels the camping areas can be inundated and it may then be necessary to camp on the higher buttongrass plains to wait for the water level to drop.

Alternative Campsites
Ironbounds High Camp There is a small rough camp in the trees beside the creek on top of the range. Stoves are essential as the range is a 'fuel stove only' area. You get superb views in fine weather but the area is exposed to storms.

Stage 6: Louisa River to Cox Bight
(18 km, 5-7 hours)
From the Louisa River crossing follow the excellent new track westwards across the buttongrass plains for six km to Louisa Creek. Cross on logs to an excellent campsite on the western bank. Continue to follow the

Top: Blizzard conditions, Bogong High Plains
Left: Bushwalkers, Major Mitchell Plateau
Right: Mt Fainter, Bogong High Plains (GvdK)

Top: Bridgewater Bay, Great South West Walk
Bottom: Glenelg River, Great South West Walk

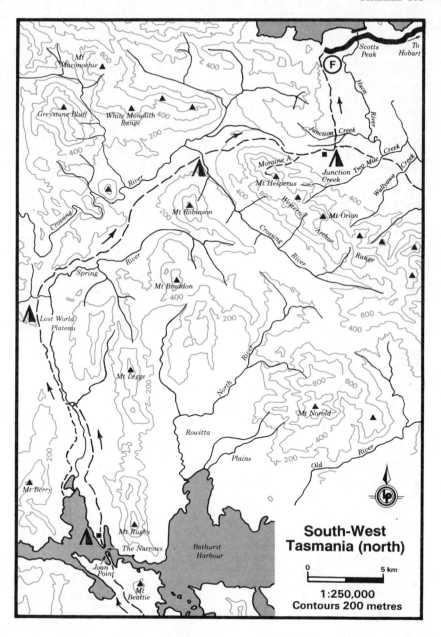

South-West Tasmania (north)

0 5 km

1:250,000
Contours 200 metres

track west over open terrain for seven km over the Red Point Hills and descend to Cox Bight. The track enters the beach at the camping area just east of Buoy Creek.

Follow the sandy beach west for three km past a rocky bluff to Point Eric. There is a sheltered camping area here and water is available from Goring Creek, 300 metres to the east.

Alternative Campsites
Louisa Creek There is an excellent sheltered campsite on the western bank beside the log crossing.

Faraway Creek There's a poor campsite and it is a 10-minute walk west from Louisa Creek.

Buoy Creek A reasonable campsite is found on the east bank of the creek.

Stage 7: Cox Bight to Melaleuca
(13 km, 3-4 hours)
Follow the track west through the forest behind Point Eric to the western beach of Cox Bight. Follow the sand to the outlet creek from Freney Lagoon where there are several good campsites. Continue west to the stones at the end of the beach where the signposted track heads inland. This follows the eastern edge of the New Harbour Range north then across the buttongrass plains for 10 km towards Melaleuca. This is a new track which is not yet marked on the *Old River* map.

Approaching Melaleuca, a log bridge crosses Moth Creek and the track leads into the mine workings. Follow the signposts which lead north to the airstrip. Halfway down the airstrip a signposted track on the right leads to the Charles King Memorial Hut. This hut and its neighbour are open for walkers to use. All other buildings in the area are private property. The mine and its workings belong to the only inhabitants of the south-west who have been very helpful to bushwalkers (they have provided the two huts). Walkers are asked not to touch the equipment or the mine workings.

Louisa Bay from the Ironbounds, South-West Tasmania

For groups who wish to use tents there are several good areas in the forest near the two walkers' huts. Light airplanes (four and six-seaters) land on the airstrip at irregular intervals throughout the summer. A flight out can be arranged with the pilots. If a food supply was organised for delivery before beginning the walk it can be collected from the shelter hut beside the airstrip.

The two walkers' huts are the only proper huts on the walk and most bushwalkers use the spare half day as an opportunity to rest, reorganise and repair equipment before continuing. In good weather fit parties can fill a day's walk by climbing Mt Counsel on the walk from Cox Bight. This is the high peak, five km north of Cox Bight, and approached by climbing the steep spur two km south of Half Woody Hill.

Creek on the South Coast Track, South-West Tasmania

Stage 8: Melaleuca to Bathurst Narrows
(14 km, 4-5½ hours)

From the walkers' huts follow the track back to the airstrip. Turn right and walk north-west along the airstrip to the signposted walking track. The track heads west for 15 minutes past old mine workings to cross Melaleuca Creek on a good bridge. There are several old tracks in this area.

The walking track has tape markers and past the bridge it swings north-west across open buttongrass plains. The plains are followed for six km to a short climb into a low saddle. The track continues north-west then north for three km sidling the lower slopes of Mt Beattie before following the long narrow promontory of Joan Point for two km to its northern end.

At the end of Joan Point there is a rowboat to cross The Narrows. This is a deep channel and care is required if there are rough seas or strong tidal currents. The crossing must be made three times so as to leave one boat on each side for the next party. The boats must be pulled clear of the water and left upside down securely tied to the trees. The northern boat is kept at the small sandy cove on the eastern side of Farrell Point. The crossing will take at least one hour to complete.

After securing the boats, follow the track north for five minutes and turn left on the signposted side track to the three-sided shelter hut. This is in the trees near the shore and an unreliable spring is found 30 metres south of the hut. It is expected that this will be removed in the near future. In dry weather it may be necessary to walk north for a further 4½ km (about 1½ hours) to the next creek where there is a campsite with water.

Alternative Campsites
Rough tent sites can be found in many places on the open plains beside the track.

Stage 9: Bathurst Narrows to Lost World Plateau
(19 km, 6-8 hours)

From the shelter hut turn left onto the main track and follow it north for four km past Lindsay Hill. Here you cross a small valley. This is a fair campsite with reasonably reliable water. The track climbs north-west onto the next ridge and provides excellent views of Manwoneer Inlet to the west. It continues north for a further three km along the faint ridge-line to a swampy plain beside a large creek.

Continue to follow the track north along the west side of Border Hill for two km and descend to the flat plain. The track swings west into the forest beside Spring River to the camping area. Follow the river upstream for 60 metres to the log bridge. Cross this with care to the west bank (this is dangerous in floods when the log is under water and a crossing in such conditions is not recommended). The track follows the bank upstream for 50 metres then climbs up to meet the benched track which is part of the original Port Davey Track cut in 1898.

The well-defined track is followed north for four km and provides easy flat walking. The track then climbs up onto the Lost World Plateau and after a further three km of undulating terrain some creeks are crossed. Some reasonable campsites exist beside the two largest creeks. All camping areas on this plateau have little shelter.

Alternative Campsites

There are plenty of fair tent sites beside all of the streams that are crossed. The larger camping areas are at the plain south of Border Hill and at Spring River.

Stage 10: Lost World Plateau to Crossing River

(19 km, 5½-7½ hours)
From the Lost World Plateau the track heads north and climbs gradually up onto the sharp ridge dividing the Spring and Crossing river valleys. The benched track then swings north-east and sidles the southern slopes of this ridge for five km until it meets the plains again. The well defined track crosses these plains and climbs gently up an indistinct ridge for four km then swings north to the plains beside the Crossing River. These plains are followed north-east for seven km past Mt Robinson to the Crossing River.

Good campsites are found on both banks

of this river and it is advisable to cross to the east bank in case the river floods overnight.

Alternative Campsites

Tent sites exist beside all of the streams along this day's walk and all sites are reasonable.

Stage 11: Crossing River to Junction Creek

(11 km, 3-4 hours)
From Crossing River the well-used track is easily followed east to pass through the broad saddle north of the Western Arthurs. As you descend from the saddle, the Moraine A track is on the right. In fine weather it is worthwhile using this track for an excellent sidetrip.

The track climbs steeply south-west up a ridge onto the top of the Western Arthurs and it will take three to five hours' return to Mt Hesperus. From the Moraine A track junction follow the eastern track for a further two km along the plains to the old hut site near Junction Creek. Continue to follow the track east for 500 metres to the signposted track junction.

If you have private transport at Scotts Peak then a further two to three hours walk north leads to the car park at the end of the track. Most walkers use the bushwalkers' bus service which departs at 12.30 pm, four days a week and as there are no pleasant camping places near the road it is better to camp the last night at Junction Creek. Campsites are located at the old hut site and also beside Junction Creek near the track junction.

Stage 12: Junction Creek to Scotts Peak

(7 km, 2-3 hours)
Follow the signs to the cable crossing over Junction Creek. From this crossing the well-defined track is easily followed north for six km to the end of the track at Red Knoll Quarry. Meet the bus near the two small sheds at the end of the track. The car park is 50 metres further along the road.

FREYCINET PENINSULA CIRCUIT

The Freycinet Peninsula is a mountainous promontory on the east coast of Tasmania.

The entire promontory is a national park and is a beautiful area. It is a popular area for bushwalking as the weather is generally better than that found on the western side of Tasmania. The park has a well-maintained track system.

Features
This rugged peninsula is composed of red granite which is exposed as spectacular headlands and as extensive slabby areas on the peaks. The extensive granite produces thin soils that support mainly coastal heathlands. Low shrubs, ti-tree, banksias, wattles and blackboys are the plants that predominate. In some gullies small pockets of forest survive in the deeper soils.

Over 100 species of orchids thrive here and a visit in spring is highly recommended for the wildflower displays. Wombats, wallabies and possums are the most common animals in the area. Weathering of the granite has left deep bays and beautiful sandy beaches. Life along the beaches is interesting – crabs, prawns, seabirds and fairy penguins are often seen. The peninsula was reserved as a national park in 1916 and is an excellent example of a coastal reserve.

Standard
This circuit walk follows maintained walking tracks which are easy to follow and well-marked with signposts at each major track junction. The walk is easy to medium in standard.

Days Required
The circuit takes two days to complete and can be made into an easy three-day walk. There is little scope for extending this walk unless you leave the tracks. The sidetrips to Bryans Beach and Mt Amos are worthwhile if you have the time.

Seasons
Any season of the year is suitable for a visit to this coastal park. Summer is the most popular time as the weather is generally warm and pleasant then. Water is generally scarce during the summer and all

bushwalkers must be prepared to carry enough for the overnight stop. Autumn temperatures are generally mild and pleasant for walking. Winter is cold but still very pleasant and the occasional winter storm provides variety and interest. Spring is the flower season and a good time to visit this park.

Equipment
No special bushwalking equipment is required to walk around this peninsula. There is a good stone hut at Cooks Beach Hut, but carry a tent as the hut may already be occupied. Runners or light boots are suitable as footwear.

Carry a stove as firewood is not always easy to find and because this peninsula is in a very high-fire-risk area. During a Total Fire Ban all open fires and stoves are totally forbidden. In hot weather food that can be eaten cold should be carried.

Waterproof jacket and pants should always be carried as it can become cold, windy and wet at times. Water containers to hold four litres per person should be carried in case the water tank at Cooks Beach Hut is empty.

Maps
The 1:50,000 special topographic map, *Freycinet National Park*, is the map to use. It is produced especially for bushwalkers and shows all the tracks and campsites which may be used within the park. On the reverse side is a set of useful notes about the park and the tracks. This map is published by TASMAP. The only other map is the 1:100,000 topographic map, *Freycinet*, which is also produced by TASMAP in Hobart. This map has less detail and should only be used if the other one is out of print.

Permits
No permits are required for bushwalking in this park but all walkers are asked to register details about their party in the book at the front of the rangers' office. The office is just inside the park near the camping ground behind Richardsons Beach. The ranger can offer advice on the current track conditions,

availability of water and current fire regulations. The ranger at Coles Bay (☎ (002) 57 0107) can be contacted in advance for this and for other information if required.

Access

The Freycinet Peninsula is on the east coast of Tasmania, 120 km north-east of Hobart. From Hobart follow the Tasman Highway east for 26 km to Sorell. This highway passes the airports. At Sorell turn left (the major road to the right leads to Port Arthur) and follow the Tasman Highway north for 113 km through Buckland and Orford to Swansea.

Continue to follow the highway north for 32 km then turn right and follow the road south for 31 km to the small town of Coles Bay. One km past the town the road enters the national park. The rangers' station is near the Richardson Beach camping area.

From Launceston the Tasman Highway can be followed east through Scottsdale and St Helens then south to Bicheno, 295 km from Launceston. The shorter but less scenic route from Launceston is to follow the Midland Highway south to Conara Junction then turn left and follow Main Road east to St Marys. Then turn to the south and follow the Tasman Highway to Bicheno, 219 km from Launceston. From Bicheno follow the Tasman Highway south-west for 11 km, turn left and follow the road south for 31 km to Coles Bay.

Access by public transport is good with a variety of small bus lines which operate along the east coast. From Hobart, buses leave the Redline Coach Terminal (☎ (002) 31 3233), 199 Collins St, Hobart, at 12.30 pm Monday to Thursday and at 2.15 pm on Friday (there are no weekend services). The bus should be left at Bicheno and the fare is $24.00 each way. A service also operates from Launceston to Bicheno departing from 112 George St (☎ (003) 31 3233) at 2 pm Monday to Thursday and 3.45 pm on Friday. Hobart Coaches (☎ (002) 34 4077) also operate services from their terminal at 60 Collins St, Hobart. Their afternoon buses run at similar times to Redlines for only $18 and

they also have a service leaving Hobart at 8.30 am on Monday, Wednesday, Thursday, Friday and Sunday.

All the major services will take you to Bicheno which is located north of Coles Bay. Travel by the afternoon buses will require you to stay in Bicheno which has a youth hostel, two caravan parks and numerous up-market villas. A local bus is used from Bicheno to Coles Bay and the fare is $5 each way. This service leaves Bicheno in the early morning at 7 am, and early afternoon at 2.45 pm, from Monday to Friday. A Saturday morning service leaves at 9 am. The timetable can vary as this is the local school bus service. It is best to inquire at the shops in Bicheno about the time of the next service to Coles Bay.

Stage 1: Coles Bay to Cooks Beach
(13 km, 3 to 4½ hours)

If the party has private transport follow the road south-east past the rangers' station for two km to a road junction. Continue straight ahead and follow the road south a further two km to the Peninsula/Wineglass Bay Track car park at Parsons Cove. If the party has no private transport then it is an extra one-hour walk to the car park. Walk south from the rangers' station through the camping area out onto Richardsons Beach. Turn left and follow the beach south-east for one km to the end of the sand. Climb up to meet the road and follow it south for 2½ km to the Peninsula/Wineglass Bay Track car park.

From the car park follow the Wineglass Bay Track south for 150 metres then turn right onto The Hazards Beach Track. This track heads west through the forest for one km to a good view point high on a ridge. It then swings south-west and sidles the western slopes of Mt Mayson for two km through thickets of ti-tree and sheoaks to Fleurieu Point.

The track then turns south-east and soon reaches Lemana Lookout. This has superb views of the southern half of the peninsula and the islands. The track then descends to the northern end of The Hazards Beach. Follow the beach south for three km to

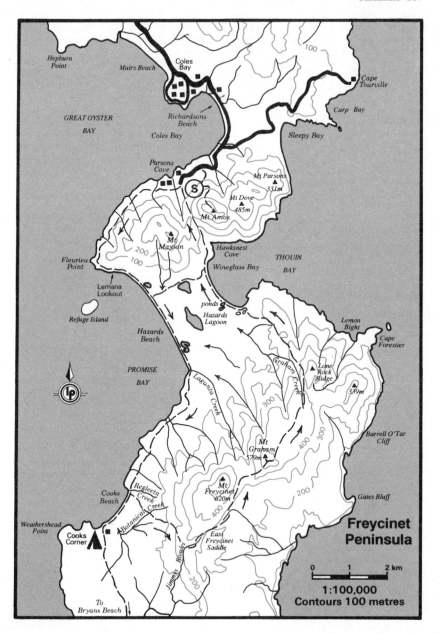

Hepburn
Point

Muirs Beach

Coles
Bay

Cape
Tourville

GREAT OYSTER
BAY

Richardsons
Beach

Coles Bay

Carp Bay

Sleepy Bay

Parsons
Cove

S

Mt Parsons
331m

Mt Dove
485m

Mt Amos

Hawksnest
Cove

THOUIN
BAY

Mt
Mayson

Wineglass Bay

Fleurieu
Point

Lemana
Lookout

ponds

Hazards
Lagoon

Lemon
Bight

Refuge Island

Cape
Forestier

Hazards
Beach

Graham Creek

Lone
Rock
Ridge

339m

PROMISE
BAY

300

Barrell O'Tar
Cliff

Laguna Creek

400

300

Mt
Graham
579m

Cooks
Beach

Regleeta Creek

200

Gates Bluff

Weathershead
Point

Cooks
Corner

Botanical Creek

Mt
Freycinet
620m

400

East
Freycinet
Saddle

Freycinet
Peninsula

Jimmys Rivulet

200

0   1   2 km

1:100,000
Contours 100 metres

To
Bryans Beach

Lagunta Creek which is at the southern end of the sand – you will pass many Aboriginal middens (kitchens) on the way. Lagunta Creek has permanent water and if the ranger has advised that the tank at the Cooks Beach Hut is low then water containers should be filled here. There are good campsites near this creek.

The track leaves the beach at this creek and heads south then south-east for four km through lightly timbered slopes to descend to the sand at the northern end of Cooks Beach. Follow the sandy shore south-west for one km passing a stand of trees virtually on the beach. Just past these trees the track heads inland for 250 metres to Cooks Beach Hut.

The hut is built of stone and is reasonably large. Collect water from the tank (sometimes empty in the warmer months of the year). There are also good campsites near the hut and close to the beach.

Sidetrip: Bryans Beach

If you have enough time, it is worth walking to Bryans Beach as a sidetrip from the campsite. This will take about two hours return. From the hut follow the walking track south for three km to the western end of Bryans Beach. Here you get great views of Schouten Island to the south. Return to the campsite by the same route.

Alternative Campsites

Lagunta Creek Good campsites are located near this permanent creek which is at the south end of The Hazards Beach.

Stage 2: Cooks Beach to Coles Bay

(18 km, 5-6½ hours)

From the hut follow the track north onto Cooks Beach, turn right and follow the shore north-east to the end of the sand at Regleeta Creek (as for the Stage 1 walk). At the track junction near the creek turn south-east and follow the track inland. This track climbs gradually for 1½ km to meet Botanical Creek where there is permanent water and a campsite. Past this creek the track climbs steeply for two km into East Freycinet Saddle.

It is worth leaving the packs here and detouring south for 500 metres to a higher knoll which has fine views to the south. Return to the track, collect the packs and walk northwards for two km to the major saddle between Mt Freycinet and Mt Graham. If you want to climb Mt Freycinet leave the packs at the saddle and scramble west up the steep slopes to the summit for fine panoramic views. Return to the saddle by the same route.

Collect the packs and follow the marked track north-east as it climbs steeply to Mt Graham. The summit is 50 metres north of the track and has fine views in all directions. From Mt Graham the track descends briefly east then heads north-east for 1½ km across a plateau to the headwaters of Graham Creek. The track swings north and follows the eastern bank of this creek downstream for 1½ km. It then leaves the creek and continues to descend for two km to the camping area at the southern end of beautiful Wineglass Bay.

Follow the curving sandy beach northwards for 1½ km to the track junction at the north end of this lovely bay. Follow the track north, climbing steeply up into the major saddle between Mt Amos and Mt Mayson. There is a lookout 100 metres south-west from this saddle which is well worth visiting for a last view of Wineglass Bay.

Continue to follow the track north for one km and descend to the car park from where the walk started. If the party has no transport it will be necessary to follow the road (then Richardsons Beach) back to Coles Bay – a further one-hour walk. If the party has sufficient time it is worthwhile climbing Mt Amos as a sidetrip from the road. The track to this peak begins one km east of the car park and takes one to two hours return. From the summit there are excellent views of Wineglass Bay.

Victoria

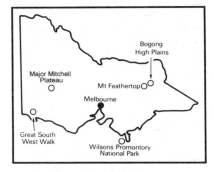

Victoria, in the south-east of Australia, is the most densely populated state in the country. A large proportion of Victoria is covered with rich farmlands but surprisingly, there are still extensive areas of bush in a natural state. Most of these are within the numerous national parks which protect a wide variety of landscapes and vegetation. They range from inland deserts, coastal strips, rainforests and alpine plateaus. All of the larger parks provide excellent bushwalking of all standards.

The largest and most important walking area is simply called The Victorian Alps. This extends from near Melbourne, north-east to the New South Wales border. This huge area is managed mainly by the Department of Conservation & Environment.

This department was formed from the amalgamation of the Forestry Commission and the National Parks & Wildlife departments. The foresters are mainly concerned with commercial timber production and the majority of the Alpine Area is managed for this purpose. An extensive network of fire trails have been constructed and the largest trees have been removed. A smaller area has been reserved in national parks but, fortunately, they include many of the more spectacular features found in the Alps. In

recent years the major parks have been connected together with thin corridor strips to form the basis of the Alpine National Park. This actually consists of several parks which will be discussed individually as they cover different types of landscape. Unfortunately the parks are not protected as well as they could be with four-wheel driving, grazing and deer hunting permitted in some areas.

The highest region of the alps is contained in the Bogong National Park. This area consists of a series of alpine meadows and plains above the tree line surrounded by deep, forested valleys. Bushwalking in this park is both pleasant and popular in summer, and there is great variation in the walks. The best walk is the circuit of the highest peaks and hills culminating in the ascent of Mt Bogong, the state's highest peak. The other classic bushwalk is to climb Mt Feathertop. This is a very steep peak separated from the plains by a deep valley and is normally visited as a separate bushwalk. Both alpine walks are described.

In the alpine area there are several other important parks for bushwalkers. The Wonnangatta-Moroka National Park is worthwhile visiting as it contains some very fine bushwalks. The area is more rugged than the Bogong National Park and requires more experience and fitness to climb its steep ridges. Several brief walking suggestions have been given for those who wish to explore further. The guide book, *Wonnongatta Moroka National Park,* by John Siseman, covers walks in this park.

On the south-western end of the Alps is the Baw Baw National Park. This is an elevated alpine plateau surrounded by thick, high forests. Bushwalking is mainly confined to the plateau which provides easy walking across grassy meadows beneath forests of snow gums.

A long-distance walking trail has been marked along the crest of the alps. This starts at Walhalla, 130 km east of Melbourne and extends for more than 400 km north-east to Canberra. There is a special guide book to this track *(Alpine Walking Track,* by John Siseman) which is essential if you intend walking it.

Another long-distance track, 'McMillans Track', passes through the southern region of the alps traversing a wide range of country. This 200-km track was first constructed in 1864 and 1865 from Woods Point to Omeo to provide access to the goldfields. It has been recut in recent years by volunteer bushwalkers. There are currently no guidebooks available which describe this track in full.

Wilsons Promontory, in the south of the state, is a large, high point of land which juts out into the stormy Bass Strait. The entire area is protected by the Wilsons Promontory National Park and is popular with a large range of visitors. It has beautiful sandy beaches and coves backed by thick forests and high granite peaks. There is a good set of well-maintained walking tracks providing easy, enjoyable overnight bushwalks.

Because of its popularity it has become necessary to impose a few restrictions relating to campsites and absolute numbers; it is best avoided during holidays. At other times there are less problems in obtaining a permit and a visit is highly recommended. The circuit walk visits both the east and west coasts and is undoubtedly the most interesting walk.

The western half of the state is covered with extensive rich farmlands. In the centre of this area is an isolated group of folded sandstone ranges known as The Grampians. They are not very high but are spectacular with extensive cliffs and rock faces that dominate the landscape. These ranges are very popular.

Most bushwalking is limited to one or two-day walks as an extensive road network covers the area. The most popular bushwalk is included in this guide and visits the Major Mitchell Plateau. It includes the highest peak in the ranges, Mt William, and passes through the greatest variety of vegetation. Navigation is reasonably easy and a visit is

particularly worthwhile in the wildflower season of spring.

In the south-west of the state there is a large area of low scrub tucked between the large, peaceful Glenelg River and the ocean beaches. The Discovery Bay and Lower Glenelg national parks protect large parts of this area and provide some very pleasant easy walking. While this park is generally not spectacular it does provide some peaceful areas without crowds.

A long-distance walking circuit of 240 km has been constructed and marked and takes 10 to 15 days to complete. This is known as the Great South West Walk and while the title may be a little over the top the track provides a pleasant easy extended walk worth seeking out. The track has been described in this guide in full as the only other information available is a useful but very brief guide.

In the north-west of the state there are a few national parks in semi-desert areas. The region near the Murray River is interesting with lakes, old river channels and stately river red gums. Hattah-Kulkyne National Park is the most popular and a good area for bushwalkers who are looking for a walk which is different to that in the more rugged areas. There are no hills and plenty of opportunities to see wildlife.

The walks included in this chapter are some of the state's best. However, they are not the only ones and there are many other enjoyable walks for bushwalkers throughout the state. There is also an abundance of information and guide books for the visitor.

Other Suggested Bushwalks
Alpine Area

The Alpine Track This is the 400-km track from Walhalla to the New South Wales border at Tom Groggin. It is a four-week, one-way walk and requires some planning regarding food supplies. A special guidebook exists.

Razor-Viking Circuit First you climb Howitt Spur then head north to Mt Speculation and over to the Razor and Viking. Descend south into the Wonnangatta Valley, climb west along the Zeka Spur to Mt Howitt and descend back to the start. A classic four-day medium to hard circuit, 50 km east of Mansfield.

Howqua Circuit Climb Eight Mile Spur to The Bluff, head east along the range to Mt Howitt then descend west and follow the Howqua River back to the start. A pleasant three to four-day medium circuit, 40 km east of Mansfield.

Lake Tarli Karng Follow the Wellington River upstream then climb Rigall Spur to the lake. Return via The Vale of Destruction and the river to the start. A very popular two-day medium bushwalk near Licola, north of Sale.

The Crinoline From Mt Tamboritha follow the ridge west over Long Hill then south over the Crinoline and down to Breakfast Creek. A medium two-day walk near Licola, north of Sale. It requires a short car shuffle.

Baw Baw Plateau Follow the track over Mt St Gwinear then head north to Mustering Flat. Return via the the Alpine Track to Mt St Gwinear and the car park. A very easy two-day walk in the snow plains of the Baw Baw National Park, 40 km north of Morwell.

Eastern Side

Croagingalong Beaches Follow the coast west from Mallacoota to Thurra River. An excellent medium five-day walk in the Croagingalong National Park in Gippsland. It requires a very long car shuffle.

Northern Wilsons Promontory From near Millers Landing follow the track west towards Barry Creek then turn left to follow walking tracks north-east to Chinaman Beach and Tin Mine Cove to camp. Next day along the track to Lighthouse Point, head south along coast to John Souey Cove then around the track to Five Mile Beach to camp. A day can easily be spent exploring this long beach. Follow the track west back to the start. A three to four-day walk in the northern section of the Wilsons Promontory National Park.

Western Area

Lerderderg Gorge From O'Brien Crossing follow the river south to the end of the gorge at Darley Ford. An enjoyable two to three-day walk, 50 km west of Melbourne. It requires a car shuffle.

Mt Difficult From Troopers Creek you climb east to Mt Difficult, north to Briggs Bluff, south-east along the ridge, then head across the Mackenzie River basin to Mt Difficult and back to the start. A popular two-day bushwalk in The Grampians north of Halls Gap.

Hattah Lakes From Lake Hattah follow the stream system north to Lake Mournpall. Walk east, then south along tracks and return via the chain of lakes east of Lake Hattah. An easy two-day circuit, 60 km south of Mildura.

Lorne Waterfalls From Allenvale walk along the well-marked trails to Phantoum Falls, The Canyon, Kalimna Falls and Swallows Cave to the coast. Return up the St George River to Allenvale. An easy two-day circuit with many possible variations, which is close to Lorne.

Mt Richmond This shorter walk, which uses part of the Great South West Walk, is suitable for those with less time. From Tarragul Camp follow the track north-west over Mt Richmond to Swan Lake to camp. Walk out to the beach and follow it southwards to camp at the Springs. Retrace your steps to Bridgewater Lakes and follow the track inland back to Tarragul. This is a two to three-day medium circuit, west of Portland.

BOGONG HIGH PLAINS CIRCUIT

The Bogong High Plains, the highest region in Victoria, consists of rolling meadows and hills which are surrounded by deep valleys and isolated mountains. Most of this area lies within the Bogong National Park and provides some of the most pleasant walking in the state. The park is well used with roads, tracks and snow-pole lines criss-crossing it.

Most of the higher peaks in Victoria are to be found within this park. The classic bushwalk is to circle around the plains, ascending many of the high peaks, and finish with an ascent of Mt Bogong, at 1986 metres, the highest mountain in Victoria. This extended walk is highly recommended for all experienced bushwalkers.

Features

The Bogong High Plains is an elevated plateau of broad ridges and plains surrounded by deep valleys. The peaks rise above these plains as rounded hills which are easily ascended. The gentle landscape is the result of the erosion of a much higher mountain range. Much of the area is open and covered only with low grasses and tussocks.

Beautiful snow gums grow in the valleys and within sheltered folds in the landscape. These tough trees are often twisted and gnarled with colourful bark; they also provide shelter for a variety of alpine shrubs. In the deeper valleys high forests of alpine ash grow. Underneath these tall, straight trees is a dense understorey of small trees and shrubs which make walking difficult.

In sharp contrast to the gentle plains is the huge solitary mass of Mt Bogong. This large mountain is separated from the plains by a deep valley. The name Bogong means 'big fella' and it is an apt description for Victoria's highest peak.

The area has been extensively used in the past by cattle owners and their huts are spread across the plains. During the summer cattle still graze on the High Plains but their numbers are now strictly controlled. The State Electricity Commission (SEC) has harnessed water from the plains for hydro-electric power and has left two dams and a sprawling network of aqueducts and tracks. A major ski resort 'Falls Creek' is located near the larger dam. The chosen route keeps away from these 'features' where possible.

Standard

The route is well marked and uses tracks which are easy to follow. Much of the walk is above or around the tree line and is exposed to the weather (sometimes severe) making it necessary to carry full wet weather equipment. Most of the walking is on gentle open terrain except for the steep ascent and descents around Mt Bogong. The standard can vary greatly depending on the itinerary chosen. The walk described is of a medium standard.

Days Required

The suggested itinerary is for a five-day bushwalk. As there are many suitable areas for camping the walk can be altered to suit the party. Six days would allow a more leisurely bushwalk. If required the walk can be abandoned by walking out to the alpine village of Falls Creek.

Seasons

Late spring, summer and early autumn are the suitable seasons of the year for this walk. The weather is usually mild but can occasionally become quite hot. Cold winds and snowfalls do occur at well-spaced intervals during the summer, but such poor weather rarely stays very long. In winter the entire area is normally covered in snow and this route then becomes an excellent ski-touring region for experienced skiers.

Equipment

In the warmer months equipment needs are fairly basic. A good tent and waterproof jacket and pants are essential. Runners/trainers are adequate as summer walking footwear. A shady hat and sunscreen are necessary for protection against the sun. Stoves should be carried and used as firewood is becoming difficult to find.

In winter this area experiences some very severe weather conditions and all parties must be well equipped for heavy snowfalls and strong winds. The huts cannot be relied upon as they may be full, may have been destroyed or you may be delayed and may not be able to reach the particular hut. Sturdy leather boots are essential in winter.

Maps

The Bogong High Plains are very well mapped in various scales. The best general purpose map to the area is the 1:50,000 'Bogong Alpine Area' which is an Outdoor Leisure Map published by the Division of Survey & Mapping. This is sold in specialist map shops and most bushwalking shops in south-east Australia. This map is very useful as it has been designed for bushwalkers. There have been some small changes to track locations which have not yet been included on the latest edition. This map is all that most bushwalkers will ever need.

For greater detail five maps are required. The 1:25,000 topographic maps, *Trappers Creek*, *Nelse*, *Fainter*, *Cope* and *Feathertop* are needed. These maps are produced by the Division of Survey & Mapping and are available at Map Sales, Information Centre Victoria, as well the map shops and some bushwalking shops. These maps are reasonably accurate in regard to the location of tracks and pole lines. There are some small errors in the location of some huts.

The Federal Government Agency, NATMAP, also produce a 1:100,000 topographic map, 'Bogong' which is a useful map to the overall area. It is not as detailed as the other maps, and it is sold in most map and bushwalking shops through south-east Australia.

A detailed guide book, *Bogong National Park* by John Siseman, covers the area and is worthwhile obtaining. It is available in most bushwalking shops and many bookshops in south-east Australia. This book is excellent, with many ideas for more walks in the area.

Permits

Permits are not required for dispersed camping within the Bogong National Park, which includes all the Bogong High Plains and Mt Bogong. Details about the party, your intended route and expected return date can be left in the log book kept at the police station (☎ (057) 57 2244), Park St, Mt Beauty.

Write details about your party in the log books at each hut as they are passed. There are two areas where camping is not permitted and they are the two alpine ski villages of Falls Creek and Mt Hotham. The popular walking tracks keep away from these two villages.

Access

The Bogong High Plains are 180 km north-east of Melbourne. The starting point for this walk is a tiny town called Bogong Village, 16 km south of Mt Beauty.

From Melbourne follow the Hume Highway north then north-east for 215 km to Glenrowan. Five km north of this town turn right at the signposted 'Snow Fields' road and follow this east for 40 km through the small towns of Oxley and Milawa to the Ovens Highway. Turn right and follow the Ovens Highway for six km into Myrtleford. Continue to follow the Ovens Highway for five km past Myrtleford to Ovens. Turn left at Ovens onto the Pretty Valley Rd leading towards Mt Beauty. Follow this road for 34 km to meet the Kiewa Valley Highway. Turn right and follow this highway for 27 km to Mt Beauty.

If you arrive late at night it is best to camp at either of the two caravan parks in the town as camping beside the road is not permitted. From Mt Beauty follow the road towards Falls Creek for 16 km to the turnoff to Bogong Village. Parking near this village is restricted and you need to get permission from the SEC. Parking is usually permitted at the very bottom of the village or at the start of the first day's walk above the main road. Petrol and some food can be purchased at the bottom of the village.

The northern approach is to follow the roads to Albury-Wodonga and then follow the Kiewa Valley Highway south to Mt Beauty.

The southern approach (from the Gippsland area) is to follow the Omeo Highway north from Bairnsdale to Omeo. Continue north for 42 km past the town of Omeo and turn left following the gravel road for 51 km across the Bogong High Plains to Bogong Village. This road is covered with snow during winter and is closed to all traffic until spring.

During the summer, access by public transport from Albury is reasonable. Albury is on the Hume Highway at the border between Victoria and NSW. A variety of bus and train services pass through this town daily. Bookings and inquiries are best made with any travel agent.

From Albury a bus runs to Mt Beauty in the afternoon, Monday to Friday. The return service from Mt Beauty to Albury leaves early in the morning. The timetable for this service varies over the summer months. The bus is operated by Pyles Coaches (☎ (057) 57 2024), Kiewa Valley Highway, Tawonga South, 3698.

From Mt Beauty to Bogong Village there is no regular bus service and a taxi or minibus can be hired from Pyles for the last 16 km. During the winter there are daily bus services from Mt Beauty to Falls Creek and these can be used for access to Bogong Village. There are also regular bus services from Melbourne to Falls Creek during the winter. These services vary according to demand and seats can be booked at most travel agents.

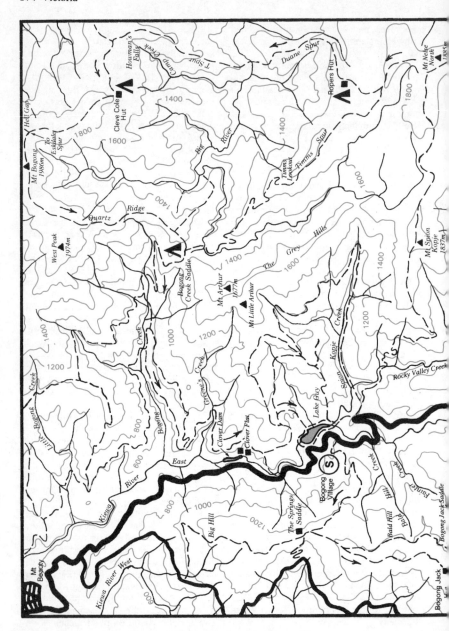

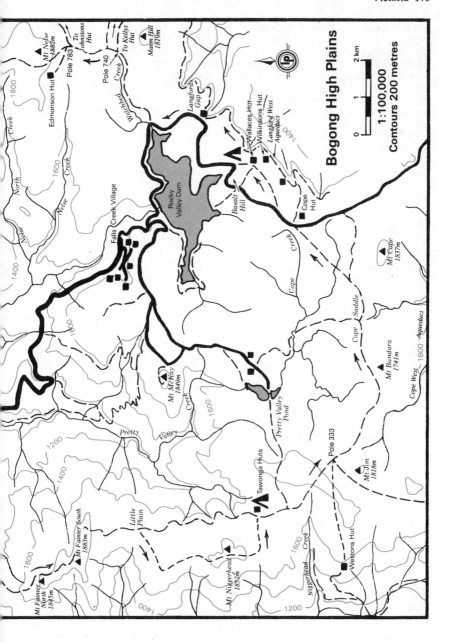

Bogong High Plains

1:100,000
Contours 200 metres

0 1 2 km

Stage 1: Bogong Village to Tawonga Huts

(20 km, 6-7½ hours)

Starting from the car park at the bottom of the village follow the road uphill through the town back to the Bogong Village turn-off on the main road. Turn left and follow the main road south for 300 metres. Turn right onto the Big Hill Fire Track. Follow the gravel track for 250 metres past some houses to a car park and a locked gate at a sharp bend. Cars can be left here or in Bogong Village. From here the track is closed to vehicles so walking is pleasant.

Follow the fire track uphill for five km (about 1½ to two hours) towards The Springs Saddle. Turn left 200 metres before the saddle onto the Fainter Fire Track. This track is followed south for 1½ km to where the track forks. Follow the right-hand track south for a further three km to the clearing at Bogong Jack Saddle.

Past the saddle the fire track climbs steeply south-west then south-east up the slopes of Mt Fainter North. The track sidles around the eastern shoulder of this peak up into a broad high valley. From here, leave the fire trail and walk a short distance north-west to the summit of Mt Fainter North. The views of the surrounding country are excellent, particularly that across the Diamantina and Kiewa valleys to Mt Feathertop.

From the summit follow pads along the open ridge south-east for one km to the rocky top of Mt Fainter South for more good views. Descend the open ridge south-east then cross the plains southwards to meet the Fainter Fire Trail on Little Plain.

From here there are two routes to Tawonga Huts. In poor visibility it is best to continue to follow the fire track south for five km. This track crosses the eastern slopes of the ridge. In good visibility the more scenic route is to follow the ridge crest over Mt Niggerhead.

To walk over the Niggerheads; at Little Plain leave the fire track and walk south-west up the slopes onto the main ridge. This ridge is covered with low trees interspersed with open grassy plains and it is followed south for two km to Mt Niggerhead's rocky

summit. Along the ridge there is a faint foot track which can be followed with care.

From the summit of Mt Niggerhead, descend south for 700 metres to a distinct saddle. Leave the ridge crest here by turning east and follow the creek downstream for one km to the large clearing at Tawonga Huts. These huts are still used by the cattlemen and some may be open for use by bushwalkers. The area is excellent for camping.

Alternative Campsites

The Springs Saddle A small hut is located in this saddle beside a clearing. Water is sometimes available in the gully west of the saddle.

Bogong Jack Saddle A small hut is located on the west side of this clearing. Fetch water from the small creek beside the fire track, 100 metres to the north.

Little Plain Excellent camping is available around the edge of this plain. Fetch water from tiny creeks and pools on the plains.

Stage 2: Tawonga Huts to Wallaces Hut

(12 km, 4-5 hours)

From Tawonga Huts, follow the fire track south (now marked with snow poles) for one km up onto the open grassy plains. When the fire track swings east, leave it and follow the snow-poled walking track south-east for 1½ km to the track junction near Mt Jim. At this junction the route joins the Alpine Walking Track and from here to Mt Bogong the snow poles are numbered.

Leave packs near the junction and walk south 700 metres across the open plains to the small steep hill called Mt Jim. The view from the top is reasonable for such little effort. Return to the packs and follow the snow pole line south-east then east for five km past Mt Bundara to Cope Saddle. There is a refuge hut beside the aqueduct in the saddle.

Several pole lines join here and the numbered pole line (don't follow the blue or green-capped poles) is followed east for one

Top: Oberon Beach, Wilsons Promontory
Bottom: Looking back to Waterloo Bay, Wilsons Promontory

Top: Stirling Range
Bottom: Lost Beach, Nuyts Wilderness

km to pole 471. To the south of the pole line stands Mt Cope (one of Victoria's highest peaks), an easy sidetrip from here to the summit. It is two-km return and will add about one hour's walk to the day. Walk up the lightly timbered slopes to the rocky summit. Return to the packs by the same route.

After collecting the packs, the pole line is then followed north-east (ignore the old road veering to the right) for 2½ km to meet the Bogong High Plains Rd near Cope Hut. This is a large hut, 200 metres south-east of the road, and is suitable for an overnight stop. To continue towards Wallaces Hut follow the main road north-east for 500 metres. The snow-poled track then leaves the road veering right (east) and follows mixed forest and plains for one km to Wallaces Hut. The slab-timber hut is 100 metres south-east of the track.

The hut was built in 1889 and is an historic landmark which is classified by the National Trust. Good campsites exist nearby and walkers are encouraged to look after it by not using it if possible. Water is available from the creek beside the main track.

Alternative Campsites
Cope Saddle A small refuge hut is found beside the aqueduct. Take water from the aqueduct. Some shelter for tents is found beside the trees well south of the saddle.

Cope Hut This is a large hut close to the Bogong High Plains Rd. Water is obtained from the creek in the valley below the hut. Other campsites can be found in many areas on the exposed plains but they are not recommended if the weather is doubtful.

Stage 3: Wallaces Hut to Ropers Hut
(13 km, 3-4 hours)
From Wallaces Hut the Alpine Track continues north to follow the main road around Basalt Hill. The more pleasant and recommended alternative is to walk south-east for 500 metres past Wilkinsons Hut down to meet the Langford West Aqueduct. Cross the aqueduct and follow the trail beside it northwards for three km to a refuge hut at Langfords Gap.

Walk north 150 metres to meet the main road. Follow the main road northwards for one km to a track junction just south of Watchbed Creek. Turn right onto the Mt Nelse Track and follow it for two km to another track junction at snow pole 740. Turn left and walk north for three km (passing some side tracks leading to huts) to Mt Nelse. This mountain is a large rounded plateau and the summit is 400 metres east of the track. Continue north across the plateau for one km to the summit of Mt Nelse North. Descend north-west for 200 metres to meet the snow poles again at a fire track junction.

In good weather a sidetrip from this junction to Mt Spion Kopje is recommended. This is a 10-km return sidetrip and will add about 2½ to three hours extra to the day. Leave the packs near the pole line and follow the fire trail leading westwards along the top of the broad ridge. This track continues for five km across very exposed country to pass just north of the summit of Mt Spion Kopje. After visiting the summit return to the packs along the same track.

After collecting the packs follow the snow poles north-east for 500 metres down to a saddle then north for one km along high ridges to a fire trail junction. Turn right following the pole line and descend to Ropers Hut near the treeline. The hut is 100 metres west of the track. The area has good campsites and water is available from the creek.

Alternative Campsites
Johnstons Hut This partially closed hut is 700 metres east of the main track near Mt Nelse. A signposted side track leads to it. The area has good water and pleasant campsites.

Edmonson Hut This is 500 metres west of the main track near Mt Nelse and at the end of a signposted side track. Good campsites are available. Water is available from the creek in the valley below the hut.

Stage 4: Ropers Hut to Cleve Cole Hut
(10 km, 4-6 hours)
From Ropers Hut follow the foot track north-east down Duane Spur. The track enters the forest and is easily followed as it descends north-east then north to a saddle two km from Ropers Hut. From the saddle the track leaves the ridge and descends north-west down the side of Duane Spur to Big River. This river must be forded and a chain is in place to help you. If the river is in flood the crossing can be difficult and dangerous. There are good campsites on the north side of the river.

From the river the track climbs steeply north for 2½ km up onto T Spur Knob. A pleasant walk north for one km leads to the clearing at Maddisons Hut site. Here the Alpine Track branches and the left-hand track is followed towards Mt Bogong. This track leads north-west down to the main creek in the valley. From here there is a short sidetrip which is worth walking.

Leave the packs near the track and follow the creek downstream for about 10 minutes to the top of Howman's Falls. The creek falls dramatically into the valley below and there are some pleasant swimming holes above the falls.

Return to collect the packs and follow the track west through the snowgums for one km to the Cleve Cole Hut. This is a solid stone hut on the ridge at the head of Camp Valley. There are numerous campsites near the hut and in Camp Valley to the east. Water is taken from the hut's tank or from Camp Creek.

Alternative Campsites
Big River There are good sheltered campsites on the north side of the river near the crossing.

Stage 5: Cleve Cole Hut to Bogong Creek Saddle
(11 km, 3-4½ hours)
From Cleve Cole Hut the snow pole line leads north for 3½ km along a high and very exposed ridge to Eskdale Point. Here a side track leads down Eskdale Spur. Continue to follow the main ridge passing another side track (which leads to Staircase Spur) as it swings west to the summit of Mt Bogong. A large stone cairn marks the top of Victoria's highest peak and on a clear day the views are excellent.

At the summit the main snow pole line ends and the remainder of the track across to Quartz Ridge is marked with an old broken down pole line. From the summit follow foot tracks west then south-west for two km to the Hooker Plateau. The track branches at a signpost and if the weather is clear the diversion to the west peak is worthwhile.

Leave the packs near the signpost and walk across the open ridge west for 1½ km to the top of the West Peak (called Mt Bogong Central on some maps). This side-trip will add about one extra hour walking to the day. Return to the packs and follow the foot track south onto Quartz Ridge. This ridge is very spectacular with rocky outcrops poised above steep slopes.

The track soon enters the trees and is followed south for three km to a track junction. Turn right (west) and walk 400 metres to meet the Big River Fire Track. Campsites exist near this junction close to the creek. Turn right and follow the fire track uphill 150 metres to Bogong Creek Saddle. Water is available from the creek or from Big River which is a one-km walk down the fire track to the south.

Alternative Campsites
The day's walk is almost entirely above the treeline. In fine weather camping on the exposed ridges can be spectacular. However, if the weather changes such a campsite can

Cleve Cole Hut, Mt Bogong

be very uncomfortable and, therefore, not recommended.

Stage 6: Bogong Creek Saddle to Bogong Village
(17 km, 3½-5 hours)
From Bogong Creek Saddle to Bogong Village it is a pleasant walk through forest along fire trails and aqueducts. From the saddle follow the fire trail north. This descends into the valley of Bogong Creek with several zigzags. After three km Bogong Creek is crossed and a further 800 metres leads to a track junction.

Turn sharp left following the fire trail to cross the creek again. The trail descends gradually for one km to the next track junction. Either track can be followed but the more pleasant route is to turn right and follow the track for 10 minutes to where it crosses the creek. Don't cross the creek but follow the south bank downstream for 200 metres to meet the Bogong Creek Race. Turn left onto this aqueduct which provides a very pleasant flat walk.

After one km, an old railway line begins and follows the aqueduct. Follow this for a further seven km to a large shed at the end of the railway line. A fire trail starts here and you follow this south-west for 300 metres to a track junction. Turn sharp left onto the Little Arthur Fire Track and follow this track (ignoring the minor side tracks) for one km to a good view point of Lake Guy and Bogong Village.

From here, it is an easy two-km walk turning right at the next three track junctions to the Lake Guy dam wall. Cross the dam using the walk way and follow the good track, along the lake shore, south to the village and the end of the walk.

Alternative Campsites
Bogong Creek Race There are several good places beside this aqueduct for campsites. Also, there are excellent camping areas at both ends of the aqueduct.

MT FEATHERTOP
Mt Feathertop, at 1922 metres, the second highest peak in Victoria, is undoubtedly the queen of the Victorian Alps. It is a classical

mountain peak guarded by very steep side slopes. All approaches to its summit are on well used walking tracks and it is very popular with local walkers. A visit to this prominent peak is a must for all bushwalkers.

Features

Mt Feathertop stands apart from most of the high country of Victoria. The deep valley of the West Kiewa River separates it from the Bogong High Plains. It is connected only to Mt Hotham by a sharp ridge known as The Razorback. The peak itself is composed of steeply dipping slates which are exposed as broken buttresses and gullies on the east face.

In winter, snow covers the peak and the strong winds blow the snow away into a feathery plume, hence the name Feathertop. The mountain has long been popular and was once used for commercial skiing activities. In recent years bushwalkers have adopted the mountain as their own and have built two huts (Federation and MUMC huts) for refuge high up the spurs of the mountain. It is now controlled by the Department of Conservation & Environment and is part of the Alpine National Park.

Standard

This walk follows well-used tracks ascending and descending the steep spurs of this mountain. The tracks are easy to follow. The summit area is exposed to the very changeable weather. The suggested walk is of a medium standard.

Days Required

The popular circuit to this peak is a two-day bushwalk. There are many possible variations. The most common variation is to follow The Razorback south towards Mt Hotham then descend Bon Accord Spur to Harrietville, the starting point. Other variations require a steep descent into the West Kiewa Valley and are less popular.

Seasons

Summer is the most popular season for visiting this peak. The days are usually warm (sometimes very hot) and the views from the summit are excellent. In autumn the weather is still very stable and is excellent for walking. Spring is also popular with snow drifts still crowning the summit.

For the hardy walkers and ski tourers winter is the challenging season, as the mountain is usually covered in a thick layer of snow. In all seasons the mountain can have very cold, windy weather and all walkers must be prepared for snowfalls at any time of the year.

Equipment

In the warmer months there is no need for any special equipment to visit this mountain. Waterproof jackets and a reasonable tent are necessary. Runners are adequate as the tracks are in fairly good condition. Take a stove as there is very little firewood left on the upper slopes of the mountain. Many thoughtless walkers have stripped branches from ancient, living snow gums for firewood.

In the cooler seasons, particularly winter, a set of excellent walking equipment is essential. Leather boots, a full set of waterproof clothing and a high quality tent, suitable for snowfalls, are required. Occasionally the mountain freezes over and an ice axe and crampons are required to reach the summit. Several deaths have occurred on the mountain and it should not be underestimated.

Maps

There are a variety of maps to this mountain and most of them are suitable. The 1:50,000 'Bogong Alpine Area' Outdoor Leisure Map is produced by the Government Of Victoria. This shows all the walking tracks and is all that most bushwalkers would ever need.

The Government of Victoria also produces a detailed series of topographic maps on a 1:25,000 scale. Three maps, *Feathertop*, *Freeburgh* and *Harrietville* are required to cover this walk. These maps are produced by the Division of Survey & Mapping and are available from Map Sales, Information Centre Victoria, and specialist map and walking shops.

The Federal Government Agency, NATMAP, produces a 1:100,000 topographic map, *Bogong*, which is a useful overall map of the area, but is not as detailed as the other available maps. This is generally on sale in most bushwalking shops in south-east Australia.

For other routes around Mt Feathertop there is a useful guide book, *Bogong National Park*, by John Siseman. This is available in most bushwalking shops and many bookshops in south-east Australia.

Permits

No permits are required for visiting Mt Feathertop at any time of the year. Bushwalkers can record their party details, intended route and expected return date in the book kept at the police station (☎ (057) 55 1444), Park St, Bright.

All parties should fill their names in the log books at the two huts on the mountain as they pass through. In the advent of any searches or accidents occurring this will help the authorities. For those who are extending their visit and walking to other areas, no camping is allowed in the Alpine Resort area on Mt Hotham. This includes all the higher parts of that mountain.

Access

Mt Feathertop is 170 km north-east of Melbourne. The starting point for this walk is the tiny town of Harrietville, 22 km south of Bright. A major road called the Alpine Rd crosses the mountains from Wangaratta to Omeo, and it provides good access to this walk.

From Melbourne follow the Hume Highway north, then north-east, for 215 km to Glenrowan. Five km north of this town turn right at the road signposted 'Snow Fields' and follow this for 40 km through the small towns of Oxley and Milawa to the Ovens Highway. Turn right and follow the Ovens Highway for 58 km through Myrtleford then Bright to Harrietville. On the north side of the bridge, turn left (to the east) and follow the gravel road for one km

Wedge-tailed Eagle

(ignoring the side roads) to the car park at the end of the road.

If you arrive late at night the car park provides very rough camping. Harrietville has a hotel, shops and a petrol station. If the party has two vehicles, a car shuffle can be made leaving one vehicle near the trout farm, four km south of Harrietville.

From the north, Harrietville can be approached via the town of Wangaratta and then the Ovens Highway, as above, or via the Kiewa Valley Highway from Albury and crossing Tawonga Gap into the Ovens Valley.

Approaching from the south, the gravel covered Alpine Rd leads from Omeo over the top of Mt Hotham to Harrietville. This approach is useful for bushwalkers coming from the Gippsland area. After heavy winter snowfalls this road may be temporarily closed. The road is normally open all year.

Access by public transport is not very good during the warmer months of the year. Wangaratta is the closest large town, easily accessible by bus or train from both Melbourne and Sydney. A local bus meets the

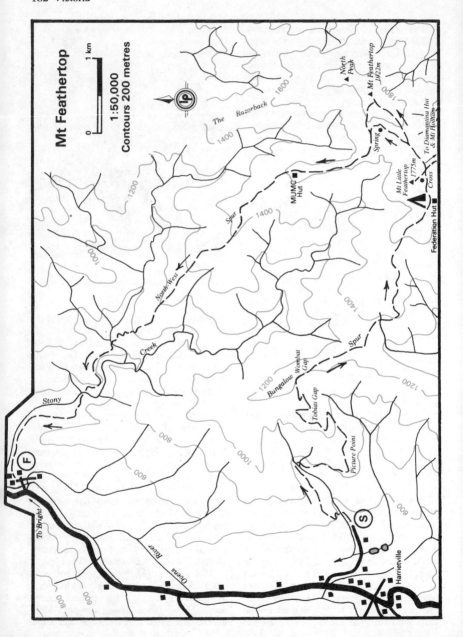

train service from Melbourne to Wangaratta on Monday, Tuesday, Thursday and Friday each week. This bus leaves in the afternoon and stops at Bright. From there to Harrietville it is another 22 km and it is necessary to use a taxi or try your luck at hitchhiking along the quiet roads.

The return bus leaves Bright in the morning on the same days for Wangaratta. During the winter months when snow covers the mountain there are plenty of bus services from Melbourne and Wangaratta to Harrietville on Monday, Friday, Saturday and Sunday. The itineraries vary considerably over the snow season, depending on demand, and bookings can be made at any travel agent.

Stage 1: Harrietville to Federation Hut
(9 km, 3-4½ hours)

From the car park the track heads east into the forest and crosses the creek. Collect water as this is the last reliable water before the campsite. Continue following the track as it climbs gently, sidling steep spurs to meet the main Bungalow Spur about half way up.

This major spur is now followed south-east past some old hut remains to the Federation Hut which is located on a saddle below Mt Little Feathertop. There is good camping on the ridge near the hut. The water tank at the hut is often empty and water can be collected at a spring south-east of the hut. It is a steep 200-metre descent to this spring, and it is therefore probably easier to obtain water from the spring on the western side of Mt Feathertop.

Sidetrip: Federation Hut to the Summit
(3 km, 1-2 hours)

If the weather is clear an ascent to the summit is recommended for the afternoon. From Federation Hut follow the well-worn tracks east to the main ridge called The Razorback. Turn left and follow the ridge north-east, ignoring the left-hand track that sidles the west face of the mountain (this is to be followed tomorrow). Continue climbing steeply up the ridge to the summit of Mt Feathertop. This has extensive views in all directions.

There is a cornice (an overhanging ledge of snow formed by the wind) on the mountain until early summer, which you should not walk on as it sometimes collapses. In poor visibility an ascent is not recommended particularly, if snow covers the mountain. Return to the campsite by the same route.

In clear weather you should complete the day with a short climb from the campsite up onto Mt Little Feathertop for the sunset.

Stage 2: Federation Hut to Ovens River
(11 km, 5-7 hours)

From the campsite follow the summit track east for 800 metres to a track junction. Turn left (the right-hand track leads to the summit) and follow the track as it crosses the western face of the mountain through the trees into the wide gully. Water can be collected here (at a spring) for most of the summer. The track continues on for another 100 metres to meet the North-west Spur.

Descend the crest of the spur west then north for 1½ km to the MUMC Hut. This is an unusual hut of geodesic dome design and is in a spectacular position on the top of the ridge. It can be used as an alternative for the overnight stop.

From the hut, the track descends very steeply for four km north-west down the spur. This track becomes steeper as the bottom is approached and it is a relief when you get to the creek. The track then climbs over the end of another spur and descends to cross Stony Creek. It then passes through a thicket of blackberries around the foot of the Bungalow Spur to enter the back of a trout farm.

The trout farm is private property and all equipment, including the fish ponds, is not to be touched. Follow the main track onto the road through the property, to the bridge across the Ovens River.

Cross the river and turn left and it is a four km walk south along the highway to Harrietville and the end of the walk. If the party has more than one vehicle a car can be left beside the bridge leading to the trout farm before beginning the walk.

MAJOR MITCHELL PLATEAU

The Grampians is a region of sandstone ranges in Western Victoria. The area is varied and very interesting with massive cliff faces, mixed forests, broad valleys and heathlands. Most of the area is protected by the Grampians National Park which is also known by its Aboriginal name, Geriwerd. In fact many of the features now have two names – the common European one as well as its Aboriginal title. To avoid confusion we use the European titles which most literature still refers to. The national park is one of the most outstanding botanical reserves in Australia with over 860 different species of plants. The ranges provide some excellent bushwalking areas and the circuit walk to the Major Mitchell Plateau and Mt William is the most popular overnight bushwalk.

Features

The Grampians is composed of a series of old sandstone rocks which have been gently folded and subsequently eroded. This weathering has left many steep cliff faces and gentle dip slopes on the ranges giving this area its characteristic landforms. The main ridges are aligned north-south and separated by broad valleys. Much of the Grampians is covered with poor sandy soils which support forests of stunted trees. These grow in open forests and make it possible for shrubs and small plants to proliferate.

Each spring the area is a mass of wildflowers for which it is famous. In some of the valleys and deeper gullies are richer soils supporting tall forests of eucalypts. On the exposed plateaus are low scrubby heathlands. This great variety of plants and flowers attracts over 200 species of birds to these ranges.

The animal life is equally varied and many of Australia's fauna can be readily found. Kangaroos, wallabies, koalas, possums and echidnas are common sights. You'll also see emus.

Originally the Grampians was managed for commercial timber production and an extensive series of roads and tracks were constructed for this purpose. In 1984 the Grampians National Park was declared to preserve 1670 sq km of this popular area. This has resulted in closure of some of the old roads which now make fine walking tracks. The area is not a wilderness, but it does provide some fine bushwalking.

Standard

This circuit is a mixture of gravel roads, constructed walking tracks and rough bushwalkers' pads. Navigation is easy if the circuit is walked in the direction described. The walk is graded medium.

Days Required

Two days are required to walk this circuit and there is little scope for variation. There are other good overnight walks in the Mt Stapylton, Mt Difficult and The Fortress areas for parties with more time.

Seasons

Spring to early summer is the best period of the year for walking this circuit. The wildflowers are in bloom and there are no problems with water at the campsite. Late summer and autumn are also suitable but there are often problems with finding water.

It can also be very hot in summer making bushwalking uncomfortable. Winter, is only for experienced walkers as the plateau and peaks are often covered in cloud and it is windy and cold. Sometimes snow falls on Mt William in winter.

Equipment

No special equipment is needed for walking this circuit but you should take a stove as firewood is becoming very difficult to find near the campsite area. Runners or very light boots are ideal footwear for this area.

In the warmer months a shady hat, sunscreen and several litres of water should be taken. If First Wannon Creek is dry (ask the rangers at Halls Gap, (☎ (053) 56 4381) then all water will need to be carried for the two days.

Maps

The best maps to The Grampians are the 1:50,000 Outdoor Leisure Maps titled *Southern Grampians* and *Northern Grampians*. The southern sheet is the only one needed for this walk and is very good showing all tracks apart from the old closed road of Stockyard Creek. This has been removed from the map to discourage vehicles from using it but bushwalkers are allowed to follow it. The map has handy notes on the back with additional walk suggestions.

The other suitable map sheet is 1:25,000 *Mt William* which is of a more detailed scale, yet shows the same information. The disadvantage of this map is that it covers only a small region and to visit other parts of the ranges you will need to buy more maps!

For other information the guide *50 Walks in the Grampians*, by Tyrone Thomas, describes lots of walks spread over the entire ranges. Most of these are one-day walks and many are only of a two to four-hour duration. Only a couple of overnight walks are included. It is available in most bushwalking and book shops in Victoria.

Permits

Permits are not required for walking across and camping on the Major Mitchell Plateau. Camping on the plateau is only allowed at First Wannon Creek and at Boundary Gap. All walkers should use stoves for cooking, not campfires. In hot weather it is best to carry food that can be eaten cold, as this area is very prone to bushfires and often declared a total fire ban area.

During a fire ban all fires and stoves (even inside tents) are prohibited from being lit. As this national park is fairly new the regulations may alter and inquiries should be made with the rangers at the Halls Gap office (☎ (053) 56 4381), Dunkeld Rd, Halls Gap. They may be able to give you information regarding the current fire danger level and the availability of water at First Wannon Creek.

Access

The Grampians Ranges are 250 km west of

Looking east from Major Mitchell Plateau

Melbourne. The starting point for this walk is the Stockyard Creek Track, on the Halls Gap to Dunkeld road, 21 km south of Halls Gap. The Grampians can be approached from all directions on good roads.

From Melbourne follow the Western Highway for 204 km to Ararat. Leave the main highway and continue straight on through the town for 16 km to Moyston. Turn right and continue north-west for 33 km through Pomonal and on to Halls Gap. This town is the main centre in The Grampians and has a petrol station, caravan and camping parks and two general stores.

Follow the main road south out of Halls Gap for 21 km towards Dunkeld, to the Stockyard Creek Track on the left. Cars may be parked on the Stockyard Creek Track close to the road. If the party has two vehicles a car shuffle can be made to leave one vehicle at the Mt William Track, six km north of

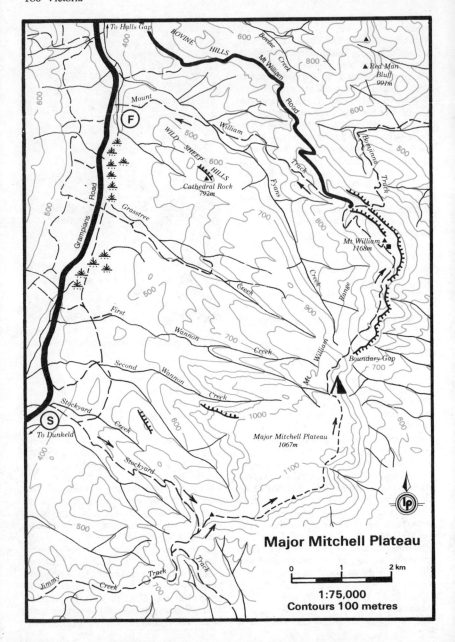

Major Mitchell Plateau

0   1   2 km

1:75,000
Contours 100 metres

Stockyard Creek, where there are several off-road parking areas.

Coming from the south, drive to Dunkeld then follow the Halls Gap road north for 45 km to the Stockyard Creek Track on the right. There are other roads which can be used to approach the start of this walk but most are gravel surfaced and not recommended.

There is no public transport to the start of this walk and the closest transport is to Halls Gap. Regular rail and bus services operate from both Melbourne and Adelaide to Stawell. There are no regular services from there to the start of the walk south of Halls Gap and a car is needed to access this walk.

Stage 1: Stockyard Creek to Major Mitchell Plateau

(10 km, 4-6 hours)

Follow the fire trail called Stockyard Creek Track past the locked gate, south-east for 10 minutes to a track junction. Continue straight ahead (to the right) on the main track. After another one km you start to climb steadily through lovely mixed forest. This climbs steadily to the crest of the Mt William Range about five km from the start (about 1½ to two hours' walking).

Leave the Stockyard Creek Track as it begins to swing south-west. Take the north-east fork through the light scrub and follow a well-defined pad which is easily followed as it climbs steeply for 30 minutes up a rocky spur to a prominent knoll covered with rocky slabs and shady trees. There is a good view of The Grampians from this knoll. From the knoll continue east following the pads along a scrubby ridge for one km to the top of the Major Mitchell Plateau.

There are fine views of the plateau and the eastern cliffs from the rocky heights at the western end of the Major Mitchell Plateau. The pads continue north-east for 1½ km closely following the eastern edge of the plateau. Some short diversions away from the edge are required to bypass some rocky obstacles.

The pads seem to peter out as the eastern edge of the plateau is approached and there are several routes. Descend north for 500 metres to the small saddle on the edge of the cliffs and the main pad again becomes well defined.

Follow the walking pad north for 1½ km to the camping area on First Wannon Creek. As you approach the creek the track branches in several places. Simply follow the main track down the gently sloping valley to the camping area. A sign downstream indicates the end of the camping area. Water is usually available from the creek except during dry summers. There are no alternative campsites on the walk.

From the campsite it is worth walking downstream into the gorge of Wannon Creek for the sunset. This is a very short and easy side trip which will take about 30 minutes return.

Stage 2: Major Mitchell Plateau to Stockyard Creek

(18 km, 5-7 hours)

From the camping area on First Wannon Creek a well-used walking track heads north for 500 metres up onto the rim of the plateau. This track follows the top edge of the cliffs very closely for 400 metres then descends steeply east through the rocks. You need to take care as the rough track passes down through the cliffs into Boundary Gap.

This will take one to 1½ hours from the First Wannon Creek campsite. Boundary Gap has a campsite on the northern side of the gap which is sheltered under tall forest. Water is not easy to find in this saddle.

From Boundary Gap the track is well defined and climbs steeply north-east for 600 metres in scrubby forest onto a prominent open knoll. The ridge is easily followed north-east up onto the next knoll where there is a radio mast. A very rough vehicle track starts here which you follow north for 1½ km to meet the sealed road at Mt William. Leave the packs at the junction and walk 200 metres north to the summit of Mt William.

This mountain is the highest in The Grampians and has extensive views. The summit area has several radio masts near it. Return to collect the packs and follow the sealed road downhill for 1½ km to the locked gate at the car park. Follow the main road a further 300 metres past the car park to the signposted walking track. Turn left onto this track and follow it north-west for 3½ km to a bridge across Fyans Creek (normally flowing).This is a good place to stop for a late lunch as it is 3½ to four hours from the overnight campsite.

From the creek crossing follow the old fire track north-west for two km to a bridge across Grasstree Creek. Cross the creek and walk 100 metres west to the sealed Halls Gap-Dunkeld Rd. If the party has two vehicles one could have been left here before commencing the walk (this will save a six-km walk). Turn left and follow the sealed road south for six km to the Stockyard Creek Track and the vehicle.

WILSONS PROMONTORY CIRCUIT

Wilsons Promontory provides some of the most scenic and enjoyable walking in Victoria. Known locally as 'The Prom' it has a great variety of rocky headlands, sandy beaches, forests and fern glades. Because of its well-maintained track system it is very popular with local bushwalkers. The classic walk is the very popular circuit which visits the beaches and bays on both the eastern and western coastlines.

Features

Wilsons Promontory is the southern most promontory of mainland Australia. It has massive granite peaks connected to the mainland by a long sandy isthmus. At various stages in its history 'The Prom' has been an island and then part of the land bridge to Tasmania. It was first declared a national park in 1905 and now protects all of the granite headlands and peaks, part of the Yanakie Isthmus and most of the off-shore islands.

The park has an area of 490 sq km. In the past The Prom was used for various activities including cattle grazing and commando training. The park has a great diversity of vegetation (with over 700 species of plants) varying from fern gullies and forests of tall trees to stunted coastal shrubs and salt marshes around the shores. The area has experienced several severe fires in the past but is recovering well.

The varied plant cover provides homes for the majority of Australia's native animals. Kangaroos, wallabies, koalas, wombats and possums all live here. The bird life is very varied with emus, seabirds, honey-eaters and parrots well represented. Around Tidal River, the start and end of the walk, the birds are very tame and are one of The Prom's most popular attractions.

Standard

This circuit walk follows maintained tracks which are well worn and easy to follow. The suggested itinerary is for two full days of walking and is graded medium. It can easily be altered to a three-day easy walk if you choose, by camping at Fraser Creek and Refuge Cove.

Days Required

The walk takes two days to complete. Alternatively it can be walked as an easy three-day walk. The itinerary must be decided before beginning the walk; note that once started the park authority will not allow variations.

Seasons

Any season of the year is suitable for a visit to this park. Summer is the most popular as it is the holiday period and it is hot enough to swim in the cold ocean. Autumn and spring are milder and better for carrying a pack. Spring, of course, is the main flower season. Winter is colder with occasional storms which provide interest and variety to the scenery. With its sheltered campsites and well-made tracks a visit in any weather is worthwhile.

Equipment

No special bushwalking equipment is required to walk at The Prom. All the campsites are sheltered and any waterproof tent will suffice. Runners are popular footwear but better still are light boots as some of the tracks are steep and slippery because of loose gravel. Fuel stoves must be carried as all fires are totally banned on the described circuit.

Maps

The best map for bushwalkers is the 1:50,000 *Wilsons Promontory National Park* Outdoor Leisure Map. This is produced by the Government of Victoria and is available from map shops, most bushwalking shops and from the store at Tidal River.

The Government of Victoria also produce some very detailed maps to The Prom. The 1:25,000 topographic sheets, *Wilsons Promontory South East* and *Wilsons Promontory South West*, are required for the circuit and while useful don't actually contain any more information than that shown on the Leisure Series Map. These are available from Map Sales, Information Centre Victoria.

A 1:100,000 topographic map, *Wilsons Promontory*, is produced by NATMAP. This map is rarely used now as it is out of date and difficult to read.

There is a series of free leaflets about The Prom, available from the rangers' office at Tidal River. These are useful as they detail the park regulations and provide some interesting information.

For more information on this park the small book, *Discovering The Prom on Foot*, details many day walks and a couple of overnight bushwalks. This book is published jointly by the Victorian National Parks Association and the National Parks Service and is available at Tidal River and in many bushwalking shops in Victoria.

Permits

Permits must be obtained for all overnight bushwalking at Wilsons Promontory. The permit details which camping area the party must stay at each night. Once the permit has been obtained it cannot be altered. The permit system is tightly enforced with regular checks by the rangers during the popular periods. Numbers are strictly controlled and there is a limit imposed.

During the summer the limit is often reached and no more bushwalkers are allowed entry. It is advisable to arrive early to obtain a permit. Mail bookings can be made a minimum of one month in advance by writing to The Ranger-in-Charge, Wilsons Promontory National Park, Tidal River via Foster, 3960 (☎ (056) 80 8538). There is an entrance fee into the park plus a moderate charge per person per night for a camping permit. The important regulations are: all fires are banned on the southern circuit; you must keep to the tracks; and, camp only at the area designated on your permit.

Access

Wilsons Promontory is 241 km south-east of Melbourne. From Melbourne follow the Princes Highway to Dandenong then follow the South Gippsland Highway through Leongatha. Leave the highway at either Meeniyan or Foster and follow the well signposted roads south to Tidal River which is well within the national park.

The rangers' office, where you get your walking permit, is at Tidal River. The display centre at the office is well worth visiting. Cars should be parked as directed opposite the display centre. At Tidal River there is also a general store, a takeaway food shop and a post office. Petrol and LP gas are available from the general store.

There is no access to this park by public transport and all visitors use private (or hired) cars. If the group has two cars a car shuffle can be made to leave one vehicle at the Mt Oberon car park four km away. The road to this is well signposted.

Stage 1: Tidal River to Little Waterloo Bay

(18 km, 4-6 hours)

Start at the rangers' office at Tidal River. Walk to the east end of the building and a signposted track 'Norman Bay South Track' starts behind the toilet block. Follow this track south- east to cross a sealed road. Continue for one km through the coastal scrub to the south end of Norman Bay Beach.

At the south end of the sand the track climbs gently through the coastal scrub belt south-west towards Norman Point. From the

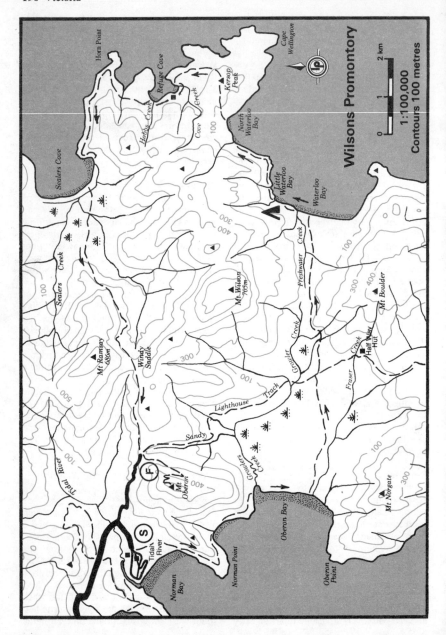

Wilsons Promontory

1:100,000
Contours 100 metres

2 km

ridge above the point there are good views of the islands and the southern half of The Prom. The track swings north-east and south-east and descends to the sand at Little Oberon Bay. Fresh water is sometimes available from the small creek in this bay.

Walk to the south end of the sand where the track begins again. This track climbs well above the ocean, but soon descends to the sand at Oberon Bay. This is six km from Tidal River.

Wade across Growlers Creek to reach the sandy beach. This creek is brackish and is usually not suitable for drinking. Walk south along the beach for 1½ km to Fraser Creek. The water from this creek is reasonable for drinking. The track leaves the beach just north of this creek.

Follow the wide track west for 3½ km to meet the sandy Lighthouse Track. Turn right and walk 100 metres to the next track junction. Turn left and follow the track west for five km to Waterloo Bay. Turn left onto the sand and walk 300 metres north to the end of the beach. Cross the creek (the depth varies with the tides) and find the track which starts on the edge of the scrub above the rocks.

This track is easily followed north for one km to the camping area at Little Waterloo Bay. There are plenty of tent sites and you can collect water from the creek 50 metres upstream of the camping area.

Alternative Campsites
Fraser Creek There is a pleasant camping area at the southern end of Oberon Bay, near Fraser Creek. Water quality here is reasonable, but the area is exposed to the westerly winds.

Half Way Hut This campsite is about one km south of the Waterloo Bay turnoff. Water is taken from a tank at the hut which is sometimes empty in the summer months.

Stage 2: Little Waterloo Bay to Oberon Car Park
(24 km, 5-7 hours)
From the campsite walk beside the creek out onto the beach. Cross the creek (the depth varies with the tides) and follow the signposted track east towards Refuge Cove. The track climbs into the forest above the coastal rocks, crosses a large gully then

North Waterloo Bay, Wilsons Promontory National Park

swings north to descend to the sand at North Waterloo Bay.

Follow the sand north-east to the small rocky headland. Walk around the rocks or, if the tide is high, use the inland track to cross to the next sandy beach. Continue along the sand to the eastern end of the beach. The track climbs up the granite rock slabs at the end of the beach and heads into the scrubby forest. You now climb gradually for 1½ km to the rocky top of Kersops Peak. In clear weather this has superb coastal views of the eastern side of The Prom.

Follow the track which descends steeply north-east then north for two km to the tiny beach at Refuge Cove. Close to the sand the track swings sharp left and is easily followed to the camping area between the two creeks. Fresh water can be collected 300 metres upstream at the end of the signposted track.

From the campsite follow the track west across the second creek to a track junction (the left-hand track is the old route which involved a steep climb). Follow the right-hand track which crosses a low ridge to the sandy beach at the northern end of Refuge Cove. Follow the track beside Hobbs Creek inland and then climb gently north for two km to the lookout above Horn Point.

After enjoying the great views, follow the track west. It generally follows the coast to the southern end of Sealers Cove.

Cross Sealers Creek to the sandy beach. This creek is fairly big and can become a deep wade at high tide so be prepared to get wet. Walk 400 metres north along the sandy beach to the signposts. The track leaves the beach and heads inland to cross Sealers Creek on a good foot bridge.

Beyond the creek the track crosses an expansive swamp with the aid of a timbered walkway. The track passes under many tall tree ferns and after two km of flat walking it begins to climb up onto the ridges of Mt Ramsay. These ridges are followed for another 4½ km to Windy Saddle.

Continue to follow the track west for three km to the Mt Oberon car park in Telegraph Saddle. Follow the sealed road downhill for three km then turn left at the road junction to walk the final one km to the rangers' office at the end of the walk. If the party has two cars one may be left at the Mt Oberon car park before starting the walk. Before leaving Tidal River all walking permits should be returned in the box provided at the rangers' office.

GREAT SOUTH WEST WALK

In the south-west of Victoria the coastline consists of long sweeping bays separated by rocky capes. Behind the coast are extensive areas of sand dunes, heathlands, marshes and lakes. With the marking and construction of extended walking tracks this area is becoming popular with bushwalkers for pleasant flat walking in natural coastal scenery. The major features of the area have been protected in the Lower Glenelg National Park and Discovery Bay Coastal Park.

There are two recognised bushwalks. The major route is called the Great South West Walk and is a 240-km circular route requiring 10 to 15 days to complete. It has been described here as the suggested walk. The shorter circuit is based around Mt Richmond and requires two or three days to complete and most of it can be incorporated into the main walk as a diversion.

Features

The Glenelg River meanders through a flat landscape of low hills in the south-western corner of the state. Despite its flatness the area is quite diverse, displaying many different aspects. The walk begins by following the shore of Portland Bay before heading inland, through farmlands, to the forests.

As the track winds its way through poorly drained forest country, messmate and stringybark gum trees are the dominant types of vegetation. Heathlands are crossed to reach the Glenelg River. This is a large, deep river which has carved an extensive gorge through underlying limestone. The river is followed until it meets the coast.

Discovery Bay is bounded by a sweeping sandy beach, 60 km in length. This is backed by sand dunes as high as 70 metres. Behind these frontal dunes are lakes and swamps which lie in depressions and extend well inland. The area is fairly flat and the only hill of any height is Mt Richmond at 225 metres. Mt Richmond is an old volcanic cone that has been covered with drifting sand and supports over 450 varieties of wildflowers on its slopes. It can be visited as a diversion to the standard circuit.

At the eastern end of Discovery Bay the large rocky peninsulas of capes Duquesne, Bridgewater and Portland extend into the Southern Ocean. These capes provide panoramic views of the surrounding bays and inland plains. The country behind the foreshore is a mixture of farmlands, forests and national parks.

The area was the first to be permanently settled in the state in the early 1800s and geographically it is relatively recent. The area's most spectacular feature is the rugged cliffs of the coastline.

Standard

The walk follows marked walking tracks which use fire trails, gravel roads, and sandy beaches. The route is easily followed as it is marked at nearly every junction and is periodically maintained by the volunteer group 'Friends of the Great South West Walk'. The notes should be carefully followed, however, as signposts do vanish or become overgrown. The markers used are generally orange triangles on treated pine posts. Some older markers displaying the black and white logo of the track still survive. The walk is graded easy to medium.

The track crosses some short sections of private land to which walkers have been granted access. You must keep to the marked track and respect the rights of the landowners. The track itself was initialised, primarily built, and maintained by volunteers who have put in a lot of work for which we can be thankful.

Days Required

The circuit takes 10 to 15 days to walk and is suitable for walkers of all standards. There are 16 established campsites each with a toilet and permanent water (which is usually

Xanothera (grass tree)

drawn from either a water tank or a bilge pump). Water can temporarily be in short supply at some of the campsites due to drought, fires or other damage so you should contact the ranger at Portland before beginning the walk.

The walk has been described in 16 easy stages and most walkers will combine sections into single days. Parcels of supplies can be posted to the Nelson post office at the half way mark if required. Nelson also has accommodation including a hotel if a break from camping is wanted half way around the circuit.

Seasons

Spring is an excellent period for walking this circuit because of the wildflowers and abundance of good water at the campsites. Walking on the beaches and headlands in summer is enjoyable, but it can be very hot on the inland section from Portland to the Glenelg River. Autumn is another excellent season for walking this circuit and has the clearest weather of the year.

Winter rains often flood long sections of

the inland route necessitating diversions and a visit then is not recommended. The coast section can then be interesting at this time, however, and worth visiting to see heavy seas crashing into the headlands and beaches.

Equipment

No special walking equipment is needed apart from a stove. Campfires are allowed at each of the designated camping areas but firewood is in very short supply at some so stoves are preferred for cooking.

Runners/trainers or very light boots are ideal footwear as the area is sandy. Good waterproof and windproof clothing is advised as it can be very cold and wet walking along a stormy ocean beach. In summer a shady hat and sunscreen are recommended. You will need containers for carrying drinking water during the day as there is usually no water between campsites. One to two litres per person is usually enough except in the summer heat when four litres is suggested.

Maps

The 1:100,000 topographic maps, *Nelson* and *Portland*, cover virtually all of the walk and are recommended. The *Casterton*, *Gambier* and *Northumberland* 1:100,000 sheets cover a small section of the walk beside the Glenelg River and are not really needed. Vicmap have been producing a detailed series of 1:25,000 maps which cover almost the entire walk. Recent editions have the track marked on them. These maps are good but there are a lot of sheets needed. If you only get some of them, then the most helpful are those which cover the inland forest section *Gorae*, *Wright*, *Lyons & Keegan Bend* as the rest of the route basically follows the river or the coastline.

The other 1:25,000 maps are *Wanwin*, *Oxbow Lake*, *Palpara*, *Lake Monbeong*, *Hedditch*, *Descartes Bay*, *Dryden*, *Cape Dequesne & Fisherman Cove*, *Chaucer*, *Grant Bay*, *Portland*, *Narrawong* and *Fitzroy River*. These maps are produced by the Division of Survey & Mapping and are

available from Map Sales, Information Centre Victoria (☎ (03) 651 4130), 318 Little Bourke St, Melbourne, 3000.

The booklet *The Great South West Walk* describes the walking tracks in general detail and includes a set of sketch maps of the route. This is currently $5 and can be purchased in Portland or in the map shops in Melbourne.

Permits

Permits are not required for walking in the Discovery Bay Coastal Park. All walkers, however, are advised to notify the Portland police (☎ (055) 23 1999) Glenelg St, Portland, or the Department of Conservation & Environment (☎ (087) 38 4051), Nelson, about their intended itinerary. This will aid them in the event of bushfires or other emergencies. While there are no fees for camping walkers are requested to restrict themselves to the designated campsites. There are several other campsites that will be passed, particularly along the Glenelg River that are reserved for car camping. Fees and bookings are required for use of these sites and better sites nearby have been provided for bush walkers.

Access

The Great South West Walk begins and ends in Portland. From Melbourne follow the Princes Highway south-west through Geelong and Warrnambool for 365 km to Portland. From Adelaide follow the Princes Highway through Murray Bridge and on to Mt Gambier, then Heywood, and turn south to Portland, 573 km from Adelaide. If arriving by car it is suggested to contact the Portland police station (☎ (055) 23 1999) for suggestions on where to park.

Portland has good public transport access. From Melbourne a regular train and bus service runs three times daily during the week and less often on weekends. This is operated by V-Line (☎ (008) 13 6109 or (03) 619 5000) and all seats must be booked in advance. This appears difficult but will guarantee a seat. Also, bookings at very short notice are usually available. The V-Line bus system continues on to Mt Gambier in South

Signpost, Discovery Bay

Australia where it connects with the bus services to Adelaide.

Kendall Airlines run regular daily flights from both Melbourne and Adelaide to Portland. This is not really that useful to walkers as the airport is located 12 km from the town.

If arriving late in the day, Portland is a large town with many caravan parks and accommodation. The best place for assistance is the tourist information centre which is located on the corner of Bentinck and Cliff Sts overlooking the foreshore.

Stage 1: Portland to Blackwood Camp
(20 km, 4½-6 hours)
The walk starts outside the tourist information centre which is near the corner of Bentinck and Cliff Streets. This overlooks the bay and the signpost gives the distance in both directions to Nelson which is about half way around the track. Turn left (north) and descend to the road parallel to the shore. Follow this to its end then continue a further 400 metres along the sand under the cliffs.

Just before the approaching bluff the track ascends the cliff by a set of steel stairs to the Ploughed Field Memorial. Turn right and follow the track behind the caravan park to the Bluff Lighthouse. This 1859 tower was resited in 1889 in an attempt to confuse a possible enemy attack. Today the bluff provides fine views over Portland Bay.

The track continues to follow the narrow grassed area between the town and the cliffs for two km then crosses the sealed road of Dutton Way into some scrub and passes under shady sheoaks. A stile is used to cross a fence into the Pioneer Cemetery at Maretimo. This is worth a stop to investigate the old headstones.

The track continues out of the cemetery by use of another stile, continues straight ahead down a short road (Cavendish St) and across another stile into a paddock. This is private land for which the owner has given permission for walkers to use so please assist by keeping to the track. This heads diagonally right and across another stile to the top of a set of steps, the Maretimo Staircase which should be descended to the foreshore.

Follow the edge of the road, Dutton Way, north as it parallels the breakwater along the

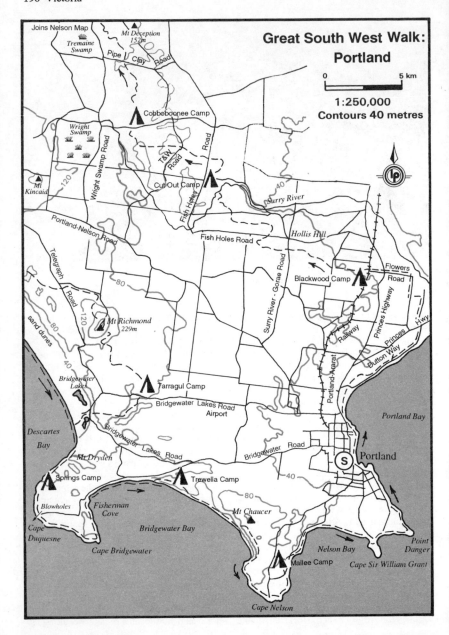

Great South West Walk:
Portland

0   5 km

1:250,000
Contours 40 metres

Joins Nelson Map
Tremaine Swamp
Mt Deception 152m
Pipe Clay Road
Cobboboonee Camp
Wright Swamp
T&W Road
Cut Out Camp
Fish Holes Road
Mt Kincaid
120
Surry River
Portland-Nelson Road
Fish Holes Road
Hollis Hill
Telegraph Road
80
Flowers Road
Surry River - Gorae Road
Blackwood Camp
Railway
Princes Highway
Princes Hwy
sand dunes
80
120
Mt Richmond 229m
40
Portland-Ararat
Dutton Way
Bridgewater Lakes
Tarragul Camp
Bridgewater Lakes Road
Airport
Portland Bay
Descartes Bay
Bridgewater Lakes Road
Bridgewater Road
40
S
Portland
Mt Dryden
Springs Camp
Trewella Camp
80
Blowholes
Fisherman Cove
Mt Chaucer
Cape Duquesne
Bridgewater Bay
Nelson Bay
Point Danger
Cape Bridgewater
Mallee Camp
Cape Sir William Grant
Cape Nelson

shore. When the breakwater ends, follow the beach north-east for three km, with some short diversions around private buildings, to meet the road again where it almost comes onto the beach. A further two km of beach leads to a sandy point with a walkers' signpost. Turn left, walk up to the road and follow it north as it heads inland to meet the Princes Highway.

Cross the highway and follow the gravel road north for two km to a marker and stile on the left leading into a paddock. Here the track enters private property. Walkers have been given permission to use the described route. You must keep to the permitted route and avoid interfering with stock if any are present. Cross the stile over the electric fence and follow the line of trees west for one km crossing seven more electric fences and a minor vehicle track by stiles to exit onto another gravel road. Follow the road north for one km then swing left and a further two km leads west to the Princes Highway.

Cross the highway and turn right to follow the fenceline north. Currently the marker is missing. After 300 metres turn left through an open gateway across the firebreak to the start of a walking track. This winds through pleasant bush for one km then crosses a stile onto a quiet country road. Turn right and follow it across the railway line, turn left, then right after only 150 metres to follow the track beside the fence line. A further 300 metres leads to the signposted left turn to Blackwood Camp. This is located on the other side of a gravel road half way up the hill. Water is obtained from a tank and there is plenty of hard, dry ground for tent sites.

Stage 2: Blackwood Camp to Cut Out Camp

(15 km, 3½-4½ hours)
Return to the walking track and turn left (west) along the fenceline. You soon veer away from the farmland to enter forest. This provides pleasant easy walking along a wide walking track which utilises old existing tracks where possible through the forest. After 1½ km the track passes through a

swampy low area which is often flooded during winter. A signposted deviation to the left leads out to a road then back again after 200 metres to bypass the area.

After five km from Blackwood Camp the track passes around the edge of Reg's Sinkhole (496688) circled by messmate and stringybark gum trees. Shortly after, turn left onto another old road to continue west to meet the sealed Surry River-Gorae Rd (487688). Cross the road and follow the minor track leading south-west from the junction (the track leading west leads to a farm). Initially this passes through some forest then briefly follows a farm fence west; the trespassing sign about the bull is worth reading! After this you enter scrubby forest west of Hollis Hill and meander northwards along disused roads towards the Surry River. This section has been extensively logged in the past and various informative signs have been placed along the route describing the forestry industry.

One km past Fish Holes Rd you will come to a four-way junction which is not marked on any map. Turn left to descend to cross Wild Dog Creek and continue west for a one km to a minor road. Cross the road and a further one km leads to a turn to the right. Soon you will cross Boiler Swamp Rd and follow the main track as it swings left at the first track junction. From here, follow the main track as it gradually descends north-west towards the Surry River.

This leads into the Surry River Gorge to the excellent timber crossing of Ralph's Bridge. Cross the bridge and climb sharply to the ridge crest following the track to the left (the right track leads to a picnic ground) and continue west for 700 metres to Cut Out Camp.

Stage 3: Cut Out Camp to Cobboboonee Camp

(9½ km, 2-3 hours)
From the camp the track continues briefly west before turning north to cross Cut Out Dam Rd. Using a series of old forestry tracks head eastwards for one km before curving around to the north, then westward again to

cross Fish Hole Rd. Continue west for two km to T & W Rd and turn left onto it. Within 50 metres turn right and continue along the walking track for four km through the Cobboboonee State Forest. A sharp right turn leads to Cobboboonee Rd. Follow this road west for 250 metres then turn north along the track for a further 400 metres to the clearing of Cobboboonee Camp.

Stage 4: Cobboboonee Camp to Fitzroy Camp
(12½ km, 3-4 hours)
Cobboboonee Camp is located on the transition from dune derived swamplands to the basaltic soils originating from Mt Deception. This is readily seen in the changes in the open forest where banksias and orchids become more common.

The track meanders northwards from the camp for six km through more forest to Pipe Clay Rd. Cross this then continue north for a further five km to meet the Mt Deception Rd. Cross over and continue north for another 700 metres to the small clearing of Fitzroy Camp. The area around this camp has been recently burnt by a bushfire and this is very evident. The camp was destroyed by the fire and was rebuilt in July 1991.

Stage 5: Fitzroy Camp to Moleside Camp
(22 km, 4½-6½ hours)
Past the camp, follow the indistinct pad north through the burnt forest for 300 metres to a track junction. Turn left and follow the track across the shallow valley of the Fitzroy River. Currently there is no bridge here but this is not a problem as the river is dry for much of the year. If the valley is flooded then turn right at the previous junction and follow the signposted deviation east out to T&W Rd, follow this north then back west on an old track to meet the track near Mt Van Dyke.

After crossing the river the main track meanders northwards to meet the flood deviation near the farmland of Mt Vandyke. Here the track swings west following the fence then enters a section of forest criss-crossed by a myriad of tracks. The track through this maze is marked by a large number of orange triangles and leads west to meet Wright Swamp Rd. If the track is lost then follow any track that leads west or south-west out onto the road.

Turn right onto Wright Swamp Rd and follow it north for 500 metres then turn left onto the walking track. This leads west into the Lower Glenelg National Park following a series of old tracks parallel to Inkpot Rd. After one km the track crosses Heath Rd then continues west a further five km across the edge of Kangaroo Heath. To the south, a glimpse through the vegetation will reveal the extent of the forest and a change of scenery.

The track swings north to meet Inkpot Rd at the junction with Harris Rd (281885). Turn left, follow Inkpot Rd for 700 metres to the first bend where the signposted walking track heads off to the right. Follow this meandering track through sandy forest to meet a fenceline on the edge of open farmlands. The fence is followed southwards and provides fine views of the Glenelg River Valley and the extensive forests to the west. As the fenceline starts descending steeply the track heads south-east into the forest to meet Inkpot Rd. Turn right and 300 metres down the road leads to the Inkpot. This is an enclosed lake with sandy shores.

Continue to follow Inkpot Rd westwards for 400 metres to a junction, follow the right-hand road for a further 100 metres then turn left onto the closed road. This descends gradually south then curves west to follow the valley of Moleside Creek to meet the sealed Nelson-Winnap Rd. Turn left, then right after 100 metres onto the walking track. This leads over a footbridge crossing Moleside Creek to a picnic area complete with tables and chairs. Some steps lead to a view of the cascade on the creek.

The signposted track continues west through the forest beside the Glenelg River to Moleside Camp. This is the only camp located beside a public road and provides access to the boat jetty.

The best camping area is on the rise at the western end of the clearing.

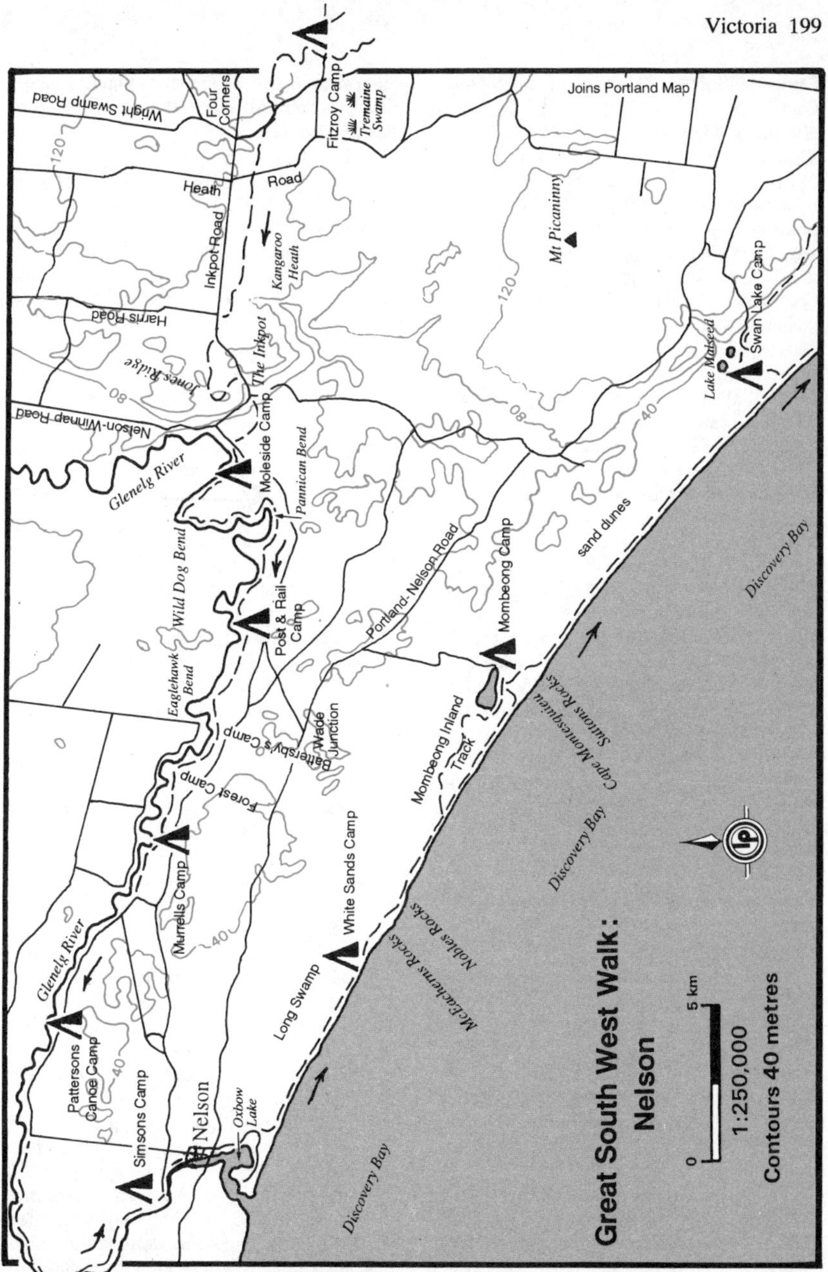

Joins Portland Map

Wright Swamp Road

Four Corners

Fitzroy Camp

Tremane Swamp

Heath

Road

Inkpot Road

Kangaroo Heath

Harris Road

Mt Picaninny

Jones Ridge

The Inkpot

Nelson-Winnap Road

120

Glenelg River

Moleside Camp

Pannican Bend

Lake Malseed

Swan Lake Camp

40

Discovery Bay

80

Wild Dog Bend

Post & Rail Camp

Mombeong Camp

sand dunes

Eaglehawk Bend

Portland-Nelson Road

Forest Camp

Battersby's Camp

Wade Junction

Mombeong Inland Track

Cape Montesquieu

Suttons Rocks

Discovery Bay

Murrells Camp

40

White Sands Camp

Long Swamp

Nobles Rocks

McEacherns Rocks

Discovery Bay

Glenelg River

40

Pattersons Canoe Camp

Simsons Camp

Nelson

Oxbow Lake

Discovery Bay

Great South West Walk: Nelson

5 km

1:250,000

Contours 40 metres

0

Stage 6: Moleside Camp to Post & Rail Camp
(12 km, 3-4 hours)

The track now follows the river for the next 50 km and uses mainly closed roads and walking tracks following the river where possible. Follow the walking track northwest for three km, through light forest beside the river, to Wild Dog Bend where there is a boat jetty and a car camping area. The river swings south and the walking track continues to follow it through varied bush for three km to Pannican Bend. This is readily identified by tall pine trees identifying the site of a former residence.

Quiet roads are now followed south-west for a short distance – turn right at each turn until you reach another walking track which leads to Saunders Landing (which is accessible by car) by the river. The track continuation is unclear; climb the steps past the toilet block to the top of the ridge, turn right and follow the markers onto closed roads. These roads provide pleasant walking for two km before joining a well used sandy road above Pritchards car camp. Continue straight ahead on the road for 30 metres and veer right onto the walking track. Follow the track for two km (there are some excellent views over the river) then descend to water level and walk into Post & Rail North Camp. This is a small sheltered clearing beside the river.

Stage 7: Post & Rail Camp to Murrells Camp
(9½ km, 2-3 hours)

Continue westwards following closed roads and some specially constructed walking tracks. The track runs parallel to the sandy surfaced river road for much of the way. It crosses it several times with some short sections following the road itself. New sections of walking track are being built and eventually the route will avoid the river road completely.

The track passes inland above the car camping areas of Battersby's and Forest camps, then leads onto a closed road. Murrells Camp is located off this, on a signposted track to the right where a short descent leads down to the small clearing beside the river.

Stage 8: Murrells Camp to Pattersons Canoe Camp
(8½ km, 2-3 hours)

The track continues west following the rim of the river valley. Closed roads then a scenic walking track leads to the boat ramp at Sapling Gully Picnic Area. Past this, there are longer sections following the sandy and tedious River Rd and a keen eye needs to be kept open for the posts and triangular markers to follow the short sections of walking track. These are well worth following as they provide excellent views of the gorge which is now beginning to become impressive as the river cuts deeper into the limestone. A longer section of walking track leads over a spur then down to meet the walkers campsite at Pattersons.

The walkers' site is provided with a table, a toilet and water tank which are located on the hill behind. Opposite are good views of one the river's many cliffs. A worthwhile side trip is to explore the Canoe Camp which is located 300 metres to the west. This comprises of a group of buildings which were built in the 1920s by the Patterson's of Warrick Station for use by the family and staff.

Stage 9: Pattersons Canoe Camp to Simsons Camp
(17 km, 4-6 hours)

The walking track is located on the hill just above the toilet block. This leads downstream through very open forest following the rim of the gorge. Good views are obtained from several vantage points along the way. The route alternates between the road and walking track. Eventually the need to follow the road will disappear as new sections of walking track are being constructed.

After five km, the river road becomes closed to traffic and the walking then becomes more pleasant along quiet roads near the river. Excellent views are obtained of the cliffs near the Princess Margaret Rose Caves. The track continues along the river road then follows a newly constructed section of walking track beside the river into South Australia. The cliffs of the gorge become even more impressive the further you progress downstream.

Eventually the gorge begins to open out as the township of Nelson is approached and the track leads into the pleasant open clearing of Simsons Camp situated away from the river.

Stage 10: Simsons Camp to White Sands Camp

(16 km, 4-5½ hours)

The track heads south through bush to the boat ramp at Simsons Landing. From here the track keeps close to the river as it follows the reserves on the bank through the town. Pass under the main bridge and continue to the post office and general store in Nelson, three km from Simsons. Toilets and picnic shelters opposite the shop provide a sheltered place to enjoy the view of the river and unpack any parcels collected from the post office. Nelson has a hotel and accommodation if a break is wanted from camping.

Continue by walking past the shelters and turning left onto the foreshore. This leads out to Beach Rd, turn right and follow the bitumen south for two km. Turn left onto the gravel side road signposted Ocean Beach and Millars Blow. Follow the constructed track through the sand dunes onto the sweeping sands of Discovery Bay. From here the walk follows the coastline the entire distance back to Portland.

Signposts show the way leading eastwards along the shore. The sand varies from firm to very soft and the easiest going is found just above the waterline where care is needed to watch for the odd rogue wave which can sweep across the beach. The continuous pounding surf creates a haze which makes it deceptive to judge distances. The first feature passed is a small sea stack called 'Shipwreck Rock' which is a favoured site for seabirds. Several small cliffs of dune limestone jut out onto the beach to break the

monotony of the sand before the signpost to White Sands is met. Follow the track inland to the sheltered campsite in the ti-tree behind the sand dune. This seems to be the favourite campsite and it overlooks the swampy land behind the dunes. Water is obtained from a bilge pump.

Stage 11: White Sands Camp to Mombeong Camp

(12 km, 3-4½ hours)

Walk back onto the beach and continue following the shore south-east. The sand soon gives way to dune limestone which rises as rough weathered cliffs above the shore. The walking surface becomes firmer and you have a choice of following the shore or walking above the rocks. At the low cliffs of McEacherns Rocks climb up onto the limestone plain and continue across it for another km to the bluff of Nobles Rocks. This provides a good view of the sweeping beach.

One km further along the shore there is a signposted alternative inland track to Lake Mombeong. This meanders through grasslands, coastal scrub then the southern shore of the lake to the campsite and is 1½ km longer than the beach route.

The beach route continues south-east for five km to where a signpost indicates the track to Lake Mombeong. Follow this inland for one km to the freshwater lake. The campsite is a public camp ground used for car camping on the southern corner of the lake.

Stage 12: Mombeong Camp to Swan Lake Camp

(16½ km, 4-5½ hours)

Walk half way back to the beach and turn left onto the track which bypasses Cape Montesquieu. This heads out onto the beach near Suttons Rocks which are the last major outcrop on the beach for the next 30 km. After five km of sand the dunes fringing the beach lose their vegetation cover and present a desert-like landscape of bare sand. The shape and height of the dunes vary as they are moving and sometimes extend as far as four km inland.

The track marker to Swan Lake is met with

some relief and this leads inland for 1½ km through the bare dunes to the large camping flat located south of Swan Lake. The main campsite is similar to lake Mombeong being for vehicle based camping and there is a walkers-only campsite 100 metres to the south-west. Water is available from taps in the main area. In this area dune buggies are permitted and you can expect to share the camping area with these noisy machines. It is worthwhile walking 500 metres north and exploring both Swan and Malseed lakes. At sunset the view from the top of the dunes above the camp should not be missed.

Stage 13: Swan Lake Camp to The Springs Camp
(21 km, 6-7½ hours)
From Swan Lake there are two tracks which can be followed to The Springs camp. The main route follows the beach along Discovery Bay to its end and is described below. The alternative track heads inland climbing over Mt Richmond then back through farmlands to rejoin the main track at Bridgewater Lakes near the end of Discovery Bay. The inland track is 11 km longer and has an intermediate campsite at Tarragul along the way.

From the campsite follow the track through the dunes back out onto the beach. It is worthwhile climbing over the highest dunes on the way as you get extensive views of the coastline.

On the beach turn left and follow the sandy beach south-east. The sand is usually very soft on this section of Discovery Bay and the firmest sand is right at the waterline. The seas must be constantly watched as larger waves occasionally sweep high onto the beach and can saturate the unwary.

After walking along the sand for two hours, you pass a small cliff of limestone. These rocks provide some shelter and a fine view from the top. This is the only feature along the 17 km of beach and a good place to enjoy a break from the sand. After the small bluff, continue to follow the sandy beach south-east for another 2½ to three hours to the Bridgewater Lakes Track which

is where the route from Mt Richmond and Tarragul Camp rejoins the main track.

Cape Bridgewater beckons and another 30 minutes leads to the end of the sand. With some relief follow the marked track up onto the top of the ridge and follow the cliff top south-west. This track has excellent views of the wide sweep of Discovery Bay. About 20 to 30 minutes from the sand the track descends into a small cove where there is a memorial to *The Marie*, shipwrecked in 1851.

The track climbs up scrubby slopes to the cliff tops again and is followed south-west for 40 to 60 minutes to The Springs Camp. This campsite is exposed, being close to the cliff edge. You can get water from a tap beside the camp area or, if it is not working, from a spring emerging from the cliffs below the camp. Take care descending to the spring. A toilet and firewood shelter are located beside the rough campsites.

Stage 14: The Springs Camp to Trewella Camp
(15 km, 3½-4½ hours)
From The Springs, follow the track south-west along the cliff tops for 40 to 50 minutes to meet the track to The Blowholes. If a heavy sea is running it is worth deviating down to the cliffs to see the waves crashing into Cape Duquesne. It is difficult to obtain good views of the blowholes but they are clearly heard in heavy seas.

Follow the walking track south-east towards the Petrified Forest. This is a series of heavily weathered limestones. The track follows the cliff edge at first then keeps about 100 metres inland to follow the farm fencelines. The cliff edge is badly eroded and dangerous and is best kept away from in this area.

The track continues for 1½ hours from The Blowholes Rd to the end of Cape Bridgewater. This cape has fine views of the coastline to the east. The track swings north and 400 metres from the cape you can see a seal colony on the rocks 80 metres below. The track follows the fence up onto the brow of a high hill which provides excellent views to the north and east.

Descend north from this hill, following the fence. About 800 metres from the hill climb over a fence, with the aid of a stile and onto private farmland. Follow the marked track down towards the shore of Fisherman Cove. Access across this farmland is by a special agreement and walkers must not interfere with stock or equipment and must keep to the track.

The markers show the track following the shore of the bay then climbing north over a scrubby ridge and down into Bridgewater Bay about one hour's walk from Cape Bridgewater. This bay has a kiosk, which is open on most days of the year. Drinks, snacks and takeaway meals are available.

From the kiosk follow the sandy beach eastwards for 2½ km to a low rocky headland. The signposted track leaves the beach near the end of the sand and climbs into the dunes to a sandy car park. Cross and follow the track east through the scrub above the cliffs. There are several excellent vantage points and one section of the track follows the actual cliff top. Care is required as it is often very windy. The track again enters the vegetation and passes through the dunes to Trewella Camp, a sheltered clearing which is located well inland from the beach. Water is obtained from a bilge pump or the newly installed water tank.

Stage 15: Trewella Camp to Mallee Camp

(17 km, 4-5 hours)

The track heads south-east from the camp and soon crosses the edge of an extensive sand blow. Poles mark the route across the shifting sands and lead onto the beach about 300 metres east of the rocks. Follow the sand east for six km to a track marker 100 metres before the rocks. Here you head inland and climb very steeply up loose sand onto the top of the ridge. Some of the poles have been buried or have fallen over but markers on top of the ridge show the route.

Initially follow a barren terrace east then pass through thick coastal scrub. A private

road is crossed and walkers must keep to the track as marked. Shortly after, cross a minor gully then walk up onto a ridge for good views of the small bay known as Murrells Beach. The track does not descend to the beach but keeps high up to contour around the bay crossing an access track. The bay is easily visited using the track.

Continue along the track following the open limestone terraces with splendid views. The track enters the Cape Nelson State Park and you keep to the right at the two junctions with the Sea Cliff Nature Walk. The cape is composed mainly of basalt rock with sheer cliffs falling into the ocean. Continue following the cliff edge and near the lighthouse meet the Lighthouse Rd.

The 24-metre-high lighthouse is built from local limestone and was first used in 1884. It is not open to visitors and walkers are requested to refrain from exploring the grounds. The track crosses the road and heads east through tall ti-tree and wattles in the lighthouse reserve. Among the rare plants found here is the soap mallee which can be identified by the soapy feel of its dark green leaves.

The track soon reaches the cliff top and follows a scenic route northwards following the cliff edge. It descends and climbs several times and is markedly different to the rest of the route which has been essentially flat. After two km of undulations, the track crosses the bitumen road and heads inland through heathland to enter Mallee Camp. This is located close to the road and overlooks the farmlands. It doesn't have the wilderness feel of the other campsites but, is probably the best site for a camp on this part of the coast.

Stage 16: Mallee Camp to Portland

(16½ km, 4-5 hours)

Heading north, the track soon crosses the main road and heads out onto the cliff top again for excellent views of Nelson Bay. Closely parallel the road for a while until the track descends below the cliff top and follows the base of an old land slip which is known as 'The Moonah'. This provides rough walking requiring some scrambling as the track winds its way around and through obstacles. The cliff base is in a sheltered location and supports very dense vegetation with tall trees. This section of track is closed from June to October due to the danger of possible rockfall and the deviation simply follows the Scenic Rd for one km and orange triangles indicates the access track to rejoin the main route.

Continue northward along a better standard track through coastal scrub. This crosses an access track near the junction of Sheoke and Scenic Rds then continues east along the open dunes above Yellow Rock. This is a particularly scenic section with almost continuous views for the next two km. The cliff edges above Crayfish Bay are followed then the track plunges through the high vegetation across the back of Cape Sir William Grant.

When another major walking track is met, turn right to walk 100 metres to the car park. Follow the Smelter Nature Walk east. This is a superb track built for wheelchairs and again offers excellent views of the coastline. This leads past the huge aluminium smelter – officials from the smelter assisted volunteers with the track construction and revegetation program. It ends at another car park near Point Danger.

The walking track heads north, passing inland of the rifle range where walkers are requested to keep to the track for their own safety. This soon leads onto the foreshore again and an excellent track heads north into Portland. This section is known as Bills Track and is surprisingly enjoyable with little hint of the town above apart from the noise generated by the smelter.

Three km from Point Danger the foreshore scrub ends and you cross Quarry Rd to the footpath near Prince Engineering. Follow the orange markers north for one km along the footpath to the old gun battery on top of the hill. Several informative signs tell you much of the history of the guns installed there and would have once had a commanding view of the port. The view is now blocked by tall silos.

The track descends gently west to the foot of the hill, so turn north to cross the road at the roundabout and follow the main street into Portland. This crosses a bridge then leads to the tourist information office where the walk began, usually about two weeks ago!

Western Australia

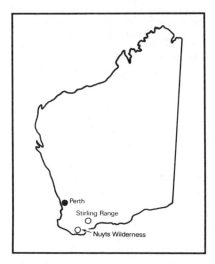

The western third of Australia forms the gigantic state of Western Australia. This immense area of 2½ million sq km is mainly uninteresting, undulating plains and deserts. For bushwalkers there are a couple of well-spaced features in the vastness of this state.

The south-west is the most fertile area of the state, and is covered with farms and forests. Rising above the plains of this area is an abrupt series of isolated peaks called the Stirling Range. These provide some spectacular, rough walking which is in sharp contrast to the surrounding area.

All of the peaks are contained in the Stirling Range National Park which is well worth crossing the continent to visit. The eastern end of this park provides the best walking and there are two popular bushwalks including a circuit walk.

Further south the rugged coastline has some worthwhile scenery and bushlands. A series of narrow parks protect much of the shore and provide some fine beach traverses.

Unfortunately, like many coastal traverses, long car shuffles are required in a region where there is no public transport. West of Albany in the Walpole-Nornalup National Park there is a single wilderness block called the Nuyts Wilderness. An easy two-day walk into this block is outlined to give a sample of the coastline.

North of Perth the undulating country continues for 600 km to the Murchison River. This stream has cut a deep gorge into the sandstone plateau and provides some good gorge walking and swimming.

A further 500 km north is the Hamersley Range National Park. Several creeks have cut gorges into the Pilbara plateau and are worth exploring.

In the north corner of the state there is a large wilderness area called The Kimberleys. This is a tropical area with a jagged coastline and inland plateaus. For the explorer, bushwalking is unlimited: The Drysdale River National Park protects the eastern side of the ranges and is one of the most isolated parks in Australia. Access to the area is very difficult to arrange.

Other Suggested Bushwalks

Bibbulman Walking Track A long-distance track that starts behind Perth and follows undulating terrain south for 500 km, staying mainly on quiet roads through forested hills. It requires four to five weeks to walk.

Fitzgerald River Start at the end of Gairdner Road, north of Bremer and follow the coast north-east to Mylies Beach. A medium to hard five-day walk in the Fitzgerald River National Park, 500 km east of Albany. It requires a long car shuffle.

Southern Coastline Traverse From Windy Harbour follow the coast south-east to Point Nuyts. This is a five to seven-day bushwalk along the coast west of Walpole. This walk requires a lengthy car shuffle.

Leeuwin-Naturaliste Coast Traverse From Augusta follow the coast north to Margaret River. This is a four to five-day bushwalk in the south-western corner of the state, 300 km south of Perth. Public transport can be used to make this a circuit.

Murchison River From Ross Graham follow the gorge downstream to The Loop. A medium to hard four to five-day walk in the Kalbarri National Park, 600 km north of Perth.

Wittenoom Gorges From Wittenoom walk south through Wittenoom Gorge to Red Gorge. Explore the canyons in this area and walk east across the plateau then follow Kalamina Gorge north to the road. Walk west back to the start. A four to six-day circuit in the Hamersley Range National Park, 1000 km north of Perth.

THE STIRLING RANGE CIRCUIT

The Stirling Range National Park is a series of abrupt isolated peaks rising above a flat agricultural plain. The range is close to the southern coast of Western Australia and dominates the area.

The park protects the entire Stirling Range, including the foothills, and is one of Australia's most outstanding botanical reserves. The peaks of this range are surprisingly rugged and well worth visiting.

Features

The Stirling Range is a single chain of peaks 10 km wide and 65 km long. For most of its length the range is composed of isolated peaks and towers separated by broad valleys. At the eastern end of the range the peaks are connected by a high ridge which is rugged and spectacular. This ridge provides the best bushwalking area in this park, with excellent views.

The exposed sedimentary rocks are a series of folded sandstones, shales and slates which have been uplifted and weathered to their present form. Underneath the sediments is a bedrock of granite which has weathered to white sands on the foothills. With the diverse rock types and sudden altitude variations the park supports an incredible variety of plant life.

There are over 500 known species of wildflowers, so in the spring it is very beautiful. Most of the park is covered with prickly shrubs and heaths which flower profusely. Orchids are numerous in the sandy soils around the foothills and there are only a few small pockets of forest on the plains.

Kangaroos and wallabies are often seen by bushwalkers, but away from the major roads. Birdlife is active and emus, parrots, magpies and currawongs are common. With the profusion of flowers the park has many honey-eating birds which are easily heard but not so easily seen. You may also see goannas, lizards and the odd snake.

Standard

This walk follows rough walking pads most of the way. There are no markers at all along the route and some care is required to take the easiest path. The walking is varied; using old fire trails and footpads you'll walk through prickly scrub with short ascents and descents through cliff lines.

The range is subject to sudden weather changes which can bring rain and thick clouds. Both days are fairly long and the suggested walk has been graded medium to hard.

Days Required

The walk is a circuit of the eastern end of the range from The Arrows to Ellen Peak. This circuit is a two-day walk. The other standard route is to walk from Bluff Knoll to Ellen Peak and it takes two to three days to walk the ridge. This requires a car shuffle or an extra day's walking along the fire trails on the northern boundary of the park to create a circuit.

Seasons

Spring is the best season for visiting this range. The wildflowers are in bloom and water is usually available at the recognised water sites. The weather is often very variable with fine, mild days interspersed with short rainy squalls, which shroud the range with thick clouds.

Winter is also very suitable as water is usually available on the crest of the range. The weather is not as good as in spring, however, as clouds often cover the peaks. In autumn the weather is very pleasant for walking but water is unreliable and parties should plan on carrying all water supplies. Summer is usually very hot and dry and it is not a good time for bushwalking here.

Equipment

A normal set of walking equipment is suitable for walking along this range. The range has a couple of camping caves which can be used for the overnight stop. It is still a good idea to carry a tent as the caves may be occupied or the party may not reach the caves before nightfall.

You'll need a waterproof jacket and pants, as short sudden storms occur fairly regularly. Long pants or gaiters and long sleeve shirts are also handy as the scrub is fairly prickly, and you'll need a shady hat in the warmer months.

All party members should plan on carrying at least four litres of water as the water supplies on top of the range are very unreliable. Fuel stoves are recommended as there is little firewood on the crest of the range. Some parties may require a short rope to assist in packhauling on some of the short rocky sections particularly on The First Arrow. Most groups don't take a rope, but it is up to the party to decide on the level of safety that is required.

Maps

The 1:50,000 topographic map, *Ellen Peak*, covers the entire route of this walk. This shows all the properties and roads that surround the park but does not show any of the fire trails within the park. This map is available from the Department of Lands & Survey.

The National Parks Service also produces a free leaflet, *Stirling Range & Porongorup National Parks*, which gives general information and shows the main roads and tracks within the park. Unfortunately, it does not show any useful information on the eastern end of the range for bushwalkers. You can get this leaflet from the Department of Conservation & Land Management (☎ (09) 367 0333), 50 Hayman Rd, Como, Perth (postal address: PO Box 104, Como, 6152), and at the ranger stations in the park.

Permits

No permits are required for bushwalking in the eastern end of the range but all walkers are asked to fill out the party's details and the intended route, in the log book provided. This book is kept near the rangers' residence (☎ (098) 27 9230) beside the Bluff Knoll road junction at the northern border of the park. In the event of a fire or other disaster the presence of walkers will influence the action taken by the rangers.

Access

The Stirling Range National Park is 400 km south-east of Perth and 80 km north of Albany. Access to this park is good from all directions and many different routes can be followed. There is no public transport available to this park and private cars (or hired vehicles) are essential.

From Perth follow the Albany Highway south-east for 250 km to Kojonup. Turn east and follow the roads for 119 km through Broomehill and Gnowangerup and turn south to Borden. From Borden continue south for 23 km on the Albany road to the service station at Amelup. This is the last petrol and food supplies before entering the park.

Leave the main road by turning left onto the Sandalwood Road and follow this south-east for 18 km. Turn left onto Gnowellen Road and follow this for four km to the park border on the right.

From Albany follow the Hasell Road (the road leading towards Esperance) north-east for 13 km then turn north. Follow the Chester Pass Road a further 73 km through the Stirling Range National Park to the rangers' station at the Bluff Knoll turn-off on the northern edge of the park. Register details of your walk in the log book then continue north towards Borden for a further eight km to the Amelup service station. Turn right onto Sandalwood Road and follow the directions outlined in the previous paragraph.

From Esperance follow Highway No 1 west for 298 km to Jeramungup then turn right and continue for 67 km, passing through Ongerup, to turn off south to Borden. From Borden follow the directions as for the Perth route.

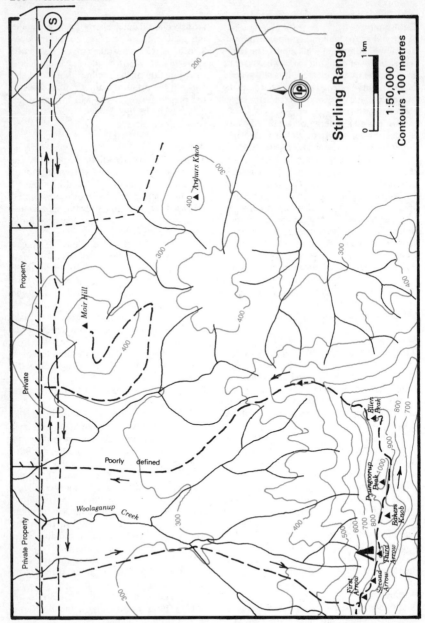

Stirling Range

1:50,000
Contours 100 metres

Stage 1: Arrows Firetrack to Third Arrow

(14 km, 5-8 hours)

From the park border follow the fire trail west, staying parallel to the border fence. There are two trails which can be followed; the southern track which is 200 metres inside the border is the more pleasant. This climbs gently for 4½ km to the the crest of a spur of Moir Hill. Continue west for a further three km across the valley of Woolaganup Creek to a fire track junction.

Turn south onto the Arrows fire trail and walk along the disused road for two km to a creek. This creek is usually flowing and is the last reliable water before ascending to the crest of the range. Continue along the fire trail for a further 1½ km to the end of the road. This is about three to four hours' walk from the start.

An unmarked walking track starts from here and follows the ridge south up onto the crest of the range. The start of the track is difficult to find so follow the walking pads south into the scrub and the track will soon become distinct.

This track is unmarked but easy to follow as it climbs steeply up the spur to meet the ridge crest on the western side of the First Arrow. This takes about one hour from the end of the road. There are several cairns and confusing pads on the crest of the range.

From here the track climbs very steeply east up onto the First Arrow. First the track climbs up some steep narrow terraces on the cliff above. You need to take great care (particularly in wet weather) in ascending this cliff. When you reach the top of the cliff the track winds around the north side of a small rock pinnacle and crosses the head of the steep gully behind the pinnacle. At this point there is a very steep track descending south-east which you do not follow.

From here several routes can be followed to the top of the First Arrow but all the routes require some scrambling. There is a cave 30 metres below the summit on the north side which can sleep about six people if necessary. However, there is no reliable water supply nearby.

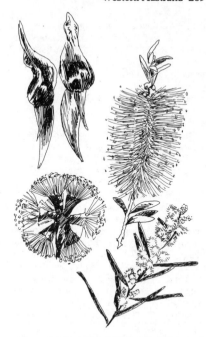

From the top of the First Arrow descend east down the crest of the ridge to the saddle before the Second Arrow – the descent is easy. You then climb steeply east, out of the saddle, up the ridge and curve south-east up over some small rock slabs to the summit of the Second Arrow. From the top descend easily east down the broad ridge to the saddle before the Third Arrow and walk 30 metres uphill to the foot of the rock faces on the Third Arrow.

The water supply is to the south and the camping cave is to the north. To find the water supply follow the rough track along the foot of the cliff, south for 40 metres. You will pass a small flat area which is suitable for several tents. The water is in the top of the gully past the flat area, reached after a steep scramble.

Several plastic containers of various types collect the drips falling from the roof of the cave at the top of the gully. The water supply is only semi-permanent. To reach the camping cave traverse along the base of the descends, then climbs up into the base of a broad gully. The cave is 10 metres above the base of the cliff, in the gully, so there is a short scramble to reach it. It has sleeping space for about eight people.

Stage 2: Third Arrow to Woolaganup Creek via Ellen Peak

(14 km, 6-7 hours)

From the camping cave you can either walk east along the cliff base for 30 metres then up into the gully above, or scramble west, then south to the eastern side of the Third Arrow (the reverse of Stage 1). This allows you to refill your water bottles on the way.

The track then climbs west into the tall chasm above on the Third Arrow. Walk through the chasm then descend westwards for 30 metres to meet the direct route from the cave. From here the route climbs a short steep gully between rocky walls, then descends east on the northern side of the ridge to the saddle between the Third Arrow and Bakers Knob. This is about a one-hour walk from the Third Arrow cave. There is a tiny campsite in this saddle.

The track then climbs steeply westward up on to Bakers Knob. The track is easy to follow and crosses the north side of Bakers Knob then gently descends to the open saddle beneath the massive cliffs of Pyungoorup Peak. This peak is bypassed on its southern side. The track follows the cliff base eastwards for 30 minutes to a camping cave.

A water drip, 30 metres west of the cave, may be used for filling your water bottles. From here the original track ascended the dangerous steep gully 20 metres west of the cave. The better track is that which continues to follow the cliff base east. About 300 metres past the cave, climb onto the ridge crest to join the other track.

If the party wishes to climb Pyungoorup Peak the scrubby ridge can be followed west without packs for 500 metres to the summit. Turn east and make the easy descent to the saddle before Ellen Peak. From this saddle there is a choice of routes. In fine weather it is recommended to climb Ellen Peak and to

descend its north-east side. In poor visibility traverse the northern slopes of Ellen Peak to the north-east ridge.

To climb Ellen Peak from the saddle, walk west in thick scrub to the base of the cliffs and follow the major gully up to the top of the ridge. This gully is well used and has several short steep steps that are easily negotiated. At the top, turn north and you'll reach the summit within five minutes. In the summit cairn there is a visitors' book contained in a metal box.

The view of the Stirling Range and the coast is excellent in clear weather. To descend from the top, climb for 20 metres on the west side to a wide terrace in the cliffs. Follow this terrace north for 80 metres along the edge of the cliff. Leave the rock face and walk 20 metres north to the saddle above a gully.

Descend steeply east down this gully. At the foot of the gully the track continues east descending some rock slabs. Near the foot of the slabs the track swings north and sidles the slopes to the north-east ridge of Ellen Peak. Look carefully for the turn to the north as some false tracks lead directly down to the east.

The two routes on Ellen Peak join on the north-east ridge and a well-formed pad is easily followed north-east down the crest of this ridge. The track passes through a timbered saddle, where there are some tent sites, then climbs onto the top of a knoll.

From the top of this knoll the track swings north-west and descends onto the plains between the two branches of Woolaganup Creek. The indistinct track can be followed northwards across these plains for 2½ km to meet a fire-break trail. If you lose the track on the scrubby plain it is easiest to push north through the scrub to cross the two fire trails instead of searching for the faint track. Once at the park boundary walk east back along the fire trail parallel to the fence for six km to the parked vehicles.

NUYTS WILDERNESS

The Walpole-Nornalup National Park is an area on the south coast of Western Australia, which has excellent coastal scenery. The region has wide ocean beaches, sharp rocky headlands and peaceful estuaries.

Much of the area has an extensive road system across it, but there is one area which has been set aside as a wilderness block with walking access only. This block has varied flora, some excellent scenery and is a pleasant, easy walking area for bushwalkers.

Features

The Nuyts Wilderness Block is one of the few wilderness areas in the southern half of Western Australia. It consists mainly of stabilised sand dunes which are covered with thick vegetation. This varies from karri and jarrah forests near Deep River to the extensive heathlands along the coastal edge. Within the area is an amazing variety of orchids. The floral symbol of Western Australia, the Kangaroo Paw, is very common also.

Rising above the rolling sand dunes are the granite tors of Point Nuyts and Mt Hopkins. These higher rises provide extensive views of the surrounding area. This region has the highest rainfall of south-west Australia and consequently supports many springs.

Lakes and marshes have formed in some of the depressions in the sand dune system and these are worth visiting. The coastline around Point Nuyts consists of steep granite faces plunging into the ocean. There are many springs in the tiny sandy coves. To the west, at Lost Beach the rocks change to jagged limestone, forming a rough shoreline. Fishing off the rocks is excellent but be careful to keep above the high wave levels.

Standard

The walk follows a well-defined track from the car park to the ocean and is graded easy. To explore the area some off-track walking is required crossing the heathlands. These are generally covered in low prickly scrub and are easily walked across.

Days Required

The walk is two very easy days, returning by the same track. It can be extended by continuing west along the coast to Mandalay Beach for a three-day walk of medium standard. This will, however, require a car shuffle as it is not a circuit walk.

Seasons

This walk is suitable for any season. As with most areas in Western Australia, spring is the time to see plenty of interesting wildflowers. Summer is an excellent period to laze on the cooler coastline away from the inland heat. Autumn is mild and pleasant. Winter is the wettest season in this park and is the least pleasant for walking although it can still be very interesting with the Southern Ocean at its roughest.

Equipment

No special equipment is needed for bushwalking in this park. Runners or very light boots are ideal footwear. You need to take a reasonable raincoat as it rains regularly throughout the year. In summer, sunburn cream and a wide-brimmed hat are advised.

Maps

The 1:50,000 topographic map, *Saddle Island*, covers the entire region of the Nuyts Block Wilderness Area. This map has excellent detail and is ideal for walking. It shows all old tracks in the area, many of which are overgrown and can no longer be followed. This map is available from the Department of Lands & Survey.

The 1:100,000 topographic map, *Rame Head*, also covers the entire route. It is not as good as the 1:50,000 map as it shows less detail. It is produced by NATMAP.

The National Parks Service also produces a free leaflet, *Walpole-Nornalup National Park*, which details the major roads and existing walking tracks in the park. This is useful as it shows the existing tracks, but has insufficient detail for use off the tracks. This leaflet is available from the Department of Conservation & Land Management (☎ (09) 367 0333), 50 Hayman Rd, Como, Perth (postal address: PO Box 104, Como, 6152).

View from Mt Hopkins, Nuyts Wilderness

Permits

No permits are required for walking in the Nuyts Wilderness Block Area. A log book is kept at the shelter near the start of the track and all bushwalkers should fill in their details and intended return date. Upon returning, remember to sign off in the book. If the party is unable to sign off in the book the ranger at Walpole can be contacted by phone (☎ (098) 40 1093).

Access

The Nuyts Wilderness Block is 400 km south of Perth and 120 km west of Albany. Access is by way of sealed highways from both Albany and Perth. Public transport to the area is a once-a-week bus service of little use to bushwalkers. It runs from Bunbury to Albany and requires booking in advance with Westrail at either Bunbury ☎ (097) 25 5564 or Albany ☎ (098) 41 0464.

From Perth follow either of the two main highways south to Bunbury then follow the South Western Highway through Bridgetown and Manjimup towards Walpole. Eight km before Walpole (418 km from Perth) turn

right onto the gravel road to Tinglewood Lodge. Follow the gravel road for three km to pass the Tinglewood Lodge and continue one km further to the Nuyts car park.

From Albany follow Highway No 1 west through Denmark to Walpole, 121 km from Albany. Follow the main highway past the town for eight km and turn left onto the road to Tinglewood Lodge. Follow the route above to the Nuyts car park. The closest petrol and food supplies are available at Nornalup or Crystal Springs and both are about 12 km from the Nuyts car park.

Stage 1: Nuyts Car Park to Thompson Cove

(7 km, 2 to 3 hours)
From the car park follow the signposted track for 300 metres to Deep River. Cross the bridge and walk 200 metres further to the information shelter where the walkers' registration book is kept. After signing the book, follow the track south through the forest for two km to a track junction on the edge of the heathlands.

Turn left as indicated by the markers and

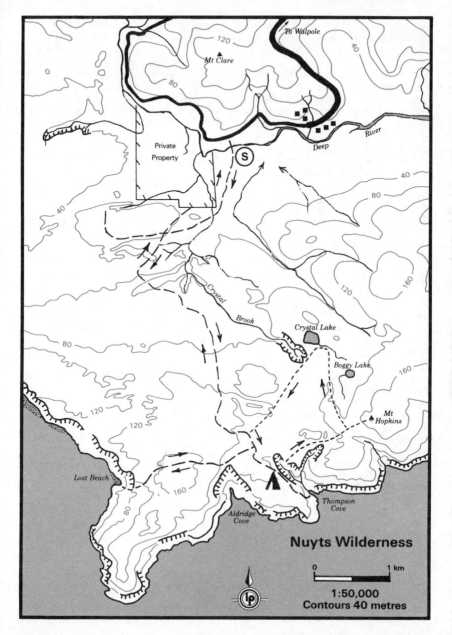

Nuyts Wilderness

0   1 km

1:50,000
Contours 40 metres

follow the old vehicle track southwards across the heathlands for four km to an indistinct track junction on top of a high ridge near the ocean. The right-hand track leads to Lost Beach. Follow the main track straight ahead for 200 metres to the next sandy ridge. A well-used track enters on the left which you follow for 100 metres to an excellent campsite under the trees in the valley. Water is obtained from the spring-fed creek beside the camp.

After establishing camp, return to the main track and follow it south for one km down to the small sandy beach at Thompson Cove. There is a small exposed campsite on the shore here. There is good fishing from the granite shoreline. Return to the camp by the same track. The creek valley is very scrubby and not worth following back to the camp.

Sidetrip: Mt Hopkins & Crystal Lake
(5 km, 2-3 hours)
Mt Hopkins and Crystal Lake are in the untracked country to the east of the campsite. The area is generally covered with low scratchy heaths. From the campsite follow a well-used pad east across the creek and up onto the heathlands. Walk east past the top edge of the second spring and follow the open valleys towards Mt Hopkins. Thick scrub covers the lower slopes of Mt Hopkins. Push through this scrub band and climb the bare rocky slabs to the final tors on the peak.

Sidle around to the eastern side of the tors and a short scramble leads onto the second highest rock. This gives you an excellent view of the coastline and the lakes to the north. The highest tor is inaccessible to walkers. Descend west back over the rock slabs and past the scrub band.

Once in the heathlands turn north and follow the higher sandy ridges past Boggy Lake to Crystal Lake. The spring near the lake is well worth visiting.

Return to the campsite by walking south-west across the heaths to meet the main track. Follow the track back to the campsite.

Stage 2: Thompson Spring to Nuyts Car Park
(11 km, 4-5 hours)
The return journey is along the same track with a diversion to Lost Beach. From the campsite follow the main track north for 10 minutes to the indistinct track junction. Leave the packs here and follow the western track. This soon becomes easy to follow and after 500 metres there is an excellent view of Aldridge Cove.

Continue for another 1½ km following the track to the top of the ridge above Lost Beach. The walking pad then heads steeply downhill to the southern end of the tiny bay called Lost Beach. A small spring enters the beach. The north end of the beach is bordered by craggy limestone pinnacles which are interesting to explore. Return to the packs using the same tracks.

Collect the packs and follow the main track north for four km to the track junction. Turn right and continue to follow the same track through the forest to the information shelter and the registration book.

After signing out in the log book, cross the river and return to the car park at the end of the walk.

Index

Guides to Australia & the Pacific

Australia - travel survival kit
The complete low-down on Down Under – home of Ayers Rock, the Great Barrier Reef, extraordinary animals, cosmopolitan cities, rainforests, beaches... and Lonely Planet!

Islands of Australia's Great Barrier Reef - travel survival kit
The Great Barrier Reef is one of the wonders of the world – and one of the great travel destinations! Whether you're looking for a tropical island resort or a secluded island hideaway, this guide has all the facts you'll need. Winner of the 1991 Pacific Asia Travel Association Gold Awards – Grand Award.

Sydney city guide
The run-down on Australia's most exciting city. Packed with information which will help you discover Sydney's many attractions. Handy pocket-sized format with colour fold-out maps.

Hawaii - a travel survival kit
Share in the delights of this island paradise – and avoid some of its high prices – with this practical guide. Covers all of Hawaii's well-known attractions, plus plenty of uncrowded sights and activities.

New Zealand - a travel survival kit
This practical guide will help you discover the very best New Zealand has to offer – Maori dances and feasts; some of the most spectacular scenery in the world; and every outdoor activity imaginable.

Fiji - a travel survival kit
Whether you prefer to stay in camping grounds, international hotels, or something in-between, this comprehensive guide will help you to enjoy the beautiful Fijian archipelago.

New Caledonia - a travel survival kit
This guide shows all that the idyllic islands of New Caledonia have to offer – from French colonial culture to traditional Melanesian life.

Solomon Islands - a travel survival kit
The Solomon Islands are the best-kept secret of the Pacific. Discover remote tropical islands, jungle covered volcanoes and traditional Melanesian villages with this detailed guide.

Rarotonga & the Cook Islands - a travel survival kit
Rarotonga and the Cook Islands have history, beauty and magic to rival the better-known islands of Hawaii and Tahiti, but the world has virtually passed them by.

Micronesia - a travel survival kit
The glorious beaches, lagoons and reefs of these 2100 islands would dazzle even the most jaded traveller. This guide has all the details on island-hopping across the north Pacific.

Tahiti & French Polynesia - a travel survival kit
Tahiti's idyllic beauty has seduced sailors, artists and traveller for generations. The latest edition provides full details on the main island of Tahiti, the Tuamotos, Marquesas and other island groups. Invaluable information for independent travellers and package tourists alike.

Tonga - a travel survival kit
The only South Pacific country never to be colonised by Europeans, Tonga has also been ignored by tourists. The people of this far-flung island group offer some of the most sincere and unconditional hospitality in the world.

Samoa - a travel survival kit
Two remarkably different countries, Western Samoa and American Samoa offer some wonderful island escapes, and Polynesian culture at its best.

Walking guides

Tramping in New Zealand
Call it tramping, hiking, walking, bushwalking, or trekking — travelling by foot is the best way to explore New Zealand's natural beauty. Detailed descriptions of 40 walks of varying length and difficulty.

Trekking in the Indian Himalaya
The Indian Himalaya offers some of the world's most exciting treks. This comprehensive guide gives advice on planning and equipping a trek, as well as detailed route descriptions.

Trekking in the Nepal Himalaya
Complete trekking information for Nepal, including day-by-day route descriptions and detailed maps — a wealth of advice for independent and group trekkers alike.

Trekking in the Patagonian Andes
The first detailed guide to this region gives thorough information on walks in Chile and Argentina, mainly through national parks or reserves, and lists other possibilities. Walking standards range from easy two-day hikes to more strenuous hikes of up to 10 days.

Trekking in Spain
This comprehensive guidebook makes the most of Spain's excellent amenities for walkers and covers a variety of terrains including mountains, vast plains, rugged coastlines and spectacular deserts.

Trekking in Turkey
Among Turkey's best-kept secrets are its superb treks, which rival those of Nepal. This book, the first trekking guide to Turkey, gives details on treks that are destined to become classics.

Where Can You Find Out.........

HOW to get a Laotian visa in Bangkok?

WHERE to go birdwatching in PNG?

WHAT to expect from the police if you're robbed in Peru?

WHEN you can go to see cow races in Australia?

In the Lonely Planet Newsletter!

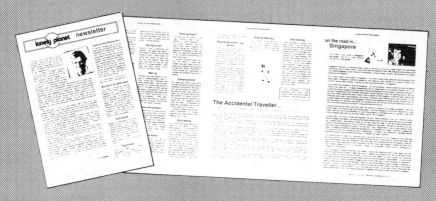

Every issue includes:

- *a letter from Lonely Planet founders Tony and Maureen Wheeler*
- *a letter from an author 'on the road'*
- *the most entertaining or informative reader's letter we've received*
- *the latest news on new and forthcoming releases from Lonely Planet*
- *and all the latest travel news from all over the world*

Lonely Planet Guidebooks

Lonely Planet guidebooks cover every accessible part of Asia as well as Australia, the Pacific, South America, Africa, the Middle East and parts of North America and Europe. There are five series: *travel survival kits*, covering a country for a range of budgets; *shoestring guides* with compact information for low-budget travel in a major region; *walking guides*; *city guides* and *phrasebooks*.

Australia & the Pacific
Australia
Bushwalking in Australia
Islands of Australia's Great Barrier Reef
Fiji
Micronesia
New Caledonia
New Zealand
Tramping in New Zealand
Papua New Guinea
Papua New Guinea phrasebook
Rarotonga & the Cook Islands
Samoa
Solomon Islands
Sydney
Tahiti & French Polynesia
Tonga
Vanuatu

South-East Asia
Bali & Lombok
Bangkok
Burma
Burmese phrasebook
Cambodia
Indonesia
Indonesia phrasebook
Malaysia, Singapore & Brunei
Philippines
Pilipino phrasebook
Singapore
South-East Asia on a shoestring
Thailand
Thai phrasebook
Vietnam, Laos & Cambodia

North-East Asia
China
Mandarin Chinese phrasebook
Hong Kong, Macau & Canton
Japan
Japanese phrasebook
Korea
Korean phrasebook
North-East Asia on a shoestring
Taiwan
Tibet
Tibet phrasebook

West Asia
Trekking in Turkey
Turkey
Turkish phrasebook
West Asia on a shoestring

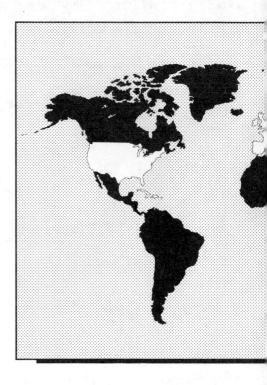

Middle East
Egypt & the Sudan
Egyptian Arabic phrasebook
Iran
Israel
Jordan & Syria
Yemen

Indian Ocean
Madagascar & Comoros
Maldives & Islands of the East Indian Ocean
Mauritius, Réunion & Seychelles

Mail Order

Lonely Planet guidebooks are distributed worldwide. They are also available by mail order from Lonely Planet, so if you have difficulty finding a title please write to us. US and Canadian residents should write to Embarcadero West, 155 Filbert St, Suite 251, Oakland CA 94607, USA, European residents should write to Devonshire House, 12 Barley Mow Passage, Chiswick, London W4 4PH and residents of other countries to PO Box 617, Hawthorn, Victoria 3122, Australia.

Europe
Eastern Europe on a shoestring
Eastern Europe phrasebook
Iceland, Greenland & the Faroe Islands
Trekking in Spain
USSR
Russian phrasebook

Indian Subcontinent
Bangladesh
India
Hindi/Urdu phrasebook
Trekking in the Indian Himalaya
Karakoram Highway
Kashmir, Ladakh & Zanskar
Nepal
Trekking in the Nepal Himalaya
Nepal phrasebook
Pakistan
Sri Lanka
Sri Lanka phrasebook

Africa
Africa on a shoestring
Central Africa
East Africa
Kenya
Swahili phrasebook
Morocco, Algeria & Tunisia
Moroccan Arabic phrasebook
Zimbabwe, Botswana & Namibia
West Africa

Mexico
Baja California
Mexico

South America
Argentina, Uruguay & Paraguay
Bolivia
Brazil
Brazilian phrasebook
Chile & Easter Island
Colombia
Ecuador & the Galápagos Islands
Latin American Spanish phrasebook
Peru
Quechua phrasebook
South America on a shoestring
Trekking in the Patagonian Andes

Central America
Central America on a shoestring
Costa Rica
La Ruta Maya

North America
Alaska
Canada
Hawaii

The Lonely Planet Story

Lonely Planet published its first book in 1973 in response to the numerous 'How did you do it?' questions Maureen and Tony Wheeler were asked after driving, bussing, hitching, sailing and railing their way from England to Australia.

Written at a kitchen table and hand collated, trimmed and stapled, *Across Asia on the Cheap* became an instant local bestseller, inspiring thoughts of another book.

Eighteen months in South-East Asia resulted in their second guide, *South-East Asia on a shoestring*, which they put together in a backstreet Chinese hotel in Singapore in 1975. The 'yellow bible' as it quickly became known to backpackers around the world, soon became *the* guide to the region. It has sold well over half a million copies and is now in its 7th edition, still retaining its familiar yellow cover.

Today there are over 100 Lonely Planet titles – books that have that same adventurous approach to travel as those early guides; books that 'assume you know how to get your luggage off the carousel' as one reviewer put it.

Although Lonely Planet initially specialised in guides to Asia, they now cover most regions of the world, including the Pacific, South America, Africa, the Middle East and Eastern Europe. The list of *walking guides* and *phrasebooks* (for 'unusual' languages such as Quechua, Swahili, Nepalese and Egyptian Arabic) is also growing rapidly.

The emphasis continues to be on travel for independent travellers. Tony and Maureen still travel for several months of each year and play an active part in the writing, updating and quality control of Lonely Planet's guides.

They have been joined by over 50 authors, 48 staff – mainly editors, cartographers, & designers – at our office in Melbourne, Australia, another 10 at our US office in Oakland, California and have recently opened an office in London. Travellers themselves also make a valuable contribution to the guides through the feedback we receive in thousands of letters each year.

The people at Lonely Planet strongly believe that travellers can make a positive contribution to the countries they visit, both through their appreciation of the countries' culture, wildlife and natural features, and through the money they spend. In addition, the company makes a direct contribution to the countries and regions it covers. Since 1986 a percentage of the income from each book has been donated to ventures such as famine relief in Africa; aid projects in India; agricultural projects in Central America; Greenpeace's efforts to halt French nuclear testing in the Pacific and Amnesty International. In 1991 $68,000 was donated to these causes.

Lonely Planet's basic travel philosophy is summed up in Tony Wheeler's comment, 'Don't worry about whether your trip will work out. Just go!'